ESSAYS IN
MONETARY ECONOMICS

HARRY G. JOHNSON

Professor of Economics in the University of Chicago

HARVARD UNIVERSITY PRESS

Cambridge, Massachusetts
1967

FIRST PUBLISHED IN 1967

PRINTED IN GREAT BRITAIN
in 11 *point Times Roman type*
BY UNWIN BROTHERS LIMITED
WOKING AND LONDON

PREFACE

This volume brings together essays and articles in the general field of monetary economics prepared for a variety of purposes over the past four years. The main reasons for collecting them in this fashion are that they appear to have been found useful for teaching purposes—as reflected in requests for offprints—and that they have been published in widely scattered and often obscure journals and conference volumes.

Part I is concerned with monetary theory proper. Chapter I is my *American Economic Review* commissioned survey of monetary theory and policy. Chapter II, which along with Chapter III originated as a survey lecture at the Instituto Torcuato di Tella in the summer of 1963, re-surveys much of the same material, but at a less difficult level, and according to a schema I believe more interesting than that imposed by the obligation to survey the field as marked out by all those actively publishing in it. Chapter III is a survey of the theory of inflation as I should have liked to approach it in a companion piece to my survey of monetary theory and policy, though unfortunately I lacked the time to invest in it as much scholarship in the literature as went into the previous survey.

Chapters IV and V, by contrast, are concerned with the theory of money itself. Chapter V, on transactions demand for money, covers the same general ground as the classic articles by Baumol and Tobin, but introduces a diagrammatic exposition that may help the non-mathematical reader to understand the main points. Chapter IV deals in what it is hoped is a relatively simple way with the complex problem of the role of money in growth models. Much of the material in this Chapter has not heretofore been published.

Part Two turns from theory to policy problems. Unlike pure theory, the economics of policy must necessarily be discussed within the institutional context of a national economy (or the international economy). Nevertheless, the essay on alternative guiding principles for the use of monetary policy in Canada does, I believe, deal with some fundamental issues concerning the autonomy of the central bank and the limitations of traditional central bank methods of operation that are of broader interest. The Chapter on issues in monetary and fiscal policy in the United States, among other things, calls attention to some recent developments in the theory of economic policy in a fixed exchange rate system and to some developments in monetary theory subsequent to those surveyed in Chapters I and II.

Part Three is concerned with monetary and fiscal problems of developing countries—as the less developed or poor countries have somewhat euphemistically come to be described. Chapter VIII analyses problems of fiscal policy and Chapter IX problems of monetary policy—which in these countries are typically problems of inflation; but in fact, as I hope the argument is careful enough to keep clear, the fiscal and monetary problems of such countries cannot really be separated. In particular, it is necessary to keep one's eye firmly on exchange rate and balance-of-payments policy, and particularly on the implications for domestic policy of maintaining a fixed exchange rate, if one is to understand rather than become confused by the problems of the less developed countries.

The final Chapter deals with an international rather than a national aspect of the monetary problems of the less developed countries, the interest of those countries in the contemporary problem of international monetary reform. I am well aware that in this Chapter I take what many of my colleagues will regard as an excessively hard line on schemes to solve the international monetary problem by methods that will channel resources to the less developed countries. My reason for refusing to endorse such schemes is not that I am opposed to the less developed countries receiving more development assistance,[1] but that I think that no useful purpose is served by misapplying economic analysis for political ends. The mathematical appendix to this chapter presents what I believe to be a novel formulation of the theory of commodity reserve money, which has been revived in the Hart–Kaldor–Tinbergen scheme for an international commodity reserve money system.

I should like to express my gratitude to the American

---

[1] See my forthcoming monograph, *Economic Policies Towards Less Developed Countries* (Washington: The Brookings Institution, and London: George Allen & Unwin, 1967), from which this Chapter is taken.

Economic Association, the Instituto Torcuato di Tella, The Royal Commission on Banking and Finance, The American Bankers' Association, The Organization for Economic Co-operation and Development, The Rehovoth Conference, and the Brookings Institution for their invitations to prepare various of the essays presented here; also to the editors of the *American Economic Review*, *Economica*, the *Federal Reserve Bulletin*, the *Indian Economic Review*, the *Indian Journal of Economics*, the Princeton University *Essays in International Finance*, and the *Malayan Economic Review*, for permission to republish material from their pages; and to the Publication Department of the Brookings Institution for permission to reprint Chapter X.

HARRY G. JOHNSON
University of Chicago
June, 1966

CONTENTS

PART ONE

MONETARY THEORY

CHAPTER I

MONETARY THEORY AND
POLICY*

In order to isolate a field of study clearly enough demarcated to
be usefully surveyed, it is necessary to define monetary theory as
comprising theories concerning the influence of the quantity of
money in the economic system, and monetary policy as policy
employing the central bank's control of the supply of money as
an instrument for achieving the objectives of general economic
policy. In surveying the field thus narrowly defined fourteen
years ago, Henry Villard [123] began by remarking on the
relative decline in the significance attached to it as compared
with the offshoot fields of business cycle and fiscal (income and
employment) theory, a decline related to the experience of the
1930's, the intellectual impact of Keynes' *General Theory* [66],
and the inhibiting effects of the wartime expansion of public
debt on monetary policy. While this division of labour has
continued, and has indeed been accentuated by the emergence
of the cross-cutting field of economic growth and development
as an area of specialization, the field of money has been
increasingly active and has received increasing attention in the
past fourteen years.

This recent activity in the money field can be explained in part
by the general logic of scientific progress, according to which
disputed issues are investigated with the aid of more powerful
theoretical tools, and the implications of new approaches are
explored in rigorous detail. Thus, in monetary theory, the issues
raised by Keynes' attack on 'classical' monetary theory have
been worked over with the apparatus of general equilibrium
analysis developed by J. R. Hicks [60] (to the gradual eclipse

* Reprinted from *The American Economic Review*, Vol. LII, no. 3, June 1962,
pp. 335–84; one of a series of survey articles sponsored by the Rockefeller
Foundation.

of the Robertsonian and Swedish period analysis once considered most promising), and Keynes' emphasis on treating money as an asset has been followed by subsequent theorists as a means of bringing money within the general framework of the theory of choice. In larger part, the revival of interest in money is a reflection of external developments—the postwar inflation, the consequent revival of monetary policy, and the persistence of inflation in the face of unemployment—together with recognition of the problems posed for both policy and theory by certain institutional characteristics of the modern economy (notably the widespread holding of liquid assets) and by potential conflicts between the diverse policy objectives now accepted as responsibilities of governmental policy.

The interest of professional economists in these matters has also been directly enlisted in the preparation of testimony and studies for a succession of large-scale enquiries into monetary policy and institutions, most recently the Radcliffe Report in Britain [127] and the Report [128] of the Commission on Money and Credit established by the Committee for Economic Development in the United States.[1] Finally, recent work on both theory and policy has been strongly influenced by the increased postwar emphasis on (and capacity for) econometric model-building and testing, and stimulated by the availability of new data— especially Raymond Goldsmith's data on saving [47] and financial intermediaries [48] in the United States, the Federal Reserve System's flow-of-funds accounts ([126] and subsequent publications), and Milton Friedman and Anna Schwartz' historical series of the United States money supply, forthcoming in [42].

While the impact of Keynes' *General Theory* has been so great that most of recent theory and research on money can be classified either as application and extension of Keynesian ideas or as counter-revolutionary attack on them, it seems preferable in a survey of the field to organize the material according to the main areas of research rather than according to the issues Keynes raised. Readers interested in the present

[1] For a list of Congressional documents bearing on monetary policy, see Friedman [34, pp. 103–40]; to Friedman's list should be added the *Staff Report on Employment, Growth and Price Levels* [129] and the accompanying *Staff Studies.*

status of Keynes' contributions to economics are referred to anniversary assessments by William Fellner and Dudley Dillard [32], James Schlesinger [102], H. G. Johnson [61], and R. E. Kuenne [71]. This survey deals with four broad topics: the neutrality of money; the theory of demand for money, which becomes the theory of velocity of circulation when the demand for money is related to income; the theory of money supply, monetary control, and monetary dynamics; and monetary policy. The theory of interest has been surveyed in a companion article by G. L. S. Shackle [105], and the theory of inflation is to be surveyed in a subsequent article in this *Review* by Martin Bronfenbrenner and Franklyn Holzman.

I. THE CLASSICAL DICHOTOMY AND THE NEUTRALITY OF MONEY

From the standpoint of pure theory, the most fundamental issue raised by Keynes in the *General Theory* lay in his attack on the traditional separation of monetary and value theory, the 'classical dichotomy' as (following Don Patinkin [94]) it has come to be called, according to which relative prices are determined by the 'real' forces of demand and supply and the absolute price level is determined by the quantity of money and its velocity of circulation. Keynes' attack has been followed by a protracted, often confused, and usually intensely mathematical investigation of the 'consistency' or 'validity' of the classical dichotomy, the requirements of a consistent theory of value in a monetary economy, and the conditions under which money will or will not be 'neutral' (in the sense that a change in the quantity of money will not alter the real equilibrium of the system—relative prices and the interest rate). In the course of the controversy at least as much has been learned about the difficulty of extracting theoretical conclusions from systems of equations as has been contributed to usable monetary theory. The argument, it should be noted, has been concerned throughout with a monetary economy characterized by minimal uncertainty, whereas Keynes was concerned with a highly uncertain world in which money provides a major link between present and future (on this point see Shackle [105, p. 211]).

A. *The Integration of Monetary and Value Theory*

The early history of what is often described as 'the Patinkin controversy' is not worth recounting in detail; an annotated bibliography of it may be found in Valavanis [122], and Patinkin's own summary in [90]. It began with Oskar Lange's argument [72] that Say's Law (which in this context is the principle that people sell goods only for the purpose of buying goods) logically precludes any monetary theory, since in combination with Walras' Law (that the total supply of goods and money to the market must be equal to the total demand for goods and money from the market) it implies that the excess demand for money on the market is identically zero regardless of the absolute price level, which therefore is indeterminate. Patinkin took up this charge, shifting the object of criticism to the classical assumption that the demand and supply functions for commodities are homogeneous of degree zero in commodity prices (that is, a doubling of all commodity prices will leave quantities demanded and supplied unchanged —in other words, quantities demanded depend only on relative prices). This criticism was refined and its mathematical formulation clarified in response to subsequent critical contributions, of which the most important was Karl Brunner's demonstration [17] that a consistent monetary theory could be constructed without assigning utility to money.

In its final form at this stage [90], Patinkin's criticism of the classical dichotomy was that there was a logical contradiction between classical value theory, in which demands and supplies of commodities depended only on relative prices and not on the real value of people's cash balances, and the quantity theory of money, in which the dependence of spending on the real value of money balances provides the mechanism by which the quantity of money determines a stable equilibrium absolute price level, a contradiction which could be removed neither by resort to Say's Law nor by abandonment of the quantity theory in favour of some other monetary theory. But, Patinkin argued, the contradiction could be removed, and classical theory reconstituted, by making the demand and supply functions depend on real cash balances as well as relative prices; while this would eliminate the dichotomy, it would preserve the basic features of classical monetary theory, and particularly the invariance of the real equilibrium of the economy (relative prices and the rate of interest) with respect to changes in the quantity of money.

The integration of monetary and value theory through the explicit introduction of real balances as a determinant of behaviour, and the reconstitution of classical monetary theory, is the main theme and contribution of Patinkin's monumentally scholarly work, *Money, Interest, and Prices* [93]. The first part of the book ('Microeconomics') develops the theory of the real balance effect (the effect of a change in the price level on the real value of money balances and hence on expenditure) in terms of a Hicksian exchange economy in which the individual starts each week with an endowment of commodities that must be consumed within the week and a stock of fiat money, and plans to exchange these for commodities to be consumed during the week and cash balances with which to start the next week. The demand for cash balances is a demand for real balances, derived rather artificially from the assumption that though equilibrium prices are fixed at the beginning of the week, cash payments and receipts are randomly distributed over the week and the individual attaches disutility to the prospect of being unable to pay cash on demand. A rise in prices lowers the real value of an individual's initial cash holding and, provided that neither goods nor real balances are 'inferior', reduces his demand for both (implying a less than unit-elastic demand curve for money with respect to its purchasing power); but a proportional rise in prices accompanied by an equiproportional increase in the individual's initial money stock does not alter his behaviour. Extended to the market as a whole, the first property ensures the stability of the money price level, the second yields the quantity theory result that a doubling of everyone's money stock will double prices but leave the real equilibrium unchanged. When lending and borrowing by means of bonds are introduced, this latter result requires a doubling of everyone's initial bond assets or liabilities as well as his money holdings. Patinkin's chief criticism of the classical economists has now been reduced to their failure to analyse the role of the real balance effect in ensuring price level stability; the charge of definite inconsistency can only be fairly pinned to a few specific writers of later vintage.

Carefully worked out as it is, Patinkin's analysis of the real balance effect is conceptually inadequate and crucially incomplete; both defects are attributable to an unsatisfactory analysis of stock-flow relationships. The conceptual inadequacy is inherent in the lumping together of the stock of cash and the week's income of goods into a total of disposable resources and the application of the conventional concept of inferiority to the possible effects of changes in this hybrid total on the quantities of real balances and goods demanded.[1] The incompleteness is inherent in Patinkin's restriction of his analysis of the effects of a disturbance to the single week in which it occurs. Archibald and Lipsey [2] have shown that over succeeding weeks an individual whose real balances differed from their desired level would accumulate or decumulate balances by spending less or more than his income until real balances attained the desired level, at which point expenditure would once again equal income. Thus, they argue, the real balance effect is a transient phenomenon, relevant only to short-run disequilibrium situations. If positions of long-run equilibrium are compared, the effect of a change in the quantity of money does not depend on its initial distribution (since individuals will redistribute it among themselves in adjusting their real balances to the desired level) and the demand for money with respect to its purchasing power has the classical unitary elasticity; finally, real balances can be dropped from the equations determining equilibrium, which can be written as functions of relative prices only.

On the basis of this last result, Archibald and Lipsey attacked the Lange–Patinkin charge of inconsistency in classical theory,

[1] For example, inferiority of real balances implies that if an individual's initial stock of real balances is reduced, his initial commodity endowment being unchanged, he will reduce his planned consumption in the current week sufficiently to increase his planned real balances. By shortening the week and reducing the individual's weekly endowment of commodities proportionately, a procedure which leaves the rate of flow of the individual's income unchanged, it can be made impossible for the individual to cut his commodity consumption sufficiently to increase his planned balances. 'Inferiority' of real balances is therefore not invariant with respect to the time-unit of the analysis. Further, inferiority of real balances would imply that any disturbance to an individual's initial equilibrium would be followed by a 'cobweb' adjustment of his real balances and consumption in succeeding weeks, a pattern difficult to rationalize. I am indebted to the oral tradition of the University of Chicago Money and Banking Workshop for these points.

and showed that a consistent system could be constructed using demand and supply functions homogeneous of degree zero in prices, supplemented by the quantity equation, though this system would not conform to Walras' Law when out of equilibrium. Earlier, Valavanis [122] had disputed Patinkin's apparent victory in the dichotomy debate, and shown that if the (in my opinion, misnamed) Cambridge equation is interpreted as an independent restraint on behaviour rather than as a behaviour relationship conflicting with Walras' Law, there is no inconsistency. J. Encarnación has since shown [31] that Lange's mathematical proof of inconsistency is invalid, and Patinkin's rests on a misuse of the term 'consistency'.

As a subsequent symposium [7] on the Archibald-Lipsey article has helped to show, these demonstrations, while justified perhaps by Patinkin's continued emphasis on the 'inconsistency' theme, are really beside the main point. While a formally consistent theory can be constructed by interpreting velocity as an externally-imposed restraint on monetary behaviour (an interpretation for which there is ample precedent in the literature) this treatment not only leaves velocity itself unexplained on economic grounds, but precludes any analysis of monetary dynamics and the stability of monetary equilibrium by its inability to specify behaviour in disequilibrium conditions. As the better classical monetary theorists saw, these problems are most easily handled by assuming that money balances yield services of utility to their holders; and Patinkin's major contribution has been to elaborate a rigorous formal theory of this approach.

B. *The Neutrality and Nonneutrality of Money*

The second part of Patinkin's book reformulates the argument in terms of a short-run macroeconomic system, Keynesian in structure[1] but based on 'classical' behaviour assumptions, and

---

[1] Goods are produced as well as exchanged; net saving and investment occur but their effects on wealth and productive capacity are abstracted from; for analysis the economy is aggregated into four markets, those for labour services, commodities, bonds, and money. Patinkin uses the dynamic development of this model to investigate Keynes' theory of involuntary unemployment, a subject not considered here; his analytical methods have been adopted by several subsequent writers.

arrives at the classical result that relative prices and the rate of interest are independent of the quantity of money. The significance of this demonstration lies mainly in the assumptions required to establish the neutrality of money [93, Ch. 12]: wage and price flexibility, inelastic expectations, absence of 'money illusion', absence of 'distribution effects', homogeneity of 'bonds', and absence of government debt or open-market operations.[1] This rarefied set of assumptions is the main object of attack in J. G. Gurley and E. S. Shaw's *Money in a Theory of Finance* [52], a central purpose of which is to elucidate the conditions under which money will not be neutral.

Mention must first be made of an earlier, and influential, article by L. A. Metzler [83], whose analysis underlies the final assumption listed above. Metzler argued that the wealth-saving relationship assumed in the use of the Pigou effect by Keynes' critics to demonstrate that price flexibility would maintain full employment in the Keynesian model[2] implied a theory in which changes in the quantity of money could affect the rate of interest (and consequently the rate of growth). Assuming for simplicity that government obligations are fixed in real terms, and that interest on government holdings of its own debt is returned as income to the community, Metzler showed that the price increase consequent on monetary expansion effected by open-market purchase of government debt would leave the

---

[1] Absence of money illusion means that behaviour depends on the real and not the money values of income, balances, and bonds; absence of distribution effects, that behaviour is unaffected by redistributions of total real income, balances, and bonds among individuals, such as result from price-level changes; homogeneity of bonds, that behaviour is affected only by the net creditor position of the private sector, not by the totals and composition of its assets and liabilities; absence of government debt or open market operations, that the net creditor position of the private sector consists in its holding of fiat money, or that, if government debt fixed in real terms is introduced (the Metzler case discussed below), its quantity does not alter when the quantity of money changes. The assumption of absence of distribution effects might seem unnecessary, on the Archibald–Lipsey argument, but that argument does not apply to this model, which by construction cannot be in full stationary equilibrium: see Ball and Bodkin's criticism of Archibald and Lipsey, which the latter accept [7, pp. 44–9].

[2] The Pigou effect in modern usage is the effect on the demand for goods of a change in private real wealth resulting from the effect of a change in the price level on the real value of net private financial assets, the latter consisting of net government debt outstanding (including fiat money) and the part of the money supply backed by gold; it is the real balance effect corrected for the presence of government debt and money issued against private debt.

community with a smaller stock of real assets and a greater willingness to save, thus lowering the equilibrium interest rate, though monetary expansion effected through the printing press would not alter the equilibrium interest rate. As Haberler shortly pointed out [54], Metzler's analysis of open-market operations implicitly rests on a distribution effect (the private sector but not the government being assumed to be influenced by a change in the latter's real debt); but subsequent writers, including Patinkin, have accepted this as a legitimate assumption, and Gurley and Shaw's analysis builds on it.

Gurley and Shaw's book is related to their earlier work on financial intermediaries in relation to economic growth and monetary policy; these aspects of their analysis will be taken up in the appropriate context. Their contribution to the neutrality discussion, apart from their insistence that rigidities, money illusion, expectations, and distribution effects may be quite important in actuality, consists in bringing back into the analysis the monetary and financial structure and the differing liquidity characteristics of different assets excluded by assumption in Patinkin's models. They begin by constructing a simple model alternative to Patinkin's, in which money is not itself government debt but is issued by the monetary authority against private debt ('inside' money, as contrasted with 'outside' money), and showing that in this model the price level is determinate[1] and money is neutral. They then show that money will not be neutral in a system containing inside and outside money, outside bonds, or a variety of securities against which money can be created. The key to these results is that in these cases an increase in the quantity of money of either variety, accompanied by a proportional increase in the prices of goods and private debts, alters the relative quantities of the various

---

[1] Their insistence on the determinacy of the price level, in contrast to what they take to be the implication of Patinkin's approach (which they term 'net money doctrine') [52, p. 76], rests on an understandable misunderstanding. Patinkin's analysis of price-level stability throws the emphasis on the wealth effect of a change in real balances resulting from a price-level change, an effect which only exists when money is a net asset; but it also provides for a substitution effect. Gurley and Shaw's demonstration that the substitution effect is sufficient to determine the price level therefore does not conflict with Patinkin's analysis (for Patinkin's views, see [91, pp. 100–9], though it does show that Patinkin's emphasis on the wealth effect is misplaced and misleading. The broader implications of this point are discussed below.

assets to be held by the public; and their significance to the neutrality debate can be reduced to any arbitrarily low level by arguing that they depend on a distribution effect, and that the appropriate test of neutrality is an equiproportional change in inside money, the assets backing it, and outside assets (see Patinkin [91, p. 108]). It may also be remarked that the results depend in no way on the presence of financial inter-mediaries.

Gurley and Shaw's analysis follows the tradition of Metzler and Patinkin in relating nonneutrality to the existence of government debt; their inside-money analysis merely makes noninterest-bearing as well as interest-bearing government debt a disturber of neutrality. This tradition leaves modern formal monetary theory rather awkwardly dependent on adventitious institutional or historical details; and the question naturally arises whether this is the best that can be done. The source of the difficulty lies in the implicit distribution effect introduced by the recognition that, unlike other debtors, the government does not have to worry about the size of its debts. For this difference there are two reasons: (1) the government can always pay its debts by issuing fresh debts, since it controls the money supply, (2) the government can always command the resources required to pay the interest on its debts, since it possesses the taxing power. The latter is the reason relevant to the level of theoretical generality of the neutrality discussion; and at that level it provides grounds for denying that interest-bearing government debt should be treated as net assets of the public. The existence of government debt implies the levying of taxes to pay the interest on it, and in a world of reasonable certainty these taxes would be capitalized into liabilities equal in magni-tude to the government debt; hence, if distribution effects between individuals are ignored, a change in the real amount of government debt will have no wealth-effect.[1] Finally, if this

---

[1] In an elegant recent article [86] R. A. Mundell, has extended Metzler's analysis by considering explicitly the tax remissions resulting from open-market purchases of government debt. He assumes that corporate taxes are capitalized in the price of equities but that personal income taxes are not capitalized (there being no market for human capital); he allows for the effect of corporate taxation on the incentive to invest; and he demonstrates that Metzler's conclusion is valid if income taxes are remitted, but reversed if corporate taxes are remitted. The nonmarketability of human capital seems an inadequate reason for assuming

logic applies to interest-bearing government debt, why should it not apply to the limiting case of noninterest-bearing government debt, which is equally a debt of the public to itself, and to commodity moneys, which are the same thing though based on custom rather than law?

This line of reasoning suggests that the more elegant approach to monetary theory lies along inside-money rather than outside-money lines, and that the foundation of the theory of monetary equilibrium and stability should be the substitution effect rather than the (in this case nonexistent) wealth effect of a change in real balances. It also has implications for the dichotomy debate: in the inside-money case the economy can be validly dichotomized into a real and a money sector, since the real-balance effect reduces to a change in the relative quantities of real balances and real debt (see Franco Modigliani [58, pp. 183–4] and Patinkin [91, p. 107]). Finally, it suggests an opportunity for a reassessment of Keynes' theory of employment, which is guiltless of the charges brought against it by Pigou and elaborated by Patinkin and others if interpreted as applying to an inside-money world.

II. THE DEMAND FOR MONEY AND THE VELOCITY OF CIRCULATION

As Villard remarked in his earlier survey [123, pp. 316–24], the equation-of-exchange approach to monetary theory was eclipsed by the income-expenditure approach[1] after 1930 largely because of the prevailing tendency to treat velocity as determined in principle by institutional factors governing the rapidity of

that people do not feel richer when income taxes are reduced; consideration of the incentive effects of tax changes introduces an interesting new aspect of the neutrality problem but one that lies at a somewhat lower level of abstraction.

[1] These terms are intended to distinguish the two main (and historically long-established) schools of thought in monetary theory, one of which formulates its analysis in terms of the quantity of money and its velocity of circulation and the other in terms of the determinants of money expenditure, without ensnaring the exposition in the rights and wrongs of Keynes' protracted quarrel with what he understood by 'the quantity theory'. As this section explains, neither the quantity theory nor the Keynesian theory is now what it was in the 1930's; in particular, the modern quantity theorist is committed to neither full employment nor the constancy of velocity, and his theory is a theory of the relation between the stock of money and the level of money income, that is, a theory of velocity and not of prices and employment.

circulation of the medium of exchange and as in practice a constant—a treatment clearly contradicted by experience in the 1930's. The alternative theory expounded by Keynes emphasized the determinants of expenditure; but it also contained a monetary theory founded on the function of money as a store of value and on the special characteristics of money as a form of holding wealth. This theory has been refined and elaborated by subsequent writers in the Keynesian tradition. In the process, Keynes' most extreme departure from previous analysis of the demand for money—his emphasis on the speculative demand for money at the expense of the precautionary—has been gradually abandoned (as has his awkward separation of the transactions and speculative demand for money), and the speculative motive has been relegated to the short run and reabsorbed into the general theory of asset holding. On the other side, the treatment of velocity as determined by payments institutions, while prominent in some expositions of the quantity theory, was by no means the core of classical monetary theory, which clearly recognized the opportunity cost of holding wealth in monetary form; and modern followers of the classical tradition, building on this foundation, treat velocity explicitly as reflecting a demand for money derived from preferences concerning the disposition of wealth.

In consequence, contemporary monetary theorists, whether avowedly 'Keynesian' or 'quantity', approach the demand for money in essentially the same way, as an application of the general theory of choice, though the former tend to formulate their analysis in terms of the demand for money as an asset alternative to other assets, and the latter, in terms of the demand for the services of money as a good. Aside from some conceptual perplexities concerning the relation between capital and income in this context, the chief substantive issues outstanding are three: first, what specific collection of assets corresponds most closely to the theoretical concept of money—an issue that arises as soon as the distinguishing characteristic of money ceases to be its function as a medium of exchange; second, what the variables are on which the demand for money so defined depends; and third, whether the demand for money is sufficiently stable to provide, in conjunction with the quantity of money, a better explanation of observed movements of money income and other aggregates than is provided by models built around income-expenditure relationships. These are essentially empirical issues, to which empirical research has as yet produced no conclusive answers; and they clearly have an important practical bearing on monetary policy.

A. *Developments in Liquidity Preference Theory*

To begin with the recent development of Keynesian analysis of the demand for money, subsequent contributions have been concerned with four aspects of Keynes' treatment of this subject: the separation of the demand into a transactions demand dependent on income and a liquidity-preference demand dependent on the rate of interest; the emphasis on the speculative element in liquidity preference; the neglect of wealth as a determinant of liquidity preference; and the aggregation of all assets other than money into bonds implicit in the use of a single (long-term) rate of interest.

The separation of the demand for money into two parts, besides being mathematically inelegant, incorporated the mechanical treatment of transactions demand that Keynes had criticized in the quantity theory. Keynesian writers (for example, Alvin Hansen [56, pp. 66–67]) began to treat transactions demand as reflecting economic behaviour and particularly as being interest-elastic, from which it was a short step to making the demand for money as a whole depend on income and the rate of interest. The logic of treating transactions demand as reflecting rational choice was subsequently provided by W. J. Baumol [9] and James Tobin [117], the former's analysis being more interesting in that it links the problem to inventory theory. Both authors show that an economic unit starting a period with a transactions balance to be spent evenly over the period, and having the opportunity of investing idle funds at interest and withdrawing them as needed at a cost partly fixed per withdrawal, will disinvest at more frequent intervals (carry a lower average cash balance) the higher the rate of interest. They also show that the average cash balance held by the unit will be higher the higher the amount of the initial transactions balance, but less than proportionately higher.[1]

[1] Ralph Turvey [121, p. 33], following Richard Selden [104, pp. 209–10], argues that the interest-elasticity conclusion does not extend to aggregate

Keynes' emphasis on the extremely short-run speculative motive as the source of interest-elasticity in the liquidity demand for money was one of the main targets of Keynes' critics. Subsequent Keynesian writing has stressed Keynes' alternative explanation of liquidity preference, which rests this interest-elasticity on uncertainty about the future interest rate rather than on a definite expectation about its level; this explanation is really the precautionary motive in disguise (see Johnson [61, p. 8]). An elegant exposition of both explanations, using the theory of portfolio management, has been provided by Tobin [115].

The introduction of the value of wealth, which itself depends on the rate of interest, as an explicit determinant of the demand for money was part of a more general process of freeing Keynes' theory from its short-period equilibrium assumptions. It implied for the theory of liquidity preference, as noticed by Lloyd Metzler [83], Ralph Turvey [120] and Frank Brechling [10], that the liquidity-preference curve would be different for a change in the quantity of money brought about by fiscal policy than for a change effected by open-market operations (these two curves, and a third corresponding to constant wealth, are discussed in Turvey [21, Ch. 2]). It also introduces the difficulty, noted earlier by Borje Kragh [69], that the speculative demand curve for money traced out by open-market operations will differ according to the size of the units in which these are conducted, since the effects on wealth will differ. The wealth effects of discontinuity in open-market operations are exploited in Sidney Weintraub's recent contention [124, pp. 156–60] that the speculative demand curve is irreversible, as Richard Davis [30] has subsequently pointed out. At a far more fundamental level, the analysis of the demand for money that emerges from these developments, in which the

behaviour because a change in the interest rate will have the opposite effect on the demand for cash of a unit facing a maturing debt and having the alternatives of holding cash in the interim or spending it and borrowing later. This argument involves an elementary confusion between saving behaviour and asset management: savings effects of interest rate changes aside, the unit in question would have the same alternative of investing its idle cash at interest, and react the same way. Turvey also argues [121, pp. 28–30] that an increase in the level of a unit's transactions will raise transactions demand only in a probability sense, since there may be an offsetting change in the timing-structures of the unit's payments and receipts.

demand for money depends on the interrelated variables income, the rate of interest, and wealth, raises important conceptual (and econometric) difficulties not always fully appreciated by monetary theorists; these difficulties will be referred to later in connection with Milton Friedman's restatement of the quantity theory.

The fourth development stemming from Keynes' theory of the demand for money has been the disaggregation of assets other than money and the elaboration of liquidity preference theory into a general theory of the relative prices of (rates of return on) assets of different types. The chief contributions in the direct line of Keynes' own thought, by Joan Robinson [98] and Richard Kahn [63], are primarily concerned with reasserting Keynes' view that the long-term rate of interest is determined by expectations about the future long-term rate, against Hicks' dismissal of it as a bootstrap theory and his attempt to explain the long-term rate as an average of expected short-term rates [60, pp. 163–4]. Robinson and Kahn both employ a division of assets into cash, bills, bonds, and equities, and a classification of asset-holders into contrasting types according to whether their asset preferences are dominated by capital-uncertainty or income-uncertainty; but Robinson is concerned to set the argument against the background of a growing economy, while Kahn concentrates on a rather subtle analysis of the interaction of the precautionary and speculative motives.

In contrast, U.S. contributions have been prompted by concern with the problems posed for monetary, fiscal, and debt-management policy by the wartime legacy of a large public debt of short average maturity; two early articles influential in subsequent thinking were those of Roland McKean [80] and Richard Musgrave [87]. The common feature of subsequent work is the treatment of assets as possessing varying degrees of liquidity, and the application of general equilibrium theory to the determination of their relative prices (yields), which are treated as the outcome of the interaction of asset preferences and the relative quantities of the different assets available. This approach (which is also central in the analysis of Robinson and Kahn just mentioned) is exemplified in W. L. Smith's study of debt management for the Joint Economic Committee [110] and Ralph Turvey's book on interest rates and asset prices [121]. The latter is notable for its explicit general equilibrium approach and its careful attention to the requirements of consistent aggregation. The formulation of monetary theory as part of a more general theory of asset holding has been carried farthest by the group working at Yale University under the inspiration of James Tobin; their 'portfolio balance' approach has been strongly influenced by Harry Markowitz's work on rational investor behaviour (notably [77a]). Unfortunately little of this group's work is yet available in print (see, however, Tobin [113] [115] [116]).

The formulation of the general-equilibrium approach to the theory of asset prices and yields in the literature just described has some implicit biases which are apt to mislead the unwary, especially in its application to the analysis of the term structure of interest rates.[1] In the first place, there is a tendency to follow too closely Hicks' original sketch of the approach [59] in identifying the typical asset-holder with a bank, borrowing for a shorter term than it lends and therefore preferring the shorter-term assets. In the second place, emphasis on the slippery and ill-defined quality of liquidity as the characteristic differentiating alternative assets tends to divert attention from the linkage of asset markets by speculation, and so to exaggerate the sensitivity of the interest-rate pattern to changes in the relative quantities of assets.[2] In this connection it is appropriate to refer briefly[3] to some recent work on the term structure of interest rates by John Culbertson [29] and Joseph Conard [24, Part III], which on its empirical side contributes to filling the gap noted by Villard [123, pp. 336–7] between the theory and the his-

---

[1] This phrase has reference to the pattern of rates on loans of successively longer maturity; statistically it is represented by the 'yield curve', which charts the yields on government debts against their maturities. In the English literature the problem appears as that of the relation between the long and the short rate of interest (the bill rate and the bond rate), a reflection of the institutional fact that the British government obtains its short-term financing predominantly by three-months bills of exchange, and has a substantial volume of perpetual debt ('consols') outstanding.

[2] The sensitivity of the rate pattern to changes in the relative quantities of short-term and long-term debt is the crucial empirical issue in some recent controversies about monetary policy, especially the 'bills only' policy.

[3] Shackle's survey of interest theory [105], to which the reader has been referred in the introduction, unfortunately makes very little reference to rate-structure theory, presumably because it has not been discussed recently in English journals. The interested reader is referred to Conard's useful book [24].

torical facts of interest-rate behaviour. Both authors arrive at essentially the same major result, that short and long rates tend to move together in a rational way, though Culbertson regards his analysis as contradicting the classical 'expectations' theory whereas Conard regards his as confirming a modified version of it. The explanation of this difference is that Culbertson identifies accepted theory with the incorrect Hicks–Lutz formulation of it, according to which the investor is depicted as choosing between holding a bond to maturity and investing in successive short-term loans over the same period, whereas Conard identifies it with the correct formulation, in which the investor compares the expected yields (including interest and changes in capital value) of alternative assets over the period for which he expects or is obliged to remain invested. A more recent study by David Meiselman [81] advances both the theory and explanation of the rate structure (and incidentally refutes one of Culbertson's main arguments against the expectations theory) by interpreting the yield curve as expressing expected future short-term rates and explaining changes in it as the market's reaction to errors of expectation.

B. *Restatement of the Quantity Theory*

While Keynes' formulation of the theory of demand for money has been evolving in the directions just described, a fundamentally very similar formulation has been developed by a group of scholars associated with the University of Chicago, inspired by Milton Friedman and claiming allegiance to the quantity theory as handed down in the oral tradition of that institution. The most complete statement of this group's basic theory— which tends usually to be mentioned only briefly in the course of presenting the results of empirical research—is contained in the condensed and rather cryptic restatement of the quantity theory by Friedman that introduces four of their empirical studies [41], a restatement that takes the reader at a hard pace from the fundamental theory to the simplifications required for its empirical application. The central points in the restatement are that the quantity theory is a theory of the demand for money, not of output, money income, or prices; and that money is an asset or capital good, so that the demand for it is a problem in capital theory. In formulating the demand for money as a form of capital, however, Friedman differs from the Keynesian theorists in starting from the fundamentals of capital theory. He begins with the broad concept of wealth as comprising all sources of income, including human beings, and relates the demand for money to total wealth and the expected future streams of money income obtainable by holding wealth in alternative forms. Then, by a series of mathematical simplifications, approximations of nonobservable variables (of which the most important is the representation of the influence of human wealth by the ratio of nonhuman to human wealth), simplifying economic assumptions, and rearrangements of variables, he arrives at a demand function for money which depends on the price level, bond and equity yields, the rate of change of the price level, income, the ratio of nonhuman to human wealth, and a taste variable; finally, he makes neat use of the homogeneity assumption to show that the demand for real balances depends only on real variables and that it can be reformulated as a velocity function depending on the same variables.

In its final form, Friedman's demand function for money is hard to distinguish from a modern Keynesian formulation, especially in view of his remark that the nonhuman to human wealth ratio 'is closely allied to what is usually defined as the ratio of wealth to income' [41, p. 8]. The apparent similarity is misleading, however, because what comes out as income originally entered as wealth, i.e. capitalized income, the process of capitalizing it being absorbed by Friedman's simplifications into the yield and wealth-ratio arguments of the function; and, as Friedman indicated by various remarks and has since demonstrated by the application of his permanent income concept to the explanation of the behaviour of velocity [38], the 'income' relevant to this equation is not income as measured in the national accounts but income conceived of as the net return on a stock of wealth, or wealth measured by the income it yields. The use of 'income' to represent what is really a wealth variable has incidentally contributed to some minor confusions of stock and flow concepts in the writings of Chicago monetary theorists, especially in the alternative formulation of the theory of demand for money as an application of demand theory developed by Richard Selden [104], where money rather than its services is described as the good demanded, the elasticity relating changes in the stock of money demanded to changes in the flow of income is described as an income-elasticity, and money is classed on the basis of the empirical magnitude of this elasticity as a luxury good.

Friedman's application to monetary theory of the basic principle of capital theory—that income is the yield on capital, and capital the present value of income—is probably the most important development in monetary theory since Keynes' *General Theory*. Its theoretical significance lies in the conceptual integration of wealth and income as influences on behaviour: Keynes ignored almost completely the influence of wealth, as was legitimate in short-period analysis; and while subsequent writers in the Keynesian tradition have reintroduced wealth they have generally followed the Cambridge practice of re-stricting wealth to nonhuman property, a practice which encourages uncritical treatment of wealth and income as entirely independent influences on behaviour. In consequence, as mentioned earlier, much of the recent monetary literature contains formulations of the demand for money relating it to income, wealth, and the rate of interest, variables which are in fact interdependent and the use of which in this way involves inelegant redundancy and promotes errors in both theoretical reasoning and empirical applications.

The most important implication of Friedman's analysis, however, concerns not the formulation of monetary theory but the nature of the concept of 'income' relevant to monetary analysis, which, as explained above, should correspond to the notion of expected yield on wealth rather than the conventions of national income accounting. This concept Friedman has elaborated under the name of 'permanent income', and em-ployed in his theory of the consumption function [35] and subsequent empirical work on the demand for money [38]. The statistical application of it has involved estimating expected income from past income, which means that empirically the theory is very similar to theories employing lagged income as a determinant of behaviour.[1] This similarity exemplifies a serious

[1] These brief remarks do justice neither to Friedman nor to other consumption theorists, a number of whom have been working towards similar theories (see Johnson [61]).

B

problem in the empirical application and testing of economic theories—the theoretical interpretation of empirical results—which is especially acute in the interpretation of empirical findings on the demand for money because of the interrelationship of income, wealth, and interest.

C. *The Distinguishing Characteristics of Money*

While the treatment of money as an asset distinguished from other assets by its superior liquidity is common ground among contemporary theorists, the transition from the conception of money as a medium of exchange to money as a store of value has raised new problems for debate among monetary theorists. These problems result from recognition of the substitutability between money (conventionally defined as medium of exchange) and the wide range of alternative financial assets provided by government debt and the obligations of financial institutions, and between money and the access to credit provided by an elaborate credit system, in a financially advanced economy. They concern the related empirical questions of the definition of an appropriate monetary magnitude, and the specification of the variables on which the demand for the selected magnitude depends, questions that pose little difficulty when money is defined as the medium of exchange and its velocity is assumed to be determined by institutional factors. These questions lead into the fundamental question of the importance of the quantity of money in monetary theory and monetary policy, since unless the demand for money—defined to correspond to some quantity the central bank can influence—can be shown to be a stable function of a few key variables, the quantity of money must be a subordinate and not a strategic element in both the explanation and the control of economic activity. Argument and opinion about these issues have frequently been clouded by confusion between constant velocity and a stable velocity function, and between elasticity and instability of the function. In discussing them, it is convenient to describe first the main schools of thought on these issues,[1] and then the empirical research bearing on them.

---

[1] To keep the bibliography within reasonable bounds, the references below are confined as far as possible to authors who have supported their theories with empirical research, or to recent writings.

At the cost of some arbitrary oversimplification, one can distinguish broadly four main schools of thought. At one extreme are those who continue to find the distinguishing characteristic of money in its function as medium of exchange, and define it as currency plus demand deposits adjusted [73]. Next to them are the Chicago quantity theorists, who define the function of money more broadly as a temporary abode of purchasing power,[1] and in their empirical work define money as currency plus total commercial bank deposits adjusted, largely to obtain a consistent long statistical series [104] [38]. Both schools believe that there is a stable demand for money (velocity function), though they define money differently. A third school, at the opposite extreme, consists of those, usually specially interested in monetary policy rather than theory as such, who carry recognition of the similarity between money and other realizable assets or means of financing purchases to the point of rejecting money in favour of some much broader concept, measurable or unmeasurable. A measurable concept is exemplified by the long-established Federal Reserve Board theory that what matters is the total amount of credit outstanding, the quantity of money exercising an influence only because bank credit is a component of total credit (see for example [57, pp. 261–3 and 272–6]). An unmeasurable concept is exemplified by the Radcliffe Committee's concept of the liquidity of the economy [127, Ch. 6], the theory of which was left unexplained in its Report but has since been expounded by Richard Sayers [101]; according to this more extreme theory velocity is a meaningless number, the economy being able to economize on money by substituting credit for it without limit [127, p. 133]. This school, in both its variants, does not so much advance a theory as assert a position that implies a highly elastic, complex, or unstable velocity function. The serious controversy of recent years has been aroused by a fourth school, in between those already mentioned, which has been concerned with the implications for velocity of the presence of a substantial volume of liquid assets closely substitutable for money. In the early years after the war, this school was mainly concerned with the influence of short-term public debt; since the mid-'fifties, the centre of attention has shifted to the liabilities of nonbank financial intermediaries.

[1] The phrase is Milton Friedman's.

The leading figures in this last development are J. G. Gurley and E. S. Shaw, who in a series of contributions [50] [51] [53] culminating in a major theoretical work [52] have developed an analysis of the role of finance and particularly of nonbank financial intermediaries in economic development which has important implications for monetary theory. Gurley and Shaw start from the fact that real economic development is accompanied by a process of financial development in which primary securities (those issued to finance expenditure) become differentiated and there emerge financial intermediaries—of which commercial banks are only one variety—whose function is to enable asset holders to hold primary securities indirectly in the more attractive forms of liabilities issued by the intermediaries. Contrary to the main stream of both classical and Keynesian monetary theory, which treats the financial structure as of secondary importance and relates the demand for money to the long-term rate of interest or to the rate of return on real capital, Gurley and Shaw maintain that monetary theory must take account of these details of financial organization and development, since they affect the demand for money. In particular, they argue that because nonbank financial intermediaries generally offer liabilities which are closer substitutes for money than for primary securities, and hold small reserves of money themselves, their growth tends to reduce the demand for money. One implication of this analysis, which comes out more strongly in their remarks on monetary policy than in their theory,[1] but to which they do not in fact commit themselves, is that the 'quantity of money' relevant for monetary theory and policy should include the liabilities of nonbank financial intermediaries.

Gurley and Shaw's work has provoked a number of critical journal articles, but those most specifically concerned with their theoretical analysis of the influence of nonbank intermediaries on the demand for money (by Culbertson [27] and Aschheim [3]) misunderstand both Gurley and Shaw's argument and the theory of credit creation.[2] The important question Gurley and

[1] Gurley and Shaw believe that present methods of credit control discriminate against banks in their competition with nonbank intermediaries, weakening the effectiveness of monetary policy over the long run, and unlike most of their critics are prepared to contemplate extensions of the central bank's regulatory powers.

[2] Patinkin's review [91] of the book translates Gurley and Shaw's argument

Shaw raise is the empirical one of whether explanation of the demand for money requires introduction of the amounts of or yields on nonbank intermediary liabilities. This requires an elaborate statistical analysis of the demand for money and other assets which they have not yet produced. In [53] they show only that the facts of financial development in the United States can be rationalized by their theory; and Gurley's independent demonstration [49] that interest rates in the postwar period can be explained on the assumption that an increase in liquid assets reduces the demand for money by half as much—that is, that a correspondingly weighted sum of money and liquid assets can be used to represent the 'quantity of money' in applying monetary theory—does not prove that money alone would do less well; indeed Gurley explains in an Appendix why money alone could have been used. The results of recent empirical research on the demand for money and velocity by other economists described below tend to contradict Gurley and Shaw's contention, since the writers concerned find it possible to explain the demand for money without reference to the variety of alternative assets and do not discover the downward trend in demand for money implied by Gurley and Shaw's thesis. This is, however, only an indirect test; and the empirical research in question is itself controversial.

D. *Empirical Research on the Demand for Money*

Prior to the *General Theory*, empirical research on velocity was primarily concerned with the measurement of the institutional determinants of transactions velocity; since then, attention has shifted to econometric explanation of income velocity and its alternative formulation, the demand for money,[1] one of the

---

into his own language and interprets the effect of financial intermediation as an increase in the liquidity of bonds which decreases the demand for money and increases its interest-elasticity. Alvin Marty's review [78] makes the interesting theoretical point that the introduction of a substitute does not necessarily increase the elasticity of demand. Neither reviewer notices that Gurley and Shaw infer increased elasticity only in the special case of an unfunding of government debt, and present a satisfactory reason for it [52, pp. 162–6].

[1] For discussion of the earlier literature, see Villard [123] and Selden [104]; a useful survey of the econometric studies preceding their own work is given by Bronfenbrenner and Mayer [13]. The more traditional type of research on transactions velocity has been continued by a number of contemporary economists, notably George Garvey [46].

prime objects being to determine the existence or otherwise of the Keynesian liquidity trap. An influential early contribution by James Tobin [114] followed Keynes' theory in estimating idle balances by subtracting from total deposits an estimate of active balances derived from the maximum recorded velocity of circulation, and found a rough hyperbolic relationship between idle balances and interest rates, implying a liquidity trap. This relationship broke down for the postwar years, one reason being its failure to include the influence of total wealth; and subsequent researchers have generally preferred to avoid its assumption of a separable and proportional transactions demand in favour of analysing the total demand for money. Tobin's method has, however, been employed in a more sophisticated form in a recent major study by Martin Bronfenbrenner and Thomas Mayer [13], which relates the demand for idle money (total money being defined as currency plus demand deposits adjusted) to the short-term interest rate, wealth, and idle balances of the previous year. They find that the last two variables explain most of the fluctuations in idle balances, and that the demand for idle balances is interest-inelastic with no tendency for the elasticity to increase as the rate falls. They interpret this last result as evidence against the liquidity trap; the validity of this inference depends on whether the liquidity trap is identified with infinite elasticity at some positive interest rate or an unlimited increase in the quantity of money demanded as the interest rate falls.

Estimates of the total demand function for money, besides avoiding arbitrary assumptions about transactions velocity, are easier to relate to income velocity than estimates of the Tobin type, since they usually use income as one of the explanatory variables.[1] Among a number of such estimates the two most important, in terms of length of period covered, simplicity of the demand function fitted, and intrinsic theoretical interest, are those by Henry Latané [73] and to Milton Friedman [38]. Latané, adopting what he called a pragmatic approach to the constant-velocity and Keynesian formulations of demand for money, found that a simple linear relationship between the ratio of money (currency plus demand deposits) to income and the

[1] An interesting exception is Harold Lydall's derivation of the demand for money from the hypothesis of a constant ratio of liquidity to wealth [77].

reciprocal of high-grade long-term interest rates fitted the historical data closely. Friedman's contribution builds on Selden's earlier finding (104) that the secular decline in velocity could be explained by the hypothesis that the demand for money (currency plus total commercial bank deposits) increases more rapidly than income (money is a 'luxury good'), a finding apparently inconsistent with the fact that income and velocity vary together over the cycle. Friedman resolves the paradox by hypothesizing that the demand for real balances is an elastic function of permanent income, and showing that the apparent inconsistency of the cyclical behaviour of velocity with this hypothesis disappears when the expected income and expected prices indicated by the theory are used instead of their observed counterparts; moreover, since this empirical analysis explains velocity without introducing interest rates into the demand function for money, it seems to dispose of the liquidity trap.

These two empirical demand functions for money apparently conflict, in that Latané's depends on both income (with a unitary income elasticity) and the long-term interest rate, whereas Friedman's depends only on income, with an income-elasticity substantially above unity. But there is no necessary conflict, since Friedman's definition of money includes time deposits, and may therefore absorb most of the substitution between demand deposits and currency and interest-bearing assets induced by interest-rate changes. The real issue is which definition of money gives the better empirical results. Latané has since shown [74] that his formulation fits the subsequent data well. He explains the difference between the income-elasticities of the two functions by the facts that over the period covered by Friedman's calculations time deposits (whose inclusion he questions on theoretical grounds) grew more rapidly than demand deposits, and the long-term interest rate declined from 6·4 to 2·9 per cent. (Latané also adduces evidence for the existence of a liquidity trap, though he prefers to explain it by the cost of bond transactions rather than by Keynes' speculative motive.) Friedman's demand function, by contrast, does not fit the subsequent data, since the secular decline in velocity has reversed itself (Latané's analysis would attribute this to the subsequent upward movement of interest rates). Friedman has since been experimenting with an extended permanent income hypothesis that allows for changes in the confidence with which expectations are held [37]. Latané's demand function, incidentally, can be used to illustrate the difficulty of interpretation mentioned earlier: if wealth is assumed to be measured by income capitalized at the long-term interest rate, the quantity of money demanded in Latané's function can be expressed alternatively as a function of interest and wealth or of wealth and income,[1] thus being consistent with a variety of theoretical formulations.

The empirical studies of demand for money just discussed have a bearing on the fundamental issue, the subject of continued controversy in the history of monetary theory: whether monetary theory is more usefully formulated in terms of the demand for and supply of money or of the influence of money on expenditure and income—the equation-of-exchange approach or the income-expenditure approach. This issue, which Keynes' promulgation of the propensity to consume as a behaviour relationship more stable than the discredited velocity of circulation seemed to have settled finally in favour of the income-expenditure approach, has become less settled with the postwar failure of the simple consumption function and the increasing complexity of Keynesian models on the one hand, and the increasing sophistication of modern adherents of the velocity approach on the other.

The counterattack on Keynesian income theory first launched by Friedman [36] [41] has been carried further in an article by Friedman and Gary Becker [43], which argues that the proper test of Keynesian theory is not the stability of the consumption function but its ability to predict consumption from investment, and produces some evidence that the investment multiplier is a poorer predictor of consumption than is the trend of consumption. In reply, Lawrence Klein [67] and John Johnston [62] have argued that a proper test should be concerned with the

---

[1] In [74] Latané uses a linear relationship between income velocity and the rate of interest, $V = 0.77r + 0.38$, where $V = Y/M$, the quantity of money divided into income. This yields the demand function for money, $M = Y/(0.77r + 0.38)$. Using the definition $W = Y/r$, this can be written equivalently as

$$M = \frac{W}{0.77 + 0.38/r} \text{ or } M = \frac{W}{0.77 + 0.38W/Y}$$

sophisticated and not the naïve version of a theory, and should test the predictive power of the complete model and not just one part of it. This preliminary skirmish probably indicates the main lines of the battle that is likely to follow publication of a major study by Friedman and David Meiselman [44], which shows by exhaustive statistical tests on U.S. data since 1897, that except for the 1930's, the quantity of money has been a better predictor of consumption than has autonomous spending.

These results pose an important theoretical problem, since they imply that a change in the quantity of money that has no wealth-effect nevertheless will have an effect on consumption even though it has no effect on interest rates. The difficulty of understanding how this can be prompted the dissatisfaction of Keynes, Wicksell, and other income-expenditure theorists with the quantity theory, and provides the hard core of contemporary resistance to it. Friedman and Meiselman's explanation of their results may therefore initiate a new and possibly fruitful debate on how money influences activity.

III. THE SUPPLY OF MONEY, MONETARY CONTROL, AND MONETARY DYNAMICS

A. *The Supply of Money*

The theory of money supply is virtually a newly-discovered area of monetary research. The general practice in monetary theory has been to treat the quantity of money as determined directly by the monetary authority, without reference to the links intervening between reserves provided by the central bank on the one hand, and the total of currency and bank deposits on the other. This treatment has rested on a mechanical analysis of the determination of money supply, very similar to the out-moded treatment of velocity, in which the money supply is related to the reserve base by a multiplier determined by the reserve ratio observed by the banking system, and the ratio between currency and deposits held by the public. In conformity with developments on the side of demand, the trend of recent research on money supply has been towards treating these ratios as behaviour relationships reflecting asset choices rather than as exogenous variables, and elaborating the analysis to include the part played by other financial intermediaries than commercial banks, in the process evolving a less mechanical theory of central bank control. In part, recent developments in this area reflect a more general tendency to formulate the dynamics of monetary change in terms of the adjustment of actual to desired stocks rather than in terms of changes in flows.

Though Keynes followed convention in treating the quantity of money as a direct policy variable, other monetary theorists (an early example is Kragh [70]) applied the notion of liquidity preference to the reserve behaviour of banks, and the same idea has been incorporated in various Keynesian models (not always consistently) by making the money supply vary with the rate of interest. Theorists concerned with the money supply have, however, tended until recently to stick to the mechanical 'money multiplier' approach, extending it to allow for the different reserve requirements against time and demand deposits and the demand for money by financial intermediaries; and empirical research has followed the same line, partitioning changes in the quantity of money among changes in the currency-deposit and reserve-deposit ratios and the reserve base, and changes in the reserve base among changes in reserve bank liabilities and assets. These techniques can be extremely fruitful—notable examples are Donald Shelby's investigation of the monetary implications of the growth of financial intermediaries [107], and Brunner's empirical study of U.S. monetary policy in the middle 1930's [15]—but asset ratios are a crude technique for representing behaviour relationships.

Philip Cagan's study of the demand for currency relative to the total money supply [19] has broken new ground in attempting an economic explanation of the ratio of currency to currency plus total deposits. Cagan examines a number of possible determining factors, and finds that expected real income *per capita* explains most of the decline in the ratio from 1875 to 1919, while changes in the net cost of holding currency instead of deposits explain most of the variation in the ratio from 1919 to 1955, though the rate of personal income tax (taken to represent the possible gain from tax evasion permitted by using currency for transactions) is required to explain the rise in the currency ratio in the Second World War.

Other researchers have concerned themselves with the response of the banking system to changes in reserves, though so far the published results have been theoretical rather than empirical. Recent work on this problem has departed from the 'money-multiplier' approach in three respects: first, in basing the analysis on the behaviour of the individual bank instead of the banking system; second, in applying economic theory to the explanation of the level of reserves desired by the bank and relating its behaviour in expanding or contracting its assets to the difference between its actual and its desired reserves; and third, in treating the loss of reserves consequent on expansion as a stochastic process. These innovations are exemplified in two recent articles, both intended as a basis for empirical research: Brunner's schema for the supply theory of money [16], the central feature of which is a relationship between a bank's surplus reserves and its desired rate of change in its asset portfolio, formulated in terms of a 'loss coefficient' measuring the (probable) loss of surplus reserves per dollar of asset expansion; and Daniel Orr and W. J. Mellon's analysis of bank credit expansion [89], which applies inventory theory to the bank's holding of reserves against cash losses (which are assumed to be random and normally distributed). Orr and Mellon show, in contrast to the results of money-multiplier analysis, that the marginal expansion ratio will be lower than the average for a monopoly bank, and lower for a banking system than for a monopoly bank; and that for a banking system the marginal expansion ratio depends on the distribution of the additional reserves among banks.

B. *Monetary Control: A Theoretical Issue*

The research just mentioned is concerned with introducing into the theory of money supply recognition of the fact that commercial banks are profit-maximizing institutions with economic behaviour patterns on which the central bank must operate to control the money supply. The fact that monetary control operates in this way is the source of one group of issues in recent discussions of monetary policy, to be described in the next section; it also poses the interesting theoretical question of what powers the central bank needs to control the price level. This question has been raised and discussed by Gurley and Shaw [52, Ch. 6], who conclude their book by contrasting monetary control in a private commercial banking system with their standard case, in which the government determines the nominal quantity of money and the deposit rate on it. Unfortunately their argument is nonrigorous and inconsistent: having shown [52, pp. 261–2] that control of the nominal quantity of bank reserves and the rate of interest paid on these reserves is sufficient for control of the price level (though they argue that this control is weaker than in their standard case because bank liquidity preferences or deposit rates may change independently of central bank action), they conclude their discussion of the technical apparatus of monetary control with the statement that 'of three indirect techniques—fixing nominal reserves, setting the reserve-balance rate, and setting members' own deposit rate—the Central Bank can get along with any two in regulating all nominal variables in the economic system' [52, pp. 274–5].[1] Patinkin [91, pp. 112–16] has shown that this statement is incorrect, and that the central bank needs to control nominal reserves and one of the interest rates.[2]

C. *Monetary Dynamics*

As mentioned above, one of the recent innovations in the theory of money supply is the analysis of bank response to changes in reserves in terms of the adjustment of actual to desired reserves. This way of stating the problem reflects a more general tendency toward the formulation of monetary dynamics in terms of adjustment of actual to desired stocks, associated in turn with the formulation of monetary theory in terms of asset choices as described in the previous section. This tendency has developed somewhat apart from, and has been concerned with more fundamental issues than, the controversy over the interrelated issues of stock versus flow analysis and liquidity-preference versus loanable-funds theories that has broken out anew since the war. Much of the relevant literature on the latter subject

[1] Gurley and Shaw also state as a prerequisite of monetary control that the authorities take steps to ensure the moneyness of bank deposits; the necessity for this is debatable.

[2] Patinkin goes on to argue that price-level determinacy requires fixity of one nominal quantity and one yield, and would be secured by fixity of the nominal quantity of (non-interest-bearing) outside money; and that therefore Gurley and Shaw should have considered the means by which the central bank changes the price level, instead of the powers required to determine it. This argument raises the question discussed earlier, of the usefulness of founding monetary theory on the real-balance effect.

has been surveyed by Shackle [105]; unfortunately, Shackle's discussion of the issues is vitiated by the erroneous belief that the presence of both a stock of old securities and a flow of new securities implies a conflict of forces—stock demand and supply, and flow demand and supply—operating on the interest rate, and that this conflict poses a dilemma for monetary theory that can only be resolved by the postulation of two rates of interest. It is therefore necessary to describe the controversy briefly, before turning to the more important development in monetary dynamics.

Modern controversy over liquidity-preference versus loanable funds theories starts from Hicks' demonstration of the formal equivalence of the two [60, pp. 160–2]; Hicks used the fact that Walras' Law permits the elimination of one of the equations in a general equilibrium system to argue that one can omit either the excess-demand-for-money equation, leaving a loanable-funds theory of interest, or the excess-demand-for-securities equation, leaving a liquidity-preference theory of interest. The omitted equations are flow equations; William Fellner and Harold Somers [33] subsequently showed that they could be identified with the desired change in the stock of money or securities over the market period, so that flow analysis and stock analysis of monetary equilibrium were equivalent. Fellner and Somers also argued in favour of the loanable-funds theory and against the liquidity-preference theory that, as the rate of interest is the price of securities, it is more sensible to regard it as determined by the demand for and supply of securities than by the demand for and supply of money. This led to a controversy with L. R. Klein [68], who objected to Fellner and Somers' assumption that the period of analysis starts with equilibrium between actual and desired stocks as begging the question of stock versus flow theory, and declared that the real difference between the liquidity-preference and loanable-funds theories was a dynamic one, liquidity-preference theory maintaining that the rate of interest would change in response to an excess demand for or supply of money, not an excess supply of or demand for securities [68, pp. 236–41].[1]

---

[1] An excess demand for money does not necessarily imply an excess supply of securities, since it may be accompanied by an excess supply of goods.

In commenting on the controversy, Brunner [68, pp. 247–51] pointed out that Fellner and Somers' analysis, while correct, evaded the real issue that Klein was raising—that there is a difference between the dynamic adjustment processes of markets in which the object of demand is primarily a stock to be held, and of those in which the object of demand is primarily a flow to be consumed; but he sided with Fellner and Somers against Klein on the dynamic determinants of interest-rate changes. Earlier, Lerner had produced a much-quoted but untraceable objection to Hicks' original argument: that if the excess demand equation for some commodity (Lerner chose peanuts) is eliminated by Walras' Law, the resulting system includes both a loanable-funds and a money equation, one of which must be used to determine the price of the excluded commodity.

Subsequent contributors to the debate can be classed as those who maintain the identity of the two theories, and those who maintain that the liquidity-preference theory is different from (and superior to) the loanable-funds theory. To clarify the issues, it is convenient to discuss these groups in order. Among the former group, S. C. Tsiang [119], W. L. Smith [111], and Don Patinkin [92] deserve mention—Smith for his compact exposition and explicit recognition of the difference between stock and flow theories of behaviour.

Tsiang objects to the Hicks–Fellner and Somers use of Walras' Law to establish the equivalence of the two theories on the Lerner grounds that this law only permits the elimination of one of the general equilibrium equations, and maintains that to establish the equivalence it is necessary to show that the individual can only demand or supply securities by supplying or demanding money. He also objects that the flow demand and supply of money in the Fellner–Somers analysis bears no relation to the stock demand and supply of Keynesian theory. To get around these difficulties (which, as Patinkin [92] shows, are of Tsiang's own creating) Tsiang chooses a period so short that the economic unit cannot plan on using its proceeds from planned sales of commodities to finance planned purchases of them; by this arbitrary device the flow and stock demands for money are equated and the only choice left to the unit is between holding cash (as an idle balance or for spending) and holding securities, so that identity of the two theories (in Tsiang's sense) necessarily follows.

Patinkin's article is an elegant restatement of the Hicksian position. Patinkin argues that the Lerner objection merely means that it is wrong to classify interest theories by the equation omitted, and that the two theories are simply alternative formulations of one general equilibrium theory of interest. He disposes of Tsiang's objection to the Fellner–Somers analysis by showing that the excess flow-demand for money is identical with the excess stock-demand for money for the period (Patinkin slips in not making explicit that to translate a desired change in a stock over a period into a flow during the period it is necessary to divide the change by the length of the period). Finally, he disposes of Klein's statement of the difference between the two theories by showing that this difference refers to the dynamic behaviour of the same market—the securities market—so that the choice of which market to eliminate is not relevant.

Patinkin goes on to argue, with the help of the apparatus of dynamic theory developed in his book, that the Klein hypothesis concerning the dynamics of the interest rate is inherently implausible, since it implies that the interest rate will fall (rise) in the face of excess supply (demand) in the securities market. This argument, appealing as it is, is restricted by its dependence on Patinkin's dynamic apparatus, which permits simultaneous disequilibrium in all markets and relates the direction of movement of individual prices to the excess demand or supply in the corresponding markets. It can be objected both that there is no reason why the movement of price in a market should be dominated by the excess demand or supply in that market (Brunner's argument against Klein recognized this point [68, p. 251]) and that a dynamic analysis of price movements in one market requires specification of how disequilibria in the remaining markets are resolved.[1] Further, in setting up a dynamic analysis—particularly a period analysis—explicitly allowing for the (temporary) resolution of disequilibrium, it is

[1] Patinkin recognized these difficulties in the discussion of dynamic stability in his book [93, pp. 157–8], and admitted that they made stability a matter of assumption rather than of proof; but he overlooked them in applying his dynamic apparatus to the liquidity-preference loanable-funds controversy.

possible and sometimes convenient to define the relationships
in such a way that Walras' Law does not hold. This is the
procedure that has been adopted (implicitly or explicitly) by
recent defenders of the liquidity-preference theory: Joan
Robinson's exposition of it [98] employs a period analysis in
which retailers confronted with unintended increases in inventories finance themselves by releasing cash or securities, and
Hugh Rose's dynamic version of Keynes' theory [100] (which
behaves according to Klein's hypothesis) uses the same model
with inventories being financed by security issues. In both
cases the demand and supply of goods are equated *ex post* by
the accommodating behaviour of retailers, but this behaviour
is not included in the *ex ante* description of disturbances to
equilibrium. F. H. Hahn's reformulation of the liquidity-
preference theory as a theory of the ratios in which cash and
securities are held [55] employs a similar but more subtle
device—a distinction between the investment-planning period,
and a shorter 'investment-financing' period during which the
loanable-funds but not the liquidity-preference theory applies—
to reconcile the two theories dynamically.

Elegant as it is, Patinkin's analysis is confined to the determination of equilibrium in a single period, and ignores the
effects of the changes in stocks determined in that period on
the equilibrium determined in the next period. Other participants in the controversy have followed him (or rather Keynes)
in abstracting from the process of accumulation of real and
financial wealth. The discussion has therefore stopped short of
the issue raised by Klein, and elaborated on by Brunner, of
the dynamics of price in a market characterized by a large
stock and small demand-and-supply flows per period. Brunner
[68, pp. 247-9] sketched a theory of such a market; in this
theory price is determined at every moment by the demand for
the existing stock, but at this price there may be a net flow
demand or supply which gradually changes the existing stock
and therefore the price; and full equilibrium requires a price
which both equates the stock demand and supply and induces
a zero net flow.[1] A very similar theory has since been elaborated

---

[1] In describing a mathematical model of this theory, Brunner admits two
possible situations of partial equilibrium—stock equilibrium and flow disequilibrium and the converse—but nevertheless asserts that the stock relation

by Robert Clower [22], who uses it to argue that productivity and thrift have only an indirect effect on interest (through the net flow of new securities) unless they affect the stock demand for security directly by changing expectations. Clower and D. W. Bushaw [23] have produced a general theory of price for an economy that includes commodities appearing only as stocks, commodities appearing only as flows, and commodities appearing as both stocks and flows; in this theory the equilibrium price in the market for a stock-flow commodity must equate both the desired and actual stock and the flow demand and supply, and in the dynamic analysis the rate of change of price depends on both the excess-stock and excess-flow demands.[2]

Neither the Brunner–Clower nor the Clower–Bushaw theory really solves the stock-flow problem: the former subordinates the flow analysis entirely to the stock, the latter simply adds stock and flow analysis together. The defect common to both is the absence of a connection between the price at which a stock will be held and the current rate of change of the stock held, and correspondingly between the price at which a stock will be supplied and the current rate of change of the stock supplied; such connections would yield a simultaneous equilibrium of stock and flow evolving towards full stock equilibrium (zero net flow.)[3] The addition of such connections would require treating savings and investment as processes of adding to stock, rather than as flows as they have customarily been treated in the post-Keynesian literature.[4]

determines momentary price in both. This inconsistency, which was presumably prompted by his intention to contrast the adjustment processes of markets dominated respectively by stocks and flows, is the source of the dilemma Shackle finds between stock and flow equilibrium as the determinant of price [105, p. 222].

[2] Cliff Lloyd [75] has argued that the presence of two equilibrium equations for a stock-flow commodity may invalidate the Hicksian proof of the equivalence of the loanable-funds and liquidity-preference theories. It may be noted that the Clower–Bushaw theory provides a formal solution to the apparent dilemma created by Brunner's alternative partial equilibria.

[3] In one passage [105, p. 223] Shackle outlines a solution to his dilemma along these lines, but does not pursue it further. The Brunner–Clower theory can (with some difficulty) be interpreted as a special case of the general theory, one in which the price at which a stock is held is independent of the current rate of change in the stock.

[4] This observation refers to the literature on the Keynesian general equilibrium system, and not to the specialist work on consumption and investment, where

This is the approach to monetary dynamics that has been emerging in the past few years, from both 'Keynesian' and 'quantity' theorists, as an outgrowth of the formulation of monetary theory as part of a general theory of asset holding. The essence of the new approach, elements of which are to be found in recent works of such diverse writers as Cagan [20], Tobin [116], Friedman [40, pp. 461–3] and Brunner [18], is to view a monetary disturbance as altering the terms on which assets will be held (by altering either preferences among assets or the relative quantities of them available), and so inducing behaviour designed to adjust the available stocks of assets to the changed amounts desired.[1] The new approach has been aptly summarized, from the point of view of monetary policy, by Brunner [18, p. 612]:

'Variations in policy variables induce a reallocation of assets (or liabilities) in the balance sheets of economic units which spills over to current output and thus affect the price level. Injections of base-money (or "high-powered" money) modify the composition of financial assets and total wealth available to banks and other economic units. Absorption of the new base money requires suitable alterations in asset yields or asset prices. The banks and the public are thus induced to reshuffle their balance sheets to adjust desired and actual balance-sheet position.

'The interaction between banks and public, which forms the essential core of money-supply theory, generates the peculiar leverage or multiplier effect of injections of base money on bank assets and deposits and, correspondingly, on specific asset and liability items of the public's balance sheet. The readjustment process induces a change in the relative yield (or price) structure of assets crucial for the transmission of monetary policy-action to the rate of economic activity. The relative price of base money and its close substitutes falls, and the relative price of other assets rises.

the treatment of saving and investment as processes of adding to stock has become well established since the war.

[1] While this approach can be described as new in relation to the time-period included in this survey, it can from another point of view be regarded as a development of certain strands in Keynes' thought [65, Vol. I, pp. 200–9] [66, Ch. 11].

'The stock of real capital dominates these other assets. The increase in the price of capital relative to the price of financial assets simultaneously raises real capital's market value relative to the capital stock's replacement costs and increases the desired stock relative to the actual stock. The relative increase in the desired stock of capital induces an adjustment in the actual stock through new production. In this manner current output and prices of durable goods are affected by the re-adjustments in the balance sheets and the related price movements set in motion by the injection of base money. The wealth, income, and relative price effects involved in the whole transmission process also tend to raise demand for non-durable goods.'

IV. MONETARY POLICY

There is probably no field of economics in which the writings of economists are so strongly influenced by both current fashions in opinion and current problems of economic policy as the field of monetary policy. In the period immediately after the war, economists writing on monetary policy were generally agreed that monetary expansion was of little use in combating depression. Scepticism about the effectiveness of monetary restraint in combating inflation was less marked, though some took the extreme view that monetary restraint would either prove ineffective or precipitate a collapse. But it was generally thought that the wartime legacy of a large and widely-held public debt was a major obstacle to the application of monetary restraint, both because it was feared that abandonment of the bond-support programme adopted to assist war financing would destroy public confidence in government debt, and because the transfer from the government to the private banking system that would result from an increase in the interest payable on the latter's large holdings of public debt was regarded as undesirable. Economists therefore divided into those who advocated schemes for insulating bank-held government debt from general interest-rate movements, as a means of clearing the way for monetary restraint, and those who argued for an extension of selective credit controls.

The inflation that accompanied the Korean War forced the

termination of the bond-support programme, and thereafter monetary policy became the chief instrument for controlling short-run fluctuations. The nonmaterialization of the disastrous consequences that some had predicted would follow the termination of the bond-support programme, together with the development of the availability doctrine (which enlisted liquidity preference on the side of monetary policy and made a widely-held public debt a help rather than a hindrance) strengthened confidence in the power of monetary restraint to control inflation, though the availability doctrine also provided ammunition to advocates of selective controls by depicting monetary policy as achieving its results through irrational and discriminatory mechanisms. Subsequent experience, together with empirical and theoretical research, has fairly conclusively disposed of the availability doctrine's most appealing feature—the proposition that the central bank can produce large reductions in private spending by means of small increases in interest rates—and research has tended to refute the contention that monetary policy operates discriminatorily. Nevertheless, the availability doctrine has left its mark on the field, inasmuch as the majority of monetary economists would probably explain how monetary policy influences the economy by reference to its effects on the availability and cost of credit, with the stress on availability. Trust in the power of monetary restraint to control inflation has been further reduced by the coexistence of rising prices and higher average unemployment in the late 1950's, and the associated revival and elaboration of cost-push theories of inflation. On the other hand, experience of monetary policy in three mild business cycles has revived confidence in the efficacy of monetary expansion in combating recessions and dispelled the belief that monetary restraint in a boom will do either nothing or far too much. In fact, the wheel has come full circle, and prevailing opinion has returned to the characteristic 1920's view that monetary policy is probably more effective in checking deflation than in checking inflation.[1]

[1] This account refers, of course, to developments in the United States (compare Paul Samuelson [57, pp. 263–9]). A parallel evolution of opinion has occurred in other countries, though in Britain prevailing opinion, as reflected notably in the Radcliffe Report [127, Ch. 6], has remained sceptical of the efficacy and usefulness of monetary policy; this difference in prevailing opinion is partly responsible for the generally critical reception of the Report by U.S.

Changing fashions in prevailing opinion apart, the revival of monetary policy as a major branch of economic policy has stimulated much controversy, thought, and research on all aspects of monetary policy. In addition, the legacy of war debt and the increased size and frequency of government debt debt operations that it has entailed, together with the difficulties created for the Treasury by 'bills only' and other Federal Reserve and governmental policies, has brought the whole subject of debt management within the purview of monetary economists as a special form of open-market operations. It is neither possible nor worth while to attempt to survey all the issues discussed in this voluminous literature: the Report of the Commission on Money and Credit [128] contains a consensus of informed professional opinion on most of them, the usefulness of which is much reduced by the absence of documentation of empirical statements and precise references to conflicting points of view; Friedman's *A Program for Monetary Stability* [34] discusses many of the issues within a consistent theoretical framework; and a 1960 *Review of Economics and Statistics* symposium [57] assembles the views of a variety of monetary specialists. The remainder of this part will instead concentrate on what seem to be the significant developments in three areas: the objectives of economic policy and the instrumental role of monetary policy; the means by which monetary policy influences the economy and their effectiveness; and the adequacy of the tools of monetary policy.

A. *The Objectives and Instrumental Role of Monetary Policy*

In pre-Keynesian days, monetary policy was the single established instrument of aggregative economic policy, and price stability was its established objective. The Keynesian revolution introduced an alternative instrument, fiscal policy, and a second objective, maintenance of full employment (now more commonly described as economic stability), which might conflict with the objective of price stability. Since the war, debt management has been added almost universally to the list of instruments; and since the middle 1950's many economists have added a third item—adequately rapid economic growth—to the

commentators. Limitations of space make it necessary to confine this section to developments in the United States.

list of objectives. In recent years the balance of-payments problem has been forcing the admission of a fourth objective—
international balance—and may eventually establish a fourth
instrument—foreign economic policy.

Recognition of several objectives of economic policy introduces the possibility of a conflict of objectives requiring resolution by a compromise. This possibility and its implications
have been more clearly recognized elsewhere (for example by
the Radcliffe Committee [127, pp. 17–18]) than in the United
States, where there has been a tendency to evade the issue by
denying the possibility of conflict[1] or by insisting that conflicts
be eliminated by some other means than sacrifice of the achievement of any of the objectives.[2] Where a conflict of objectives
has been clearly recognized—notably in the criticisms directed
at the anti-inflationary emphasis of Federal Reserve policy
in 1957–60—the arguments about alternative compromises
have been qualitative and nonrigorous; rigorous theoretical
exploration and quantitative assessment of the costs and
benefits of alternative compromises between conflicting policy
objectives remain to be undertaken.

The availability of alternative policy instruments introduces
the question of their absolute and comparative effectiveness;
research on this range of problems has been undertaken by a
number of economists, but has not progressed far towards an
accepted body of knowledge. As already mentioned, monetary
policy since 1951 has resumed a large part of the responsibility
for short-run economic stabilization—a consequence of both
the inadaptability of the budgetary process to the requirements
of a flexible fiscal policy and the domination of the budget by
other objectives of national policy than stabilization. Reliance

[1] This can always be done by giving priority to one objective and defining the
others in terms that implicitly impose consistency with the favoured objective;
an example is the concept of 'sustainable economic growth' promulgated by the
Federal Reserve System.

[2] One example of this type of evasion is the affirmation that balance-of-
payments difficulties should not be allowed to hinder the achievement of domestic
policy, an affirmation rarely accompanied by specification of any obviously
efficacious solution to these difficulties. Another is the expression of trust that
policies designed to increase the competitiveness and efficiency of the economy
will eliminate the possibility of conflict between high employment, price stability,
and adequate growth. Both are contained in the Report of the Commission on
Money and Credit [128, p. 227, p. 45].

on monetary policy for this purpose has raised the question of how effectively the task is likely to be performed. The argument for using monetary policy is usually expressed in terms of the 'flexibility' of monetary policy, by which is often meant no more than that monetary policy can be changed quickly. But the real issues are whether the monetary authorities are likely to take appropriate action at the right time, and whether the effects of monetary action on the economy occur soon enough and reliably enough to have a significant stabilizing effect.

As to the first question, there is general agreement that the Federal Reserve has committed errors in the timing, extent and duration of policy changes. Most economists seem inclined to trust the System to improve its performance with experience and the benefit of their criticism. Some, however, are so distrust-of discretionary authority in principle, or so sceptical of the feasibility of effective stabilization by monetary means, as to advocate that the Federal Reserve should not attempt short-run stabilization, but should confine itself (or be confined) to expanding the money supply at a steady rate appropriate to the growth of the economy (for variants of this proposal, see Friedman [34, pp. 84–99], Angell [57, pp. 247–52], and Shaw [106]). The proposal to substitute a monetary rule for the discretion of the monetary authority is not of course new—Henry Simons' classic statement of the case for it [108] appeared in the 1930's—but the definition of the rule in terms of the rate of monetary expansion rather than stability of a price index reflects both the modern concern with growth and a more sophisticated understanding of the stabilization problem.

Whether such a rule would have produced better results than the policy actually followed in the past is a difficult matter to test. Friedman [34, pp. 95–8] discusses the difficulties and describes some abortive tests that tend to favour his (4 per cent annual increase) rule. Martin Bronfenbrenner has devised a more elaborate series of tests of alternative rules, including discretionary policy; his results for annual data 1901–1958 (excluding the Second World War) [11] show that a 3 per cent annual increase rule comes closest to the 'ideal pattern' defined by price stability, though his subsequent tests on quarterly data from 1947 on [12] suggest the superiority of a 'lag rule' relating changes in the money supply to prior changes in the labour force, productivity and velocity. These tests are subject to statistical and theoretical objections, but they open up an interesting new line of research. In the absence of a definitely specified standard of comparison, discussions of the appropriateness of the central bank's monetary policy tend to fall back on textual criticism of its explanation of its actions or the exercise of personal judgment about what policy should have been (see, for example, the contributions of Weintraub, Samuelson, and Fellner to [57]).

The question of the extent of the stabilizing effect that monetary action may be expected to achieve was first raised, at the formal theoretical level, by Friedman [39], who argued that policies intended to stabilize the economy might well have destabilizing effects because of the lags involved in their operation. Subsequent work and discussion on this aspect of monetary policy has concentrated on the length and variability of the lag in the effect of monetary policy, and has become enmeshed in intricate arguments about the proper way of measuring the lag. Two alternative approaches to the measurement of the lag have been employed, direct estimate and statistical inference. The outstanding example of the first is Thomas Mayer's study of the inflexibility of monetary policy [79]. Mayer estimates the lag in the reaction of investment expenditure and consumer credit outstanding to monetary policy changes, sector by sector, and, taking into account lags in monetary-policy changes and the multiplier process, concludes that monetary policy operates on the economy much too slowly for its effects to be quickly reversed; from a computation of the effect that an optimally-timed monetary policy would have had on the stability of industrial production over six business cycles, he concludes that monetary policy is too inflexible to reduce the fluctuation of industrial production by more than 5 to 10 per cent on the average [79, p. 374]. W. H. White [125] has since argued that Mayer seriously overestimates the average lag, and that the correct estimate would provide almost ideal conditions for effective anticyclical policy; White also remarks that Mayer's results do not show the destabilizing effects indicated as possible by Friedman's analysis.

Statistical inference is the basis of Friedman's contention that monetary policy operates with a long and variable lag, a

contention which figures largely in his opposition to discretionary monetary policy. Friedman's preliminary references to his
results, which are yet to be published in full [42], made it
appear that this contention rested mostly on a comparison of
turning points in the rate of change of the money stock with
turning points in National Bureau reference cycles (that is,
in the level of activity); this comparison automatically yields
a lag a quarter of a cycle longer than does a comparison of
turning points in the level of the money stock with reference-
cycle turning points, the comparison that Friedman's critics
regard as the proper one to make. In reply to criticisms by
J. M. Culbertson [26], Friedman has produced a lengthy
defence of his measure of the lag, together with other supporting
evidence [40]. This defence indicates that the measurement of
the lag raises much more subtle and fundamental theoretical
and methodological issues than appear at first sight; but the
majority of monetary economists competent to judge is likely
to agree with Culbertson [28] in finding Friedman's arguments
unpersuasive.

Statistical inference is also employed in the study of lags in
fiscal and monetary policy conducted for the Commission on
Money and Credit by Brown, Solow, Ando and Kareken [14].
These authors claim that Friedman's comparison of turning
points in the rate of change of the money stock with turning
points in the level of activity involves a methodological *non
sequitur*, and find from a comparison of turning points in the
rates of change of money with the rate of change of aggregate
output that the money stock and aggregate output move
roughly simultaneously over the cycle. Their own work attempts
to estimate the lag between the indication of a need for a change
in monetary policy and the effect of the resulting change in
policy on output, and finds that a substantial stabilizing effect
is achieved within six to nine months. They also find that fiscal
policy operating on disposable income is a more powerful
stabilizer, achieving as much as half of its effect within six
months.

This research on the lag in effect of monetary policy has been
orientated towards determining the efficacy of monetary
policy as a stabilizer, on the assumption that monetary policy
is decided with reference to contemporaneous economic

conditions. Little if any research has been devoted to the more ambitious task of designing optimal systems of changing monetary policy in a response to movements of relevant economic indicators. A. W. Phillips [95] and more recently W. J. Baumol [8] have shown that what seem like sensible procedures for changing a policy variable in response to changing conditions may well aggravate instability; Phillips has applied the theory and concepts of control systems to the analysis of the effects of alternative operating rules of stabilization policy.

B. *The Effectiveness of Monetary Policy*

To turn from the instrumental role of monetary policy to the related but broader questions of how monetary action influences the economy, and how effectively, the prevailing tendency has been to approach these questions by analysing how monetary policy, and particularly open-market operations, affect the spending decisions of particular sectors of the economy. This formulation of the problem is a natural corollary of Keynesian theory, and the evolution of the analysis since the war has closely reflected the evolution of monetary theory, though with a perceptible lag; but the analysis has also been strongly influenced by the availability doctrine. That doctrine, the formulation of which was largely the work of Robert Roosa [99], emerged in the later years of the bond-support programme as a solution to the conflict between the belief that a large widely-held public debt obliged the central bank to confine interest-rate movements to narrow limits and the belief that large interest-rate changes were necessary to obtain significant effects on spending.

The doctrine comprised two central propositions. The first was that widespread holding of public debt, particularly by financial institutions and corporations, facilitates monetary control by transmitting the influence of interest-rate changes effected by open-market operations throughout the economy. The second was that small interest-rate changes could, by generating or dispelling uncertainty about future rates and by inflicting or eliminating capital losses that institutions were unwilling to realize by actual sales ('the pinning-in effect'), achieve significant effects on spending even if the demands of spenders for credit were interest-inelastic—these effects being achieved by influencing the willingness of lenders to lend or, put another way, by influencing the availability of credit to borrowers by altering the terms of credit and the degree of credit rationing. The second proposition has turned out on subsequent investigation to depend on incorrect empirical assumptions about institutional behaviour, particularly with respect to 'the pinning-in effect' (see Warren Smith [112]) and on a doubtful asymmetry between the reactions of lender and borrower expectations to interest-rate changes (see Dennis Robertson [97]), as well as to involve some logical inconsistencies (see John Kareken [64], and for a theoretical defence of the availability doctrine, Ira Scott [103]). Nevertheless, the doctrine and discussion of it have helped to popularize the concept of 'availability of credit' as one of the main variables on which monetary policy operates.

'Availability' actually comprises a number of disparate elements—the liquidity of potential lenders' and spenders' assets, the terms on which lenders will extend or borrowers can obtain credit, and the degree to which credit is rationed among eligible borrowers (see Kareken [64]). Emphasis on these factors as influences on spending has provided new arguments for those who favour selective credit controls—specific arguments for controls where the terms of credit rather than the cost of credit seem the effective determinant of spending decisions, as in the case of instalment credit, and a general defensive argument based on the discriminatory character of credit rationing. The most powerful attack on the discriminatory character of allegedly general methods of economic control has come from J. K. Galbraith [45], who has maintained that the use of monetary and fiscal policy has favoured the monopolistic at the expense of the competitive sectors of the economy to an extent comparable to repeal of the antitrust laws. Others have maintained that monetary restraint discriminates against small business. Empirical studies by Bach and Huizenga [6] and Allen Meltzer [82] show that this is not true of bank credit; Meltzer's study finds that while small firms have greater difficulty in obtaining nonbank credit in tight periods than large firms, this discrimination tends to be offset by extension of trade credit from large firms to small.

The emphasis on the availability of credit as a determinant of expenditure has led to a critical re-examination of the business-attitude survey findings that formerly were used as evidence that business investment is insensitive to monetary policy. In addition, monetary theorists have tended to raise their estimates of the sensitivity of business investment to changes in the cost of credit. These reassessments have been based on the opinion that investors' expected profits are more finely and rationally calculated than used to be thought, rather than on any impressive new empirical evidence of such sensitivity. The most definite new empirical evidence there is confirms the long-time theoretically established sensitivity of residential construction to interest-rate changes, and even this sensitivity has been attributed in part to the influence of ceiling rates on federally-guaranteed mortgages on the willingness of institutional lenders to lend on such mortgages [128, p. 51]. The failure of empirical research to disclose such sensitivity may, as Brunner has suggested [18, p. 613], be the consequence of too simple a theoretical approach, the attempt to relate a flow of expenditure on assets to the cost of credit without adequate recognition of the range of alternative assets or the complexities of stock-adjustment processes. The new approach to monetary dynamics described in the previous part suggests . that a more sophisticated theory of real investment is necessary for successful empirical work; on the other hand, some of the empirical work described in Part II suggests that better results might be achieved by working with changes in the quantity of money than by attempting to determine the influence of changes in interest rates on particular categories of spending.

The discussion of the effectiveness of monetary policy just described has been concerned with monetary policy operating in a given institutional environment. Since the middle 1950's a new debate has been opened up, concerned with the fact that traditional methods of monetary control are primarily directed at commercial bank credit, and the possibility that institutional change stimulated by monetary restriction may reduce the effectiveness of traditional techniques of monetary control. The main debate has been concerned with Gurley and Shaw's contention [50, pp. 537–8] that the growth of financial intermediaries, prompted in part by the competitive handicaps imposed on commercial banks for purposes of monetary control, progressively provides close substitutes for money the presence of which weakens the grip of monetary policy on the economy; and with their suggestion that the controlling powers of the central bank should be extended beyond the commercial banks to other financial institutions.[1] The debate has ranged over a wide territory, including such matters as whether existing controls over commercial banks are really discriminatory, given that banks enjoy the privilege of creating money (Aschheim [3] and Shelby [107]) and whether imposition of credit controls on financial intermediaries would in fact improve the effectiveness of monetary policy or the competitive position of the banks (David Alhadeff [1]). From the point of view of monetary policy, the central issue is not whether financial development leads to a secular decline in the demand for money—by itself, this would increase the leverage of monetary policy (Shelby [107]) and could readily be assimilated by the monetary authorities ([128, pp. 80–1] and Axilrod [5])—but whether the liabilities of financial intermediaries are such close substitutes for money that monetary restriction is substantially offset through substitution for bank deposits of other financial claims backed by only a small fractional reserve of money—in short, whether financial intermediaries substantially increase the interest-elasticity of demand for money. This is an empirical question; and the empirical evidence so far is that shifts by the public from money into thrift assets in periods of monetary restraint have not had a significant influence on velocity ([128, pp. 78–80]; see also Smith [110]).

C. The Adequacy of the Tools of Monetary Policy

The revival of monetary policy as an instrument of short-run stabilization has provoked a great deal of discussion not only of the use and effectiveness of monetary policy, but also of the use and efficiency of the Federal Reserve's traditional instruments

---

[1] A related but different argument has been advanced by Hyman Minsky [85], to the effect that monetary restriction stimulates financial innovations that progressively reduce the demand for money, increase the velocity of circulation, and threaten to make the money market unstable; Minsky recommends extension of the lender-of-last-resort function to the whole market and not merely the commercial banks. Arguments similar to those of Gurley and Shaw and Minsky may be found in Smith [112].

of monetary control—open-market operations, rediscount rates, and reserve requirements. Controversy about open-market operations has centered on the 'bills only' policy—the policy of conducting open-market operations in Treasury bills only, adopted by the Federal Reserve in 1953, modified later to 'bills usually', and abandoned in 1961. Both the availability doctrine and the assets approach to the theory of interest rates imply that the central bank can obtain differential effects on credit conditions according to the maturity of government debt in which it chooses to conduct open-market operations, and can alter the structure of interest rates by switching between short and long maturities. The bills-only policy therefore appeared to most academic economists as an undesirable renunciation by the central bank of an important technique of monetary control, and the reason given for it—the desire to improve the 'depth, breadth and resiliency' of the government bond market by eliminating arbitrary central bank intervention in it—as a shallow excuse masking the unwillingness of the Federal Reserve to risk unpopularity with the financial community by overtly subjecting it to capital losses. The surrender of power entailed in bills-only was probably greatly exaggerated by many of its opponents: Winfield Riefler [96] has pointed out that the central bank's choice of securities only contributes about one-eighth of the total effect of its open-market operations, the remaining seven-eighths being determined by the asset choices of the banks whose reserves are altered by the operations; and has produced some evidence that substantial changes in the maturity composition of the public debt have had little effect on the rate structure. On the other side of the argument, Dudley Luckett [76] has shown that the empirical evidence fails to indicate any improvement in 'depth, breadth and resilience' since bills-only was adopted.

While much of the discussion of bills-only has been concerned exclusively with Federal Reserve policy, the fundamental issue involved was the division of responsibility for the maturity composition of government debt held by the public between the Federal Reserve and the Treasury. Bills-only assigned this responsibility, and the associated responsibility for smoothing the impact of debt-management operations on the market, to the Treasury. One school of thought, represented for example by A. G. Hart [57, pp. 257–8], has maintained strongly that this is an inappropriate division of responsibility, since the Federal Reserve has both the powers and the continual contact with the market required for the purpose and the Treasury has not. (The limited ability of the Treasury to conduct open-market operations has been demonstrated by Deane Carson's study [21] of debt management after the adoption of bills-only.) Others have seen the source of the trouble in the Treasury's debt management practices, particularly the practice of issuing debt in large blocks at irregular intervals, at fixed prices and with maturities 'tailored' to market requirements. Carson [21] and Friedman [34, Ch. 3] have proposed similar schemes for replacing present practice by a system of auctioning long-term government debt issues; Culbertson [25] and Friedman [34, Ch. 3] have propounded plans for regularizing the timing and composition of debt issues to reduce the market disturbance of government financing. The difficulties the Treasury has experienced with debt management in the postwar period, in consequence not only of bills-only but of other developments adverse to easy Treasury financing,[1] have led many economists to become sceptical of the practicability of a countercyclical debt-management programme. Such a programme, which would involve issuing long-term debt in booms and short-term debt in depressions, would in any case have a countercyclical influence only in so far as the interest-rate structure is sensitive to change in the composition of the debt, and this sensitivity seems to be too small to yield important stabilizing effects (see Riefler [96] and Meiselman [81]).

Though the growth of the public debt has definitely established open-market operations as the chief instrument of day-to-day monetary control, the revival of monetary policy has been accompanied by a revival of rediscounting and the use of rediscount rates as a control instrument. Controversy over rediscount policy has mainly been concerned with whether rediscount policy is a useful auxiliary instrument of control or whether the possibility of rediscounting creates an unnecessary and troublesome loophole in the control over member banks afforded by reserve requirements and open-market operations. It can be argued (see Friedman [34, pp. 34–5])

[1] For a comprehensive survey of these developments see Erwin Miller [84].

that rediscount rates are a treacherous control instrument, since their restrictiveness depends on their relationship with shifting market rates of interest, and that the growth of bank holdings of public debt and the postwar development of the federal funds market make it unnecessary for the Federal Reserve to continue to perform the function of lender of last resort for its members.[1] There has also been some argument about whether control of the rediscounting privilege gives the Federal Reserve undesirable arbitrary authority over member banks.

Apart from the debate concerning the desirability of re-discounting, a number of writers have criticized the asymmetry of the present reserve-requirement and rediscount-rate system, under which member banks receive no interest on reserves or excess reserves but pay a penalty rate on reserves borrowed to meet deficiencies, and have proposed payment of interest on reserves or excess reserves. Tobin, for example [57, pp. 276–9], has recommended payment of interest at the discount rate on excess reserves, and coupled this with the recommendation to terminate the prohibition of demand-deposit interest and the ceilings on time- and savings-deposit interest, arguing that the justification for intervention in the fixing of deposit rates—to protect depositors by preventing excess competition among banks—has been removed by federal deposit insurance.[2]

The power to change reserve requirements gives the central bank a method of changing the quantity of bank deposits alternative to open-market operations. The chief differences between the two methods[3] are, first, that reserve-requirement changes, being discontinuous, are apt to have disturbing effects on securities markets requiring auxiliary open-market operations; and second, that credit expansion by open-market

---

[1] The controversy has aroused some interest in the Canadian innovation of setting the discount rate at a fixed margin above the weekly average tender rate on Treasury bills. In England, where the rediscount rate is the chief instrument of monetary policy, recognition of the loophole in monetary control afforded by rediscounting has led to the promulgation of the theory that the liquidity ratio of the commercial banks and the supply of bills, rather than the cash ratio and the quantity of central bank deposits, determine the amount of commercial bank deposits.

[2] The fact that this justification was fallacious to begin with has not prevented the Commission on Money and Credit from endorsing the continuation of control of these rates [128, pp. 167–8].

[3] For a fuller analysis, see Aschheim [4, Ch. 2].

purchases is less costly for the government and less profitable for the banks than credit expansion by reduction of reserve requirements (and vice versa). The discontinuity and disturbing effects of reserve-requirement changes, dramatically exemplified by their misuse in 1936-7 (see Brunner [15]), have led most economists to believe that they should be used sparingly if at all, especially in restraining credit expansion. The differential effects of the two methods of control on governmental interest costs and bank profits have been the focus of controversy over the policy of lowering reserve requirements followed by the Federal Reserve since 1951. In the course of time the balance of the argument has tilted in favour of reduction of reserve requirements, as the postwar sentiment against high bank profits derived from interest on the public debt has given way to the more recent fear that banks are unduly handicapped by reserve requirements and interest ceilings on deposits in competing with other financial intermediaries.

The controversy has raised the more general issue of how the secular growth of the money supply should be provided for. George Tolley, who first raised this issue [118], has shown that the choice between open-market operations and reserve-requirement variation involves some intricate theoretical issues, since in addition to its implications for debt management and the ease of government financing this choice influences the efficiency of allocation of resources to the provision of the supply of deposit money.

Some attention has also been given to the efficiency of the present system of reserve requirements as an instrument of monetary control. Frank Norton and Neil Jacoby [88] have revived the 1930's Federal Reserve proposal to relate required reserve ratios to deposit turnover rates as a means of introducing an automatic offset to changes in the velocity of circulation. The preponderance of professional opinion, however, seems opposed to any system of reserve requirements that discriminates between banks or affects their profits differentially, and in favour of the removal of inequities among banks by the standardization of reserve requirements.

C

v. CONCLUDING REMARKS

The main impression that emerges from this survey of monetary theory and policy is not only that the field has been extremely active, especially in the past few years, but that it has been on the move towards interesting and important new developments. To summarize what is already a summary is a difficult task, and prediction of the direction of future scientific progress is a risky business; but in the literature surveyed in the preceding sections, two broad trends are evident. One is the trend towards the formulation of monetary theory as a part of capital theory, described in Part II (and implicitly in Part I). As mentioned in Part III, this trend has only just begun to manifest itself in the formulation of monetary dynamics. More important, almost nothing has yet been done to break monetary theory loose from the mould of short-run equilibrium analysis, conducted in abstraction from the process of growth and accumulation, and to integrate it with the rapidly developing theoretical literature on economic growth (important exceptions are the models of Tobin [113] and Enthoven [52, App.]). The other trend is that toward econometric testing and measurement of monetary relationships. As is evident from Part IV, econometric methods have barely begun to be applied to the study of relationships relevant to the management of monetary policy.

REFERENCES

1. D. A. ALHADEFF, 'Credit Controls and Financial Intermediaries', *Am. Econ. Rev.*, September 1960, **50**, 655–71
2. G. C. ARCHIBALD and R. G. LIPSEY, 'Monetary and Value Theory: A Critique of Lange and Patinkin', *Rev. Econ. Stud.*, October 1958, **26**, 1–22.
3. J. ASCHHEIM, 'Commercial Banks and Financial Intermediaries: Fallacies and Policy Implications', *Jour. Pol. Econ.*, February 1959, **67**, 59–71.
4. ——, *Techniques of Monetary Control*. Baltimore 1961.
5. S. H. AXILROD, 'Liquidity and Public Policy', *Fed. Res. Bull.*, October 1961, **47**, 1161–77.
6. G. L. BACH and C. J. HUIZENGA, 'The Differential Effects of Tight Money', *Am. Econ. Rev.*, March 1961, **51**, 52–80.

7. W. J. BAUMOL, R. W. CLOWER and M. L. BURSTEIN, F. H. HAHN, R. J. BALL and R. BODKIN, G. C. ARCHIBALD and R. G. LIPSEY, 'A Symposium on Monetary Policy', *Rev. Econ. Stud.*, October 1960, **28**, 29–56.

8. W. J. BAUMOL, 'Pitfalls in Contracyclical Policies: Some Tools and Results', *Rev. Econ. Stat.*, February 1961, **43**, 21–6.

9. ——, 'The Transactions Demand for Cash: An Inventory Theoretic Approach', *Quart. Jour. Econ.*, November 1952, **66**, 545–56.

10. F. P. R. BRECHLING, 'A Note on Bond-Holding and the Liquidity Preference Theory of Interest', *Rev. Econ. Stud.*, June 1957, **24**, 190–7.

11. M. BRONFENBRENNER, 'Statistical Tests of Rival Monetary Rules', *Jour. Pol. Econ.*, February 1961, **69**, 1–14.

12. ——, 'Statistical Tests of Rival Monetary Rules: Quarterly Data Supplement', *Jour. Pol. Econ.*, December 1961, **69**, 621–5.

13. —— and T. MAYER, 'Liquidity Functions in the American Economy', *Econometrica*, October 1960, **28**, 810–34.

14. E. C. BROWN, R. M. SOLOW, A. ANDO and J. H. KAREKEN, *Lags in Fiscal and Monetary Policy*. Forthcoming publication of the Commission on Money and Credit.

15. K. BRUNNER, 'A Case Study of US Monetary Policy: Reserve Requirements and Inflationary Gold Flows in the Middle 30's', *Schweizerische Zeitschrift für Volkswirtschaft und Statistik*, 1958, **94**, 160–201.

16. ——, 'A Schema for the Supply Theory of Money', *Internat. Econ. Rev.*, January 1961, **2**, 79–109.

17. ——, 'Inconsistency and Indeterminacy in Classical Economics', *Econometrica*, April 1951, **19**, 152–73.

18. ——, 'The Report of the Commission on Money and Credit', *Jour. Pol. Econ.*, December 1961, **69**, 605–20.

19. P. CAGAN, 'The Demand for Currency Relative to the Total Money Supply', *Jour. Pol. Econ.*, August 1958, **66**, 303–28.

20. ——, 'Why Do We Use Money in Open Market Operations?' *Jour. Pol. Econ.*, February 1958, **66**, 34–46.

21. D. CARSON, 'Treasury Open Market Operations', *Rev. Econ. Stat.*, November 1959, **41**, 438–42.

22. R. W. CLOWER, 'Productivity, Thrift and the Rate of Interest', *Econ. Jour.*, March 1954, **64**, 107–15.

23. R. W. CLOWER and D. W. BUSHAW, 'Price Determination in a Stock-Flow Economy', *Econometrica*, July 1954, **22**, 328–43.

24. J. W. CONARD, *Introduction to the Theory of Interest*. Berkeley 1959.

25. J. M. CULBERTSON, 'A Positive Debt Management Program', *Rev. Econ. Stat.*, May 1959, **41**, 89–98.

26. ——, 'Friedman on the Lag in Effect of Monetary Policy', *Jour. Pol. Econ.*, December 1960, **68**, 617–21.

27. ——, 'Intermediaries and Monetary Theory: A Criticism of the Gurley-Shaw Theory', *Am. Econ. Rev.*, March 1958, **48**, 119–31.

28. ——, 'The Lag in Effect of Monetary Policy: Reply', *Jour. Pol. Econ.*, October 1961, **69**, 467–77.

29. J. M. CULBERTSON, 'The Term Structure of Interest Rates', *Quart. Jour. Econ.*, November 1957, **71**, 485–517.

30. R. M. DAVIS, 'A Re-examination of the Speculative Demand for Money', *Quart. Jour. Econ.*, May 1959, **73**, 326–32.

31 J. ENCARNACIÓN, 'Consistency between Say's Identity and the Cambridge Equation', *Econ. Jour.*, December, 1958, **68**, 827–30.

32. W. FELLNER and D. DILLARD, 'Keynesian Economics after Twenty Years', *Am. Econ. Rev., Proc.*, May 1957, **47**, 67–87.

33. W. FELLNER and H. M. SOMERS, 'Note on "Stocks" and "Flows" in Monetary Interest Theory', *Rev. Econ. Stat.*, May 1949, **31**, 145–6.

34. M. FRIEDMAN, *A Program for Monetary Stability.* New York 1960.

35. ——, *A Theory of the Consumption Function.* Princeton 1957.

36. ——, 'Price, Income and Monetary Changes in Three Wartime Periods', *Am. Econ. Rev., Proc.*, May 1952, **42**, 612–25.

37. ——, 'The Demand for Money', *Am. Phil. Soc. Proc.*, June 1961, **105**, 259–64.

38. ——, 'The Demand for Money: Some Theoretical and Empirical Results', *Jour. Pol. Econ.*, August 1959, **67**, 327–51.

39. ——, 'The Effects of a Full-Employment Policy on Economic Stability: A Formal Analysis', in *Essays in Positive Economics*, Chicago 1953, pp. 117–32.

40. ——, 'The Lag in Effect of Monetary Policy', *Jour. Pol. Econ.*, October 1961, **69**, 447–66.

41. ——, 'The Quantity Theory of Money—A Restatement', in M. Friedman, ed., *Studies in the Quantity Theory of Money*, Chicago 1956, pp. 3–21.

42. —— and A. J. SCHWARTZ, *The Stock of Money in the United States 1867–1960* and *The Secular and Cyclical Behavior of the Stock of Money in the United States, 1867–1960*, forthcoming publications of the National Bureau of Economic Research.

43. —— and G. S. BECKER, 'A Statistical Illusion in Judging Keynesian Models', *Jour. Pol. Econ.*, February 1957, **65**, 64–75.

44. —— and D. MEISELMAN, *The Relative Stability of Monetary Velocity and the Investment Multiplier in the United States, 1898–1958*, forthcoming publication of the Commission on Money and Credit.

45. J. K. GALBRAITH, 'Market Structure and Stabilization Policy', *Rev. Econ. Stat.*, May 1957, **39**, 124–33.

46. G. GARVEY, *Deposit Velocity and its Significance.* New York 1959.

47. R. W. GOLDSMITH, *A Study of Saving in the United States.* Princeton 1955.

48. ——, *Financial Intermediaries in the American Economy Since 1900.* Princeton 1958.

49. J. G. GURLEY, *Liquidity and Financial Institutions in the Postwar Economy.* Study Paper 14, Joint Economic Committee, 86th Cong., 2nd sess. Washington 1960.

50. —— and E. S. SHAW, 'Financial Aspects of Economic Development', *Am. Econ. Rev.*, September 1955, **45**, 515–38.

51. J. G. GURLEY and E. S. SHAW, 'Financial Intermediaries and the Saving-Investment Process'. *Jour. Finance*, May 1956, **11**, 257–76.
52. —— and ——, *Money in a Theory of Finance*. With a mathematical appendix by A. C. Enthoven. Washington 1960.
53. —— and ——, 'The Growth of Debt and Money in the United States, 1800–1950: A Suggested Interpretation', *Rev. Econ. Stat.*, August 1957, **39**, 250–62.
54. G. HABERLER, 'The Pigou Effect Once Again', *Jour. Pol. Econ.*, June 1952, **60**, 240–6.
55. F. H. HAHN, 'The Rate of Interest and General Equilibrium Analysis', *Econ. Jour.*, March 1955, **65**, 52–66.
56. A. H. HANSEN, *Monetary Theory and Fiscal Policy*. New York 1949.
57. S. E. HARRIS, J. W. ANGELL, W. FELLNER, A. H. HANSEN, A. G. HART, H. NEISSER, R. V. ROOSA, P. A. SAMUELSON, W. L. SMITH, W. THOMAS, J. TOBIN, and S. WEINTRAUB, 'Controversial Issues in Recent Monetary Policy: A Symposium', *Rev. Econ. Stat.*, August 1960, **42**, 245–82.
58. H. HAZLITT, ed., *The Critics of Keynesian Economics*. Princeton 1960.
59. J. R. HICKS, 'A Suggestion for Simplifying the Theory of Money', *Economica*, February 1935, **2**, 1–19; reprinted in F. A. Lutz and L. W. Mints, eds., *Readings in Monetary Theory*, Homewood, Ill. 1941, pp. 13–32.
60. ——, *Value and Capital*. Oxford 1939.
61. H. G. JOHNSON, '*The General Theory* after Twenty-five Years', *Am. Econ. Rev., Proc.*, May 1961, **51**, 1–17; reprinted in H. G. Johnson, *Money, Trade and Economic Growth*, London 1962.
62. J. JOHNSTON, 'A Statistical Illusion in Judging Keynesian Models: Comment', *Rev. Econ. Stat.*, August 1958, **40**, 296–8.
63. R. F. KAHN, 'Some Notes on Liquidity Preference', *Manchester School Econ. and Soc. Stud.*, September 1954, **22**, 229–57.
64. J. H. KAREKEN, 'Lenders' Preferences, Credit Rationing, and the Effectiveness of Monetary Policy', *Rev. Econ. Stat.*, August 1957, **39**, 292–302.
65. J. M. KEYNES, *A Treatise on Money*. London and New York 1930.
66. ——, *The General Theory of Employment Interest and Money*. London and New York 1936.
67. L. R. KLEIN, 'The Friedman-Becker Illusion', *Jour. Pol. Econ.*, December 1958, **66**, 539–45.
68. ——, W. FELLNER, H. M. SOMERS, and K. BRUNNER, 'Stock and Flow Analysis in Economics', *Econometrica*, July 1950, **18**, 236–52.
69. B. KRAGH, 'The Meaning and Use of Liquidity Curves in Keynesian Interest Theory', *Internat. Econ. Papers*, 1955, **5**, 155–69.
70. ——, 'Two Liquidity Functions and the Rate of Interest: A Simple Dynamic Model', *Rev. Econ. Stud.*, February 1950, **17**, 98–106.
71. R. E. KUENNE, 'Keynes's Identity, Ricardian Virtue, and the Partial Dichotomy', *Can. Jour. Econ. and Pol. Sci.*, August 1961, **27**, 323–36.
72. O. LANGE, 'Say's Law: A Restatement and Criticism', in O. Lange, F. McIntyre, and T. O. Yntema, eds., *Mathematical Economics and Econometrics*, Chicago 1942, pp. 49–68.

73. H. A. LATANÉ, 'Cash Balances and the Interest Rate—A Pragmatic Approach', *Rev. Econ. Stat.*, November 1954, **36**, 456–60.

74. ——, 'Income Velocity and Interest Rates: A Pragmatic Approach', *Rev. Econ. Stat.*, November 1960, **42**, 445–9.

75. C. L. LLOYD, 'The Equivalence of the Liquidity Preference and Loanable Funds Theories and the *New* Stock-Flow Analysis', *Rev. Econ. Stud.*, June 1960, **27**, 206–9.

76. D. G. LUCKETT, ' "Bills only": A Critical Appraisal', *Rev. Econ. Stat.*, August 1960, **42**, 301–6.

77. H. F. LYDALL, 'Income, Assets and the Demand for Money', *Rev. Econ. Stat.*, February 1958, **40**,, 1–14.

77a. H. M. MARKOWITZ, *Portfolio Selection: Efficient Diversification of Investments*. New York 1959.

78. A. L. MARTY, 'Gurley and Shaw on Money in a Theory of Finance', *Jour. Pol. Econ.*, February 1961, **69**, 56–62.

79. T. MAYER, 'The Inflexibility of Monetary Policy', *Rev. Econ. Stat.*, November 1958, **40**, 358–74.

80. R. N. MCKEAN, 'Liquidity and a National Balance Sheet', *Jour. Pol. Econ.*, December 1949, **57**, 506–22; reprinted in F. A. Lutz and L. W. Mints, eds., *Readings in Monetary Theory*, Homewood, Ill. 1951, pp. 63–88.

81. D. MEISELMAN, *The Term Structure of Interest Rates*. Englewood Cliffs, N.J., forthcoming.

82. A. H. MELTZER, 'Mercantile Credit, Monetary Policy and Size of Firms', *Rev. Econ. Stat.*, November 1960, **42**, 429–37.

83. L. A. METZLER, 'Wealth, Saving and the Rate of Interest', *Jour. Pol. Econ.*, April 1951, **59**, 93–116.

84. E. MILLER, 'Monetary Policies in the United States Since 1950: Some Implications of the Retreat to Orthodoxy', *Can. Jour. Econ. and Pol. Sci.*, May 1961, **27**, 205–22.

85. H. P. MINSKY, 'Central Banking and Money Market Changes', *Quart. Jour. Econ.*, May 1957, **71**, 171–87.

86. R. A. MUNDELL, 'The Public Debt, Corporate Income Taxes, and the Rate of Interest', *Jour. Pol. Econ.*, December, 1960, **68**, 622–6.

87. R. A. MUSGRAVE, 'Money, Liquidity and the Valuation of Assets', in *Money, Trade and Economic Growth*, in honour of John Henry Williams, New York 1951, 216–42.

88. F. E. NORTON and N. H. JACOBY, *Bank Deposits and Legal Reserve Requirements*. Los Angeles 1959.

89. D. ORR and W. J. MELLON, 'Stochastic Reserve Losses and Expansion of Bank Credit', *Am. Econ. Rev.*, September 1961, **51**, 614–23.

90. D. PATINKIN, 'Dichotomies of the Pricing Process in Economic Theory', *Economica*, May 1954, **21**, 113–28.

91. ——, 'Financial Intermediaries and the Logical Structure of Monetary Theory', *Am. Econ. Rev.*, March 1961, **51**, 95–116.

92. ——, 'Liquidity Preference and Loanable Funds: Stock and Flow Analysis', *Economica*, November 1958, **25**, 300–18.

93. ——, *Money, Interest and Prices*. Evanston, Ill. 1956.

94. D. PATINKIN, 'The Indeterminacy of Absolute Prices in Classical Economic Theory', *Econometrica*, January 1949, **17**, 1–27.

95. A. W. PHILLIPS, 'Stabilization Policy in a Closed Economy', *Econ. Jour.*, June 1954, **64**, 290–323.

96. W. RIEFLER, 'Open Market Operations in Long-Term Securities', *Fed. Res. Bull.*, November 1958, **44**, 1260–74.

97. D. H. ROBERTSON, 'More Notes on the Rate of Interest', *Rev. Econ. Stud.*, February 1954, **21**, 136–41.

98. J. ROBINSON, 'The Rate of Interest', *Econometrica*, April 1951, **19**, 92–111; reprinted in Joan Robinson, *The Rate of Interest and Other Essays*, London 1952.

99. R. V. ROSA [ROOSA], 'Interest Rates and the Central Bank', in *Money, Trade and Economic Growth*, in honour of John Henry Williams, New York 1951, pp. 270–95.

100. H. ROSE, 'Liquidity Preference and Loanable Funds', *Rev. Econ. Stud.*, February 1957, **24**, 111–19.

101. R. S. SAYERS, 'Monetary Thought and Monetary Policy in England', *Econ. Jour.*, December 1960, **70**, 710–24.

102. J. R. SCHLESINGER, 'After Twenty Years: The General Theory', *Quart. Jour. Econ.*, November 1956, **70**, 581–602.

103. I. O. SCOTT, 'The Availability Doctrine: Theoretical Underpinnings', *Rev. Econ. Stud.*, October 1957, **25**, 41–8.

104. R. T. SELDEN, 'Monetary Velocity in the United States', in Milton Friedman, ed., *Studies in the Quantity Theory of Money*, Chicago 1956, pp. 179–257.

105. G. L. S. SHACKLE, 'Recent Theories Concerning the Nature and Role of Interest', *Econ. Jour.*, June 1961, **71**, 209–54.

106. E. S. SHAW, 'Money Supply and Stable Economic Growth', in *United States Monetary Policy*, New York 1958, pp. 49–71.

107. D. SHELBY, 'Some Implications of the Growth of Financial Intermediaries', *Jour. Finance*, December 1958, **13**, 527–41.

108. H. C. SIMONS, 'Rules versus Authorities in Monetary Policy', *Jour. Pol. Econ.*, February 1936, **44**, 1–30; reprinted in H. C. Simons, *Economic Policy for a Free Society*, Chicago 1948, pp. 160–83.

109. W. L. SMITH, *Debt Management in the United States*. Study Paper No. 19, Joint Economic Committee, 86th Cong., 2nd sess. Washington 1960.

110. ——, 'Financial Intermediaries and Monetary Controls', *Quart. Jour. Econ.*, November 1959, **73**, 533–53.

111. ——, 'Monetary Theories of the Rate of Interest: A Dynamic Analysis', *Rev. Econ. Stat.*, February 1958, **40**, 15–21.

112. ——, 'On the Effectiveness of Monetary Policy', *Am. Econ. Rev.*, September 1956, **46**, 588–606.

113. J. TOBIN, 'A Dynamic Aggregative Model', *Jour. Pol. Econ.*, April 1955, **63**, 103–15.

114. ——, 'Liquidity Preference and Monetary Policy', *Rev. Econ. Stat.*, May 1947, **29**, 124–31.

115. J. TOBIN, 'Liquidity Preference as Behavior Towards Risk', *Rev. Econ. Stud.*, Feb. 1958, **25,** 65–86.
116. ——, 'Money, Capital and Other Stores of Value', *Am. Econ. Rev. Proc.*, May 1961, **51,** 26–37.
117. ——, 'The Interest-Elasticity of Transactions Demand for Cash', *Rev. Econ. Stat.*, August, 1956, **38,** 241–47.
118. G. S. TOLLEY, 'Providing for Growth in the Money Supply', *Jour. Pol. Econ.*, December, 1957, **65,** 465–85.
119. S. C. TSIANG, 'Liquidity Preference and Loanable Funds Theories, Multiplier and Velocity Analysis: A Synthesis', *Am. Econ. Rev.*, September 1956, **46,** 539–64.
120. R. TURVEY, 'Consistency and Consolidation in the Theory of Interest', *Economica*, November 1954, **21,** 300–7.
121. ——, *Interest Rates and Asset Prices.* London 1960.
122. S. VALAVANIS, 'A Denial of Patinkin's Contradiction', *Kyklos*, 1955, **4,** 351–68.
123. H. H. VILLARD, 'Monetary Theory', in H. S. ELLIS, ed., *A Survey of Contemporary Economics*, Philadelphia 1948, pp. 314–51.
124. S. WEINTRAUB, *An Approach to the Theory of Income Distribution.* Philadelphia 1958.
125. W. H. WHITE, 'The Flexibility of Anticyclical Monetary Policy', *Rev. Econ. Stat.*, May 1961, **43,** 142–7.
126. 'A Flow-of-Funds System of National Accounts: Annual Estimates, 1939–54', *Fed. Res. Bull.*, October 1955, **41,** 1085–124.
127. Committee on the Working of the Monetary System (Chairman: The Rt. Hon. The Lord Radcliffe, G.B.E.), *Report.* London 1959.
128. *Money and Credit: Their influence of Jobs, Prices and Growth.* Englewood Cliffs, N.J. 1961.
129. U.S. Congress, Joint Economic Committee, *Staff Report on Employment, Growth, and Price Levels.* Washington 1959.

CHAPTER II

RECENT DEVELOPMENTS IN
MONETARY THEORY*

I. INTRODUCTION

The field of monetary theory has been developing very rapidly during the past 10 years, as a result of a variety of influences. These influences include the attractive theoretical intricacy of monetary problems, particularly the incentive to formulate monetary theory in terms of more modern general equilibrium concepts. That particular strand of development goes back to the effort of Oscar Lange to translate Keynesian theory into general equilibrium theory, and continues through the work of Lloyd Metzler, Don Patinkin, R. M. Clower and a number of other primarily mathematical economists.[1] The most important influence on the field, however, has been the fact that monetary policy has been revived as a major instrument of economic policy. The revival of monetary policy in postwar circumstances has raised a great many evident problems—questions of how monetary policy works (if it works), what it can do, and so forth—which have given a policy orientated edge to interest in the field. In particular, there have been three major inquiries into monetary policy: by the Radcliffe Committee in England, the Commission on Money and Credit in the United States, and the Royal Commission on Banking and Finance in Canada.[2]

* This chapter is a revised version of the first of two survey lectures in monetary theory delivered to la Reunión de Centros Argentinas de Investigación Económica, at the Instituto Torcuato di Tella, Buenos Aires, Argentina, in the summer of 1963. Reprinted with revisions from the *Indian Economic Review*, Vol. 6, No. 3, February 1963, pp. 29–69 and Vol. 6, No. 4, August 1963, pp. 1–28.

[1] Oscar Lange, Price Flexibility and Employment, Bloomington, 1944; Lloyd A. Metzler, 'Wealth, Saving and the Rate of Interest', *Journal of Political Economy*, LIX, no. 2, April 1951, 93–116; Don Patinkin, *Money, Interest and Prices*, Evanston 1956.
[2] Committee on the Working of the Monetary System (Chairman: The Right Hon. The Lord Radcliffe, G.B.E.), *Report*, London 1959; *Money and*

All of these have meant that economists either have been persuaded or have been bribed to turn their attention to the question of how monetary policy works; and the result has been a very rapid development of theoretical concepts and of econometric studies, as well as of general knowledge about how monetary affairs are conducted.

To summarize all of this work would involve a tremendous effort, going beyond the scope of an essay; I shall instead concentrate on what I think has been the main line of the development in monetary theory. This can be described in terms of two general tendencies. The first and most important from the theoretical point of view has been the application of capital theory to monetary theory—the effort to work out the theory of money in terms of the theory of capital, regarding money as an asset which is alternative to other assets, and the choice as to how much money to hold as a problem whose solution requires capital theory concepts. The second has been a shift of interest from static equilibrium theory to analysis in terms of processes of adjustment over time. This is a natural extension, given the extension of general theory into dynamics; but it is particularly important for any monetary theory that claims to have some relevance to the world of affairs and to policy, because as soon as one starts to think seriously of economic policy, one's main problem is not the direction of the influence of changes in various economic variables, but the timing relationships involved. In other words, any really concrete economic policy has to be concerned primarily with timing, timing both of changes of policy and of the working out of the policy; so that the emphasis on dynamic adjustment processes fits the revival of monetary policy as an instrument of economic control.

Within the general framework of the application of capital theory and the increased attention to processes of adjustment over time, I have chosen six topics for discussion in this essay. There are of course various alternative ways of surveying monetary theory. In my survey article on monetary theory for the *American Economic Review*,[1] I attempted to organize the

---

Credit: Their Influence on Jobs, Prices and Growth, Englewood Cliffs 1961; *Report of the Royal Commission on Banking and Finance*, Ottawa 1964.

[1] Harry G. Johnson, 'Monetary Theory and Policy', *American Economic*

material from the strict standpoint of monetary theory. But for the purposes of a general survey of recent developments one ought to cast the net wider than that, and for this reason I have chosen six problems which originate in Keynes' *General Theory* as the core of this essay. I shall discuss how monetary theory has developed since the *General Theory* in respect to each of these problems.

The first of these problems is the role of money in the economy. The second concerns the theory of the propensity to consume or the consumption function. The third is concerned with the theory of investment, the fourth with the theory of demand for money, and the fifth with the theory of the supply of money. Finally, I shall comment on some current ideas on monetary policy. I do not propose to deal at length with the propensity to consume and the propensity to invest, since these are problems which extend far outside the range of monetary theory and into general economic theory; but I shall discuss briefly the way in which those areas have developed, because they fit into the general pattern of the application of capital theory to monetary theory.

II. THE ROLE OF MONEY IN THE ECONOMY

The *General Theory* poses the role of money as a major problem in two ways: first as a general proposition, and secondly as a more specific concrete analytical proposition. The general proposition, which is not only stated in the Preface to the *General Theory* but is implicit in the whole book, is that a monetary economy is essentially different from a barter economy. This proposition is defended in Keynes' attack on Say's Law and in other parts of the book; it is a general proposition which underlies the concrete, and therefore more striking, contentions of the *General Theory*, and the argument about it has been carried on in a separate context from the argument about the more concrete proposition of the book. That proposition concerns the possibility of underemployment equilibrium in a monetary economy; the specific proposition is that a

Review, LII, no. 3, June 1962, 335–84, reprinted as Chapter I above. See also *ibid.*, 'The General Theory After Twenty-five Years', *American Economic Review, Proceedings*, LI, no. 2, May 1961, 1–17.

monetary economy will come into equilibrium within a range
of possibilities of which full employment is only one extreme.

The concrete proposition about underemployment equilibrium has been the main focus of the subsequent debate
between the Keynesian and the so-called 'classical' or 'orthodox'
economists, and much of the recent theoretical development has
concentrated on that particular proposition. The argument of
the *General Theory* was developed on the assumption of a
given level of money wages. On that assumption the quantity of
money is fixed in real terms, and this fact in conjunction with
the other elements of the Keynesian system gives rise to the
possibility of underemployment equilibrium. The analytical
question is whether the possibility of underemployment
equilibrium depends essentially on that assumption of rigid
wages. If it does then Keynes was merely maintaining that we
must assume that wages are rigid; this makes a difference to
our analytical conclusions, but it does not change our theory,
since all it implies is a switch from the assumption of flexible
wages to the assumption of rigid wages. If, on the other hand,
the possibility of underemployment equilibrium exists in spite
of the assumption of flexible wages, then there is a definite
difference in the theory. If I have a theory which relates equilibrium to flexible wages and prices, and I then assume that
wages and prices are not flexible, I need simply to invert the
theory; I obtain a different kind of equilibrium, but I have not
changed the theory; I have simply changed the factual assumption that I am employing. If, on the other hand, my theory
says that there will be an equilibrium with certain characteristics, and there is another theory which says that under precisely
the same factual assumptions the equilibrium will have different
characteristics, then that other theory is really a different
theory.

The question, then, is whether the Keynesian theory simply
amounts to saying that in reality wages are fixed, or close
enough to fixed to justify treating them as fixed, or whether it
differs from previous theory in a more fundamental sense. To
answer this question, it is necessary to consider what happens
if one allows wages to be flexible in the Keynesian system; and
one quickly arrives at the result that the system will get to full
employment with flexible wages, with two exceptions. The one

exception is where consumption and investment are not at all responsive to changes in the rate of interest. The other exception is where the demand for money becomes infinitely elastic with respect to the rate of interest at a level higher than would be consistent with full employment.

The basic analysis here proceeds by relating the effect of flexible wages and prices to that of changes in the quantity of money. Starting from a given quantity of money measured in nominal terms, a reduction in wages and prices will increase the real quantity of money (the amount of money measured in wage units, as Keynes measured it, or the amount of money measured in purchasing power). The question is whether this increase in the real quantity of money will increase demand enough to move the system to full employment; the way in which it will do this is through the effect of lower interest rates on demand. So obviously there are two blocks which may prevent the economy from reaching full employment. The first occurs when the nature of the demand for money is such that interest rates will not fall as the quantity of money increases, in other words, people simply absorb more and more money at a given level of interest rates which will not secure full employment. The other block occurs when even though interest rates can be reduced to a minimal level (clearly one cannot have negative interest rates, but one can get interest rates down towards zero) this does not increase investment or increase consumption sufficiently to increase aggregate demand to the full employment level. Both of those cases are obviously special cases, and empirical possibilities rather than theoretical novelties; but still they constituted the Keynesian reply to the argument that the possibility of underemployment equilibrium depends on rigid wages.

The counter-argument which was produced concentrated on the effects of the increased wealth that results from an increased real value of the money supply. This argument is that regardless of what happens to interest rates and the demand for money, as the price level falls the real value of money increases, people become wealthier, and eventually this will lead to increased consumption or increased investment, even though there is no change in interest rates. This argument calls in the so-called 'Pigou effect'; and it has, I would judge, been accepted by most economists as a refutation of the Keynesian under-employment equilibrium proposition, so that the theory is reduced to one which concentrates on the rigidity of wages. In the more recent interpretations of the Keynesian theory it is argued that what Keynes was really doing was to assert, with the very crude theoretical technique of that time, that though in fact there are wage adjustment processes in the economy, these work so slowly that one might as well forget about them for practical purposes. In other words, fundamentally he was asserting that it is much more realistic to assume that wages are rigid, than to assume that they are flexible enough to bring about full employment via the Pigou effect within any reasonable period of time. The modern tendency therefore, is to interpret the Keynesian theory not as resting on the unrealistic assump-tion that wages are rigid when they are not, but as emphasizing that in the period of time with which we are concerned for most practical purposes the flexibility of the system is too small to allow the processes of adjustment to maintain a consistently high level of employment.

What I have just discussed is the practical or semipractical analytical proposition of the *General Theory*. The general proposition concerns the question of the role of money in the economy. Here I think that the subsequent literature on this question has departed very widely from what Keynes really meant when he insisted that a monetary economy is different from a barter economy. In my judgment, Keynes was trying to draw attention to the facts that in a monetary economy behaviour is based on expectations about the future, and that an important part of that behaviour relates to the demand for money, the hoarding of money and therefore the determination of interest rates. The line of analysis that started from that proposition, however, has been concerned with a rather different problem, namely: suppose an economy which uses money, but which is basically the same kind of economy as a barter economy, in the sense that it operates in an environment of fairly high certainty about the future, so that the problem is not uncertainty but simply the fact that people have an asset, money, as well as current supplies of commodities that they can exchange; then what difference does the presence of money make to the way that economy functions? Thus there is a wide separation between what Keynes was analysing, which was an advanced industrial economy dependent on the use of money, contracts, and so forth, and this theoretical problem, which concerns an economy which is as close as possible to a barter economy without quite getting there so that money still has a role to play.

The problems involved here, as they have been cast particularly by Don Patinkin, whose main work has been concerned with this problem, are of two sorts.[1] Both sorts relate to the structure of classical theory, which treated relative prices as being determined by real demands (tastes) and real supplies (production conditions), and the money price level as depending on the quantity of money in relation to the demand for money. The first problem concerns what is called the classical dichotomy, which I have just described, where there is a real theory for relative prices and a monetary theory for the level of prices, and these are treated as being separate problems, so that in analysing what determines relative prices one does not have to introduce money, whereas in analysing what determines the level of money prices, one does not have to introduce the theory of relative prices. The problem here is how these two theories can be reconciled. Once this has been done, the second problem arises: whether the reconciliation permits one to arrive at the classical proposition that an increase in the quantity of money will increase all prices in the same proportion, so that relative prices are not dependent on the quantity of money. That particular property is described technically as the 'neutrality' of money. If money is 'neutral', an increase in the quantity of money will merely raise the level of money prices without changing relative prices and the interest rate (which is a particular relative price). In Pigou's terminology, money will be simply a 'veil' covering the underlying real operations of the system.

The classical dichotomy poses the problem of how, if demands for goods are determined entirely by their relative prices, a change in the quantity of money can lead to a change in the price level. The standard explanation offered by classical monetary theory was that if people receive an increase in their money balances they will try to spend this increase, and this

[1] Don Patinkin, *op. cit.*

will put up prices. But as soon as one produces that explanation, one is saying that the demands for goods depend not only on relative prices, but also on the amount of money people have. The question that then arises is how this assumption can be reconciled with the assumption made in price theory, that quantities demanded are determined simply by relative prices. The solution to this problem, as Patinkin develops it, is to introduce the stock of real balances held by individuals as an influence on their demand for goods; it should be stressed that what is involved here is real balances, that is, the real purchasing power of people's money holdings. The consequence of making demands depend on real balances as well as relative prices is that if there is, say, a chance increase in the price level, this will reduce people's real balances and therefore lead them to try to rebuild their balances by spending less; this in turn will force prices back down, so that the presence of real balances as an influence on demands ensures the stability of the price level. Also the assumption that what people demand is *real* balances rather than nominal balances implies the classical 'neutrality' of money, and the proportionality of the money price level to the quantity of money, because if everyone's money balances and the money price level are simultaneously doubled, relative prices and individual real balances will be unchanged so that the equilibrium of the system will not be disturbed. Thus the introduction of the 'real balance effect' disposes of the classical dichotomy, that is, it makes it impossible to talk about relative prices without introducing money; but it nevertheless preserves the classical proposition that the real equilibrium of the system will not be affected by the amount of money, all that will be affected will be the level of prices.

This is Patinkin's solution to the problem; but it has not been completely accepted. The basic disagreements centre on whether or not it is necessary to retain this real balance effect in the real analysis; in my view it is clear that if the real analysis is confined to equilibrium situations, the real balance effect can be omitted. Its only function is to keep the price level at the level which ensures equilibrium between the demand for money and the supply of it, so that if all one is concerned with is what determines relative prices and quantities, one does not need the real balance effect because one can simply assume that the monetary behaviour of the system has adjusted itself to equilibrium. What one needs the real balance effect for is to ensure the stability of the price level; one does not need it to determine the real equilibrium of the system, so long as one confines oneself to equilibrium positions. This is the conclusion established by Archibald and Lipsey in a famous article in *The Review of Economic Studies*,[1] though their methods of establishing it are not entirely satisfactory. Archibald and Lipsey show that Patinkin's analysis of the real balance effect is inadequate, inasmuch as Patinkin confines himself to the impact effect of a change in prices and does not work the analysis through to the long-run equilibrium. The result of the debate, in my judgment, is that the real balance effect must be considered not as a necessary part of general equilibrium theory but as a part of the analysis of monetary stability; in that context it performs the function of ensuring stability of the price level.

Even in this context there has been some questioning of Patinkin's argument, on the grounds that though some kind of monetary effect is necessary, it need not be a real balance effect. The real balance effect assumes that people are interested in the real value of their money balances; in other words, they do not suffer from 'money illusion', they hold money for what it will buy, and what determines their behaviour is the real value of their money holdings. This assumption yields the classical monetary proposition that a doubling of the money supply will lead to a doubling of prices, and no change in the real equilibrium. But a recent article by Cliff Lloyd[2] has shown that the stability of the price level can be obtained without assuming the real balance effect, but simply by assuming that there is a finite quantity of money and that people want to hold money for some unspecified reason. Why they want to hold it does not matter; nor does whether they are concerned with its real purchasing power or simply the nominal amount of it. The mere fact that they want to hold money and that the available quantity is fixed will ensure the stability of the price level; but

[1] G. C. Archibald and R. G. Lipsey, 'Monetary and Value Theory: A Critique of Lange and Patinkin', *Review of Economic Studies*, XXVI (1), no. 69, October 1958, 1–22.

[2] Cliff Lloyd, 'The Real Balance Effect: *Sine Qua* What?' *Oxford Economic Papers*, XIV, no. 3, October 1962, 267–74.

it will not produce the 'neutrality of money' of the classical theory.

One other piece of work needs to be mentioned in this context; this is the work of Gurley and Shaw.[1] These authors' main claim to fame is through their discovery of and emphasis on the fact that in a growing economy, along with the process of economic growth in real terms there is a proliferation of financial institutions—banks, savings institutions, and so forth —and their insistence that this fact makes a difference to monetary analysis. In support of this contention they have produced a large theoretical work, in which they develop the theme that financial intermediaries are important in the framework of the questions set by Patinkin as to whether or not money is neutral, and under what circumstance money will be neutral. In the course of the analysis they develop a variety of theoretical models; in particular, they draw an important distinction between what they call 'inside' money and 'outside' money.

Outside money is the kind of money that is assumed in the Patinkin kind of model; it is money which comes from outside the private sector and simply exists. Inside money, which Gurley and Shaw emphasize, is money created against private debt. One can think of outside money as being gold coins in circulation in a country that does not have any gold mines, these gold coins being a heritage from the past, or as paper currency printed by the government. In either case, outside money represents wealth to which there corresponds no debt. On the other hand, inside money is typified by bank deposits created by a private banking system, the deposits on the one side of the balance sheet corresponding to loans to private individuals on the other side, so that for every dollar of assets there is a dollar of somebody's debt. The difference between these two is that if money consists of a given quantity of gold coins, the real value of these coins, and therefore the wealth people think they have in the form of gold coins, will vary inversely with the price level. As prices go up the real value of this monetary wealth goes down. But with inside money, when prices go up a person who holds a dollar bill is poorer but a

[1] J. G. Gurley and E. S. Shaw, *Money in a Theory of Finance*, Washington 1960.

person who owes a dollar is richer in real terms, so that the money price level has no effect on the real wealth of the community as a whole.

Gurley and Shaw show with their different models that if the money supply consists of a combination of inside and outside money, the classical 'neutrality' of money does not hold. A money supply consisting of a combination of inside and outside money implies that changes in the quantity of money will not simply produce a movement up or down in the general price level, but will also produce changes in relative prices. The origin of this conclusion is easy enough to understand: whenever the public holds a combination of these kinds of money, a change in the quantity of one of them without a change in the other will change the ratios in which people are obliged to hold assets and owe liabilities. If there is a change in the amount of outside money without a change in the amount of inside money, there must be a change in the ratio of the debt that backs the inside money to the outside money, so that a change in the quantity of money involves a change in the real variables of the system. By contrast, if there were only one kind of money, say only outside money, a change in the price level could preserve the real value of the outside money with no real change in anything else.

To illustrate, suppose we start with a system which has only outside money, that is to say gold coins, and we double the amount of gold coins and simultaneously double the price level; then we get back to the initial real situation—that is, all relative prices are the same and the ratio of real balances to everything else is the same as it was before. Now suppose there are two kinds of money—gold coins and bank deposits—and suppose we double the amount of gold coins but do not change the amount of bank deposits; then if we double the price level we can restore the real value of gold coins, but we will reduce the real value of bank deposits and the assets backing them, so that the community cannot get back to the situation it started from; consequently there must be some change somewhere else in the system to reconcile people's desires for assets and liabilities with the changed amounts there are available.

This analysis takes Gurley and Shaw several hundred pages

to develop; but the key to it is the devising of a situation in which the ratios of assets change. The whole purpose of this is to show that money is not neutral; but this result is obvious once one appreciates what assumptions are necessary to make money neutral. To begin with, changes in the price level will always have redistribution effects; in addition there will always be expectations problems in any realistic kind of model. Consequently, if the effect of a monetary change is 'neutral', this will be only a coincidence. The Gurley and Shaw book may therefore be regarded, in a sense, as an effort to play the Patinkin game and make the answer come out different from Patinkin's answer; naturally Patinkin, in his review of the book,[1] shows that it is really not a different answer at all, but merely the consequence of a different set of assumptions.

To complete this part of the exposition, let me say that I do not think that this particular controversy is of great relevance to practical work on monetary policy or monetary analysis, or even I think to monetary theory, because most of the model building has been concerned with static models with no growth in them, and this makes it not too useful for the design of models intended to fit a world in which growth is actually going on. But there is one implication which is important for the field of pure monetary theory, and that comes out of the Gurley and Shaw construction of a model using inside money. Recall the argument on the possibility of underemployment equilibrium, where the real balance effect (the Pigou effect) is introduced as a means of disproving the possibility of under-employment equilibrium with flexible wages and prices. The disproof rests on the assumption that the fall in the money price level increases wealth by increasing the real value of money. This result obviously assumes that the money involved in this system is outside money, in other words, money which is an asset for someone without being a debt for anyone else. If one builds a model with inside money only, then money is always created against some other kind of debt, and this result does not follow. As the price level falls, some people (those who own money) become richer, others (those who owe money to banks) become poorer, but on balance the economy has not

[1] Don Patinkin, 'Financial Intermediaries and the Logical Structure of Monetary Theory', *American Economic Review*, LI, no. 1, March 1961, 95–116.

become richer, so that there is no Pigou effect and consequently that argument against the Keynesian position does not hold.

From the standpoint of devising a monetary theory that is intended to be relevant to the modern world, the inside money model is in my judgment a much more useful one than the outside money model, inasmuch as most modern monetary systems do involve money that is backed by the debt of somebody or other: either it is created against private debt or it is created against government debt. The Patinkin kind of analysis reinforces the real balance effect by assuming that people regard government debt as an asset but not as a liability, so that government debt gets thrown in with paper currency and gold coins or money backed by gold reserves as outside money. This assumption, however, does not make fundamental economic sense, at the level of abstraction at which the model is used. If there is government debt, the government will have to pay interest on that debt, and to get the money to pay that interest the government will have to levy taxes. In any kind of rational model people will realize that when the government debt increases their future taxes will also increase; consequently, we cannot assume that, if they are rational, they will feel richer than they would if the government debt were smaller and taxes were also smaller. This consideration leaves the outside money model's relevance dependent on the importance of gold and paper currency in the money supply; and to my mind the relatively greater importance of deposit money in modern monetary systems makes the inside money model a more reasonable one for the purpose of monetary theory than the outside money model used in the Patinkin kind of analysis.

III. THE PROPENSITY TO CONSUME

The concept of the propensity to consume plays an essential part in the whole Keynesian system. Nevertheless, this concept, which is so important in the Keynesian model, according to Keynes' own description of it rests on very little support: it rests mostly on the assertion that there is a fundamental psychological law according to which as income rises consumption rises but not as much. This is a rather crude way of constructing an economic theory, though economists ever since Adam Smith have relied at various crucial points on men's 'propensities', such as the natural propensity to truck, barter and exchange, and concepts of this kind, to disguise the fact that they are relying on observation rather than advancing an explanation of behaviour. This original concept of the propensity to consume was very strongly influenced by national income accounting (in fact, the development of the Keynesian theory can be related fairly closely to the development of national income accounting), and it rests on a very simple view of human nature—a person receives so much money income in a year and spends so much on consumption, consumption being determined by a simple relation between the money received and the money spent.

The attempt to use that kind of simple theory to forecast what would happen after the war broke down completely. It was forecast that there would be eight million unemployed in the United States, and this prediction completely failed to come true. One consequence of the traumatic shock of this failure in prediction was an effort to look more closely into consumption behaviour in order to formulate a better theory. Some of the early attempts involved trying to relate consumption to assets as well as to income, or to build in the persistence of habit and what are called ratchet effects; the latter effects incorporate the assumption that once a person has achieved a certain level of consumption he is reluctant to descend from it, but that his consumption behaviour as he moves up to a higher level of income is different. These modifications of the theory can best be viewed as rather crude attempts to get away from the simple idea of income as so much cash receipts and consumption as so much cash outflow towards a more comprehensive theory of consumption behaviour as determined by 'normal' income or 'wealth'. They were followed closely by much more sophisticated attempts to analyse consumption behaviour, attempts which were based on a more detailed analysis of the relation between income and capital. There are two of these attempts which I consider particularly interesting.

The first is Friedman's permanent income hypothesis.[1] Friedman's argument starts from a criticism of the measures

[1] Milton Friedman, *A Theory of the Consumption Function*, Princeton 1957.

of income and consumption that had been used so far. The criticism is that one's income is not one's cash receipts in a particular period, otherwise say the average worker would have zero income on four days of the week and a big income on the fifth, and if one tried to develop a consumption function based on that concept of income one would find that on four days he was spending without receiving any income and on the fifth day he was receiving income and spending very little of it. Consequently, Friedman's argument is concerned with the proper definition of income, and also with the proper definition of consumption. Friedman's analysis develops the concept of permanent income, that is of normal income as distinct from whatever current cash receipts may be, and also refines the concept of consumption to comprise the current using of goods rather than purchases.

The problem of defining consumption arises because a great deal of consumption expenditure is the purchase of capital assets of various kinds. The purchase of a loaf of bread is one thing, the purchase of an automobile is another; and the purchase of an automobile can be regarded as a form of investment in consumer capital, so that a distinction is necessary between consumption expenditure, in the sense of expenditure on flow items, things that are used up, and saving, which includes not only cash saving or purchase of financial assets but also the accumulation of consumer capital. Friedman's theory is that consumption in this sense is determined by 'permanent' (normal) income and is a constant proportion of it; that cash receipts are made up partly of 'permanent' income and partly of 'transitory' income (the excess or deficiency of cash receipts as compared with permanent income); and that people save all of their transient income, positive or negative. Space limitations forbid discussion of the statistical testing of this theory; but it is worth emphasizing that Friedman's analysis is essentially a way of trying to refine the income concept until it becomes the equivalent of a wealth concept. The idea of permanent income is essentially a concept of wealth, because one can always regard wealth as a source of permanent income. And, similarly, if one defines income as permanent income, one is in fact defining wealth rather than income.

The other approach, which is in some ways more interesting than Friedman's, is the Modigliani-Brumberg-Ando attempt to relate consumption behaviour to the life-cycle of income and expenditure.[1] The essence of the permanent income hypothesis is the notion of 'normal' income, which the individual is assumed to derive from his cash receipts of recent years, whereas the Modigliani-Brumberg-Ando model looks at the individual's behaviour as determined by his whole life-cycle. In the early part of his life he is consuming without earning income, in the middle part he is earning income and consuming less than the whole of it, the purpose being to accumulate assets so as to support him in the final stage of his life-cycle after the completion of his working life. In other words, the individual over his life cycle is trying to regularize the uneven flow of his cash receipts into a more regular flow of expenditure and to rearrange the receipts and expenditure pattern into one which supports his preferred flow of consumption. The simplest model of this theory leads to the conclusion that the average individual will do no net saving over his lifetime. All his savings will be temporary savings, made at the time when he is earning most money and destined to be used to support him later in his life; the rational individual in this theory would expire clutching his last penny in his hand, that penny being necessary to pay the last instalment on his funeral. But the theory can easily be modified to allow for the desire to leave assets to one's heirs. And it gives some interesting results—for example, that the rate of net saving in an economy will depend on the growth-rate of the population and the rate of increase of productivity. Each individual will be planning to use up his savings over his life, but if there are more and more individuals all the time, obviously at each point of time there will be more people saving than dissaving; similarly, if the new generation has higher incomes than the old generation, its savings will exceed the dissavings of the previous generation. One of the interesting aspects of this analysis is that by giving reasonable

[1] Franco Modigliani and Richard Brumberg, 'Utility Analysis and the Consumption Function: An Interpretation of Cross-Section Data', 383–436 in K. K. Kurihara (ed.), *Post-Keynesian Economics*, New Brunswick, 1954; Albert Ando and Franco Modigliani, 'The "Life-Cycle" Hypothesis of Saving: Aggregate Implications and Tests', *American Economic Review*, LIII, no. 1, March 1963, 55–84.

magnitudes to the parameters of the model one obtains predictions of rates of savings that test out fairly well against the observed values. This theory again is an attempt to move away from the simple Keynesian notion of income as cash receipts to a notion of income related to wealth and related also to the choice between accumulation of assets or decumulation of assets and the enjoyment of current consumption.

Finally, reference should be made to an interesting piece of work in this same general area, by Alan Spiro.[1] Spiro's work is interesting for two reasons. First, he attacks the Keynesian assumption that the marginal propensity to consume is less than one; and secondly, his model essentially is a real-balance model of the Patinkin type, but with an Archibald and Lipsey mechanism. His argument starts from the assumption that people save to build up their assets. Clearly there will be some limit to the quantity of assets they will want to accumulate, *given* the level of income they have. In other words, ignore the fact that assets yield income; if income were constant, people would want to build up a stock of assets appropriate to that level of income. Given enough time, they would build up their stock of assets to the desired level, and thereafter they would consume all their income. Similarly, if their incomes were to fall, they would gradually decumulate assets, consuming more than their incomes until eventually their assets were reduced to a level commensurate with the reduced level of income. This theory implies a unit marginal propensity to consume out of income, if income is held constant over a long enough run. Spiro has tested this theory against the US data and found that it works very nicely. His theory, again, is an attempt to sophisticate the theory of saving by relating it to capital theory instead of relying on the simple Keynesian assumption that people consume some of their income and save some of it. All of these theories attempt to relate saving behaviour to the motives for saving; and the Modigliani-Brumberg-Ando model and the Spiro model in particular are interesting for their attempt to relate consumption theory to the fundamentals of capital theory.

[1] Alan Spiro, 'Wealth and the Consumption Function', *Journal of Political Economy*, LXX, no. 4, August 1962, 339–54.

IV. THE PROPENSITY TO INVEST

My discussion of this problem will be very brief. The main development has followed the line of going beyond the Keynesian, or perhaps I should say more accurately the Hansen-Hicks,[1] 'flow' approach to investment to a more sophisticated theory of investment as a process of capital accumulation. The simplest Keynesian model, which is not actually Keynes' model but a simplification of it, asserts the existence of a propensity to invest which relates the rate of investment expenditure to the rate of interest. Behind the propensity to invest lies the real rate of return on investment, but that has to be related to the current rate of interest to determine how much investment will take place. The model may also be extended to allow investment to depend also on the level of income; but the essential notion is that investment is a *flow* of spending which depends simply on the rate of interest, and possibly on the level of income.

This treatment of investment assumes that the desire to invest is fundamentally the same as the desire to eat bread. If the economy can go on day after day eating bread, then it can go on day after day investing. But such a treatment of investment is not reasonable, given that the purpose of investing is to create a capital stock which is to exist as a stock and is not to be used up immediately—the essence of capital is precisely that it is a stock. The modern approach is to regard investment as a process of accumulating capital stock, of adjusting an actual level of stock to the level desired. In other words, it is not the rate of investment but the desired capital stock that is a function of, say, the rate of interest and the level of income. Other determining variables may also be introduced; but the basic notion is that what is desired is a certain stock of capital, not a rate of investment, and that investment is the process of moving from the actual stock towards that desired capital stock, the actual rate of investment being at any time a function of the difference between desired and actual stock. Expression of the rate of investment as a fraction

[1] J. R. Hicks, 'Mr. Keynes and the "Classics"; A Suggested Interpretation', *Econometrica*, V, no. 2, April 1937, 147–59; Alvin H. Hansen, *Monetary Theory and Fiscal Policy*, New York, 1949.

of this difference is the simplest kind of econometric formulation one can use, but obviously this is not necessary and one could have a much more complicated theory of the relationship. In any case, the central notion is that the level of actual investment is a by-product of the relation between the desired stock and the actual stock, so that instead of investment being simply a flow—comparable to consumption—it is a series of stages in an adjustment process, which stages do not necessarily repeat themselves. On this basis one can develop a rather elaborate accelerator or capital-stock-adjustment model of economic fluctuations and growth. Suppose that income rises; this will raise the desired capital stock; this in turn will raise investment, as people try to make up the desired stock; and then, depending on the relationships between the economic variables in the model, eventually the economy may reach the desired capital stock. But that desired stock is dependent on the level of income; and as soon as the economy stops accumulating capital stock, or even slows down the rate at which it is accumulating capital, the level of income drops and the capital stock that formerly was appropriate becomes excessive, so that the economy moves from upswing into downswing. The mechanism, with appropriate magnitudes of the parameters, yields a business cycle model, and can also be developed to give a growth model with oscillations in the process of growth.[1]

V. THE DEMAND FOR MONEY

I return now to problems of monetary theory narrowly defined, beginning with the theory of demand for money. The Keynesian theory left the demand for money in a rather unsatisfactory state. Before the Keynesian theory, the general approach to the demand for money tended to be a rather mechanistic one, assuming that money is used for circulating goods and that there are various technical factors which determine how much money is needed for this purpose—the length of the pay period, for example, and the degree of development of banking —and which therefore determine the relation between money and income. That kind of theorizing broke down disastrously in the 1930's, when velocity proved to be quite variable instead

[1] For an early example of such a model, see N. Kaldor, 'A Model of the Trade Cycle', *Economic Journal*, L, no. 197, March 1940, 78–92.

of being the rigid constant it was assumed to be; and part of the Keynesian attack on classical theory was directed at the notion that there is a rigid relationship between the quantity of money and the level of income.

Keynes formulated the demand for money in a new way, in terms of two major motives for holding money—the transactions demand and the assets demand. The assets demand was formulated as a quite sophisticated speculative theory of demand for money, but the transactions demand retained the old assumption that the amount of money needed to circulate income is technically fixed by the conditions and customs of society. Keynes' theory of demand for money is therefore a rather awkward hybrid of two theoretically inconsistent approaches, with the transactions demand being regarded as technologically determined, and the assets demand being treated as a matter of economic choice. In expounding this theory Keynes also threw most of the emphasis in the analysis of the asset demand for money on liquidity preference and the speculative motive for keeping assets in monetary form.

The subsequent tendency has been to depart from this mechanistic treatment of transactions demand in two ways. The first has been to aggregate the demand for money, on the grounds that the public does not hold two stocks of money, but instead holds just one stock of money, though it holds this stock for various purposes, which include the transactions motive and the asset motive. The second has been to develop a capital-theory approach to the transactions demand, the idea being that money is a kind of working capital, an inventory serving that function in the processes of production and consumption, and that just as there is maximizing behaviour with respect to inventories of goods, so there is maximizing behaviour with respect to the inventory of money. Baumol and Tobin have developed a formal analysis of transactions demand on this basis.[1] The problem of inventory theory is that

[1] W. J. Baumol, 'The Transactions Demand for Cash: An Inventory Theoretic Approach', *Quarterly Journal of Economics*, LXVI, no. 4, November 1952, 545–56; James Tobin, 'The Interest-Elasticity of Transactions Demand for Cash', *Review of Economics and Statistics*, XXXVIII, no. 3, August 1956, 241–7; see also Harry G. Johnson, 'Notes on the Theory of Transactions Demand for Cash', *Indian Journal of Economics*, XIV, Part I, no. 172, July 1963, 1–11 (Chapter 5 below).

it costs more to hold more inventory, but the more inventory you hold the less likelihood there is of costly interruptions in production, so that the choice of an optimal inventory involves balancing the cost of extra inventory and the advantages of extra inventory in terms of facilitating production. When transactions demand is analysed in this way, it turns out to follow the same sort of rule as optimum inventory policy; in particular the money needed for transactions will be inversely related to the interest rate and will not vary proportionately to the quantity of transactions but according to a complex relation involving the square root of the total of transactions. This development of the theory of demand for money has therefore brought the transactions demand into the fold of capital theory, thus removing the awkwardness and inconsistency of Keynes' mechanical treatment of transactions demand.

Another development of the theory of demand for money since Keynes' time has been the extension of the theory to take account of the differentiation among assets. The Keynesian theory assumes for simplicity only two assets, money and bonds; and the demand for money is viewed as the choice to hold money instead of bonds on the basis of the current yield of the bonds and prospective changes in that yield. One obvious line of development was to allow for the variety of assets, particularly to distinguish between short term securities, long term securities and equities. One consequence of this has been to reduce the emphasis Keynes placed on the purely speculative motive for holding money—liquidity preference proper. Once one recognizes the existence of short term securities, the speculative motive for holding money becomes not a speculative motive for holding money instead of bonds but a speculative motive for holding short term securities instead of bonds. In other words, the Keynesian analysis carries the implication that if an asset-owner is worried about a possible fall in bond prices he will put all his wealth into a bank. Speculators actually do not do that; instead they move from longs into shorts, so that all of that elasticity of demand for money that emerges from the Keynesian analysis ceases to refer to the demand for money specifically and instead refers to the demand for liquid assets in general. By similarly allowing other kinds of differences among assets than maturity, one arrives at a general theory of asset holding in which the rates of return on assets with differing characteristics determine the quantities of them that people want to hold; and in the general equilibrium context, the amounts of the different assets available determine the relative rates of return on these assets. This particular development has been pushed forward particularly at Yale University, under the description of 'portfolio-balance' theory, by James Tobin and his group, towards a theory of monetary behaviour and monetary management that stresses substitutions among assets, and views monetary policy as operating initially by changing the relative quantities of money and of other securities, these changes causing a ripple all through the chain of substitutable assets and eventually reaching the end of the chain and influencing decisions to invest or not to invest in real assets.[1]

Along with this theoretical development has gone a great deal of experimentation with the fitting of empirical demand curves for money. In this connection there has been a great deal of argument about how money should be measured, because empirical research requires a definition, and once one abandons the concept of money as a means of making trans-actions in favour of the concept of money as an asset, one is faced with the difficulty of defining money as distinct from non-monetary liquid assets. Once 'money' ceases to be defined as something the individual needs for making payments with, and becomes instead an asset alternative to securities, it becomes difficult to define empirically. At one extreme the purists maintain that money is only that which can be used for im-mediately making payment: that is, money is only currency plus bank deposits withdrawable by cheque. Others maintain that money is anything that serves the function of money, in the sense of being an asset whose capital value is safe, and they will include in money time deposits, savings deposits or even such far-fetched items as borrowing power on life insurance policies or tax deposit receipts.

These issues as to what money is are closely associated with the question of whether there is a stable demand function for

[1] For an outline of this approach, see James Tobin, 'Money, Capital and Other Stores of Value', *American Economic Review, Proceedings*, LI, no. 2, May 1961, 26–37.

money. This is an important question both for theory and for policy. Obviously there is no point in monetary theory if we cannot define what it is we are theorizing about; and there is no point in talking about monetary policy if whatever money is is something the Central Bank cannot get a grip on. The issues here are therefore deeper than might appear at first sight.

There have been many efforts to fit demand functions for money, for many different economies. Some of these have been motivated by the desire to test the Keynesian proposition that there is a liquidity trap—that is that at some low rate of interest people will absorb money indefinitely. Others have simply been concerned with determining whether there is a demand function for money that is stable enough to form a basis for monetary theory and for policy. There are three major empirical studies that are worth mentioning. One is by Friedman, and uses the permanent income hypothesis; it arrives at a demand function for money which is not interest elastic.[1] The second is a rather simple demand function fitted by Latané, which finds that the ratio of money to income is a function of the long term interest rate.[2] The interest of this empirical result is that, unlike most econometricians, Latané estimated the same thing twice with five years in between and—an outcome practically unparalleled in the history of econometrics—obtained a better result the second time than he did the first. The third piece of work, by Allan Meltzer, attempts to relate the demand for money to wealth rather than to income, and finds a substantial interest elasticity of demand for money.[3]

Whether the demand for money is interest-elastic or not is a more important question than appears at first sight, because it is fundamental to many issues in both monetary theory and monetary policy. Clearly the question of interest-elasticity of demand for money is crucial to the relevance of the Keynesian under-employment equilibrium trap. If it can be demonstrated

[1] Milton Friedman, 'The Demand for Money: Some Theoretical and Empirical Results', *Journal of Political Economy*, LXVII, no. 4, August 1959, 327–51.

[2] H. A. Latané, 'Cash Balances and the Interest Rate—A Pragmatic Approach', *Review of Economics and Statistics*, XXXVI, no. 4, November 1954, 456–60; 'Income Velocity and Interest Rates: A Pragmatic Approach', *Review of Economics and Statistics*, XLII, no. 4, November 1960, 445–9.

[3] Allan H. Meltzer, 'The Demand for Money: The Evidence from the Time Series', *Journal of Political Economy*, LXXI, no. 3, June 1963, 219–46.

that the demand for money is not interest-elastic at all, then one is back with the classical quantity theory with a constant velocity of circulation; and this implies that monetary policy must be tremendously effective, because by controlling the quantity of money the authorities are directly controlling money income—either real income and employment, or prices. If, on the other hand, the demand for money is interest-elastic, expansion or contraction of the money supply may simply change interest rates without having any significant influence on the level of income. Consequently, the results of the attempts to fit empirical demand functions for money raise some crucial issues about the effectiveness of monetary—and fiscal—policy.

VI. THE SUPPLY OF MONEY

The theory of money supply is a field in which there has been almost no work done until very recently; and yet it is a very important aspect of monetary theory. Keynes, and most monetary theorists, simply assumed that the Central Bank has control of the money supply, and worked out their theory in terms of a given quantity of money and what would happen if that quantity were changed. But obviously the fact is that the Central Bank does not have control of the money supply in that direct a sense. What it does control is the quantity of reserve money ('base' money), and this influences the total money supply through the behaviour of the public in determining the ratio of currency to deposits, and of the commercial banks in determining their reserve ratios of base money to deposits. There is, of course, a long-standing theory of the money supply which relates the total quantity of money to the amount of Central Bank money through a 'money multiplier' involving two coefficients, the one being the ratio in which the public holds currency and deposits and the other being the reserve-to-deposit ratio held by the commercial banks. If one is content to assume these two coefficients to be constant, obviously one can proceed to theorize about the influence of money on activity by simply assuming that the Central Bank's control of the reserves of the system is sufficient to control the total money supply.

The defect of that procedure, however, is that both of these ratios are not technically-determined or legally fixed coefficients, but are instead behaviour relationships. The decision as to whether to carry currency or hold a bank deposit is influenced, at least in principle, by the rate of return available on bank deposits as compared with the zero rate of return on currency. Similarly, the reserve ratio held by the banks is determined not only by legal requirements but also by their calculations of how much they want to hold in relation to their deposits additional to such requirements; and this in turn will depend on their expectations about future developments, their competition with other banks, and so forth, which will influence the probability of outflows of cash. Consequently the most recent tendency in theorizing about the supply of money has been to develop a theory of the supply of money more or less parallel with the theory of the demand for money, relating the money supply to the behaviour of the Central Bank, to the reserves desired by the commercial banks, and to the behaviour of the public, so that the theory of money supply becomes basically another exercise in capital theory.[1] The division of the public's assets between currency and deposits is obviously a question of capital theory, and similarly the amount of reserves desired by banks is another question of capital theory because these reserves are in effect an inventory that they hold against the possibilities of a cash withdrawal, just as a business holds inventories of its products against possible unexpected orders. The supply theory of money is therefore now being developed in the same way as the theory of demand for money.

One particular consequence is that the theory of the influence of monetary policy becomes very complicated, inasmuch as the desired relation of reserves to deposits will be influenced by the banks' expectations of what the Central Bank is going to do. If the banks experience an increase in reserves because the Central Bank has bought securities on the open market, they are faced with the problem of deciding whether this is a purely temporary increase in reserves or whether it is the first of a succession of increases; their view on this question will influence their behaviour, because it will determine their decision whether simply to hold the increased reserves in the form say of short-

---

[1] See, for example, A. J. Meigs, *Free Reserves and the Money Supply*, Chicago 1962.

D

term securities, or whether to expand their longer-term lending operations. Thus the money supply side of the picture involves just as great difficulties as the money demand side, and particularly raises the difficult problems of expectations and of reactions based on expectations.

The behaviour relationships involved in the supply of money also raise a problem for the analysis of demand for money. Most of the work on the latter problem has assumed that the amount of money in existence is given exogenously—that is, that money holdings, interest rates and so forth can be assumed to reflect only demand behaviour. Once one begins to view the monetary situation as reflecting the interaction of the demand of the public for money and the supply of money by the banks, the picture becomes much more complicated. In particular some questions arise about both the validity of the econometric work that has been done on the demand for money, most of which has employed single-equation regression techniques, and about how one should formulate a demand-supply model, a simultaneous equilibrium model, with these interacting adjustments in it.[1]

VII. MONETARY POLICY

The approach to the demand for money in terms of asset choices obviously involves a view of how monetary policy operates. The view that has been emerging from the writings of a variety of different monetary theorists, both Keynesians and classical quantity theorists, stresses the influence of monetary policy changes on the composition of assets that have to be held by the public, and the influence of these changes on the rates of return on these assets and ultimately on the rate of return from investing in the creation of new physical assets. In other words, the effect of a change in monetary policy is initially to change the composition of assets that the public has to hold. Monetary expansion increases the money that the people have to hold and reduces the government debt they have to hold. Conversely a monetary contraction forces them to hold

---

[1] For such a model, see Ronald Teigen, 'Demand and Supply Functions for Money in the United States: Some Structural Estimates', *Econometrica*, XXXII, No. 4, October 1964, 476–509.

more public debt and less money. This, according to the analysis, sets off a chain of adjustments as people reshuffle their portfolios of assets; and here it is necessary to take account not only of marketed assets but also of personal assets—consumers' durables, and other forms of wealth yielding returns not observable in the markets. The reshuffling of assets portfolios leads to a new set of rates of return on such assets, and this in turn makes it more profitable or less profitable to invest and create more real assets—including both consumer and producer capital.

The new approach to monetary theory therefore involves a new view of how monetary policy works. This new analysis raises some questions, incidentally, about the many efforts that have been made to determine just how monetary policy affects the economy. It is very easy to describe how monetary policy affects the economy if one starts from a simple view of investment as a flow of expenditure which depends on the rate of interest and possibly on the level of income. Also, on this view, to study the influence of monetary policy one needs simply to set up a regression equation with those variables in it, possibly with lags, and see whether investment expenditure is sensitive to changes in the rate of interest. But if on the other hand the process of investment is a process of capital accumulation which depends on the relations between the rates of return on all these different assets, many of which rates of return are not observable in the market place, then one's view of how investment is influenced by monetary policy has to be much more sophisticated, and in particular it is a much more difficult problem to get at that influence by econometric work. One can summarize the difficulty by saying that the same rate of interest on government debt can be either high or low according to circumstances; and that what influences investment is not the level of that interest rate, but its level relative to returns on alternative ways of investing money. This difficulty makes a great deal of the effort to measure the influence of monetary policy on the economy of doubtful validity, because most of that effort has started from much too naïve a conception of how monetary policy influences activity to be able to quantify the influence of money on activity in any reliable way.

The second point of interest is that once one seriously thinks of economic policy as a means of controlling the economy, what becomes important is not the direction of influence of policy on the economy, but the timing and the lags in the timing of the influence. There has been a great deal of work done recently on the influence of time lags on the efficiency or otherwise of policy, and on the design of efficient systems of policy management.

The one thing that becomes crystal clear from all this work is that the traditional method of operating central bank policy is probably the worst that could be devised from the standpoint of efficient stabilization. Central banks usually emphasize the 'flexibility' of monetary policy, the technique of 'probe and withdraw', the need for 'feel and flair', and other descriptions according to which policy is determined by looking at current information and implemented by making small adjustments in policy. In other words, the policy is always following the current development. Now if there is a lag between the change in the situation and the change in the policy, and another lag between the change in the policy and the effect on the economy, the delay involved between the change in the situation in the economy and the effect of the resulting change in policy might be so great that the policy consistently takes effect only after the need for it has disappeared, so that things are actually made worse rather than better. There have been various calculations made on how far lags in the economy might have this effect. One calculation by Thomas Mayer suggested that monetary policy as currently operated could only stabilize the economy by about 10 per cent of the actual variation because of these lags.[1] I made some calculations for the Royal Commission on Banking and Finance in Canada[2] on the influence of the first of these lags—between a change in the situation and a change in policy—on the effectiveness of monetary policy in 1958–62. In some months monetary policy was operating in the right direction, and in some months in the wrong direction; by subtracting the number of months in the second category from the number in the first and taking

[1] Thomas Mayer, 'The Inflexibility of Monetary Policy', *Review of Economics and Statistics*, XL, no. 4, November 1958, 358–74.

[2] Harry G. Johnson and John W. L. Winder, *Lags in the Effect of Monetary Policy in Canada* (Working Paper, Royal Commission on Banking and Finance), Ottawa 1964.

the result as a proportion of the total months, I obtained the result that monetary policy was doing more good than harm for about one month in twelve. This kind of performance will obviously not take a country far towards effective stabilization policies; the way in which such policies are usually operated is pretty certain, under the existing theory of stabilization policy, to lead to bad results.

Finally, let me say something further about the question of discovering econometrically the effects of monetary policy on the economy. There have been two views on how this problem should be approached: the Keynesian view and the Quantity Theory view, recently revived at the University of Chicago. I have stressed the difficulty of designing relationships which actually correspond to the way in which monetary policy operates; the difficulty here is precisely that the rates of return which are going to influence investment decisions are not for the most part observable. Now the Keynesian way of going about the problem involves trying to relate particular categories of spending, notably investment of various kinds but also consumption, to change in interest rates; and the problem is that the interest rates that must be used may not reflect the relevant costs and profits of investment. An alternative view, which has been put forward by Milton Friedman and his disciples,[1] is (and this is my own interpretation of it) that because of the difficulty of sorting out the relevant rates of return one cannot hope to obtain useful results by looking at relations between interest rates and categories of spending, and that a much more promising approach lies along the line of trying to relate changes in income directly to changes in the quantity of money.

The argument is that monetary policy operates through a complicated rearrangement of asset patterns, so complicated that one cannot trace down any particular path that it follows, but that one should be able to find some relationship between changes in the quantity of money and changes in income, this relationship operating with some sort of lag. In other words, the Keynesian theory pictures the influence of money as operating on income in a causal sequence that runs from the

[1] Milton Friedman, 'The Lag in Effect of Monetary Policy', *Journal of Political Economy*, LXIX, no. 5, October 1961, 447–66, especially, 461–3.

quantity of money to demand for money to rates of interest
and then to investment, and then through investment to income
by the multiplier. The Friedman view is that this whole process
is so difficult to trace that one should proceed instead by the
direct route from money to income, using the proposition that
there is a stable relationship between income and money.
Notice that the question of interest elasticity of demand for
money is of crucial importance to this alternative view, because
if the demand for money is not influenced significantly by the
interest rate, there will be a very simple relation between money
and income, whereas if the demand for money depends on the
rate of interest, one cannot hope to find a relationship unless
one specifies an independent theory of what determines the
interest rate. (There is therefore a certain suspicious appropriateness in the Friedman treatment of the cyclical behaviour
of velocity, which assigns interest rates only a small residual
role.)

Friedman and Meiselman conducted a major study for the
Commission of Money and Credit, testing the predictive power
of the theory that the quantity of money explains consumption
against the theory that investment determines consumption;
for the period from 1897 until recently they found that the
quantity of money worked better than the multiplier for all
periods but the 1930's.[1] The significance of this result depends
on which period one considers to be the right one for conducting such a test; any Keynesian can well argue that the 1930's
was the period for which the Keynesian theory was designed,

[1] Milton Friedman and David Meiselman, 'The Relative Stability of Monetary
Velocity and the Investment Multiplier in the United States, 1897–1958', in
Commission on Money and Credit, *Stabilization Policies*, Englewood Cliffs
1963, 165–268.

This research has provoked considerable controversy. See: D. D. Hester,
'Keynes and the Quantity Theory: A Comment on the Friedman-Meiselman
CMC Paper', *The Review of Economics and Statistics*, Vol. XLVI, no. 4, No-
vember 1964, pp. 364–8; M. Friedman and D. Meiselman, 'Reply to Donald
Hester', *ibid.*, pp. 369–76; D. D. Hester, 'Rejoinder', *ibid.*, pp. 373–7; A. Ando
and F. Modigliani, 'The Relative Stability of Monetary Velocity and the Invest-
ment Multiplier', *American Economic Review*, Vol. LV, no. 4, September 1965,
pp. 693–728; M. De Prano and T. Mayer, 'Tests of the Relative Importance of
Autonomous Expenditures and Money', *ibid.*, pp. 729–52; M. Friedman and
David Meiselman, 'Reply to Ando and Modigliani and to De Prano and Mayer',
ibid., pp. 753–85; A. Ando and F. Modigliani, 'Rejoinder', *ibid.*, pp. 786–90;
M. De Prano and T. Mayer, 'Rejoinder', *ibid.*, pp. 791–2.

a period in which there could be fluctuations in the level of employment and output, and that in showing that the Keynesian theory works better for that period Friedman and Meiselman have vindicated the Keynesian Revolution.

Incidentally, in my own work for the Canadian Royal Commission on Banking and Finance, my colleague and I tried approaches of the Friedman type. We could not find any influence of the quantity of money on particular expenditure categories; we also found that though we could explain total income as a lagged function of the money stock to some extent, we could do even better if we simply assumed that income this year depends on income last year—in that case the introduction of money did not improve the explanation of income at all. I conclude that this whole area is still in something of a state of flux, and that there is much work still to be done before definitive knowledge can emerge.

In this essay I have surveyed recent developments in monetary theory with respect to six major questions originating in Keynes' *General Theory*. The survey has been conducted within the general framework of two main aspects of development: one, the emphasis on capital theory, and two, the growing interest in time patterns of adjustment, both of which I think are central characteristics of modern monetary theory. Much has been going on in the field of monetary theory, and much has had to be omitted from this survey; but the survey has attempted to indicate the nature of the most important developments.

CHAPTER III

A SURVEY OF THEORIES
OF INFLATION*,1

I. INTRODUCTION

For the purposes of this survey I define inflation as a sustained
rise in prices. (There are other definitions which I shall discuss
subsequently.) While the definition of inflation as a sustained
rise in prices is a simple one, one encounters problems of
some difficulty as soon as one tries to apply it in practice. The
first such problem is that there may be price rises which are
not inflationary but are merely part of the normal working of
the competitive system. For example, it is obvious that if there
is a crop failure or something of that kind, there will be some
rise in prices to ration the reduced supply; again, if the economy
is moving upwards from the bottom of a recession to a higher
level of employment, there will inevitably tend to be some rise
in prices due to the increased demand for goods and labour.
In both cases, the rise of prices ought not to be regarded as
inflationary: first, because in the nature of things it will be
self-limiting, and second, because it does not in itself represent
any serious policy problem.

A second problem arises when one begins to consider what
prices (or price index) should be referred to as indicating the
presence or absence of inflation. For example, if one chooses a

* Based on the second of two survey lectures delivered to la Reunión de
Centros Argentinas de Investigación Económica, sponsored by Centro de
Investigaciones Económicas, Instituto Torcuato di Tella, Buenos Aires, Summer
1963; reprinted from the *Indian Economic Review*, Vol. VI, no. 4, August
1963.

1 For an officially-sponsored survey, including an extensive bibliography, see
Martin Bronfenbrenner and F. D. Holzman, 'Survey of Inflation Theory',
American Economic Review, Vol. LIII, no. 4, September 1963, pp. 593–661.
This article appeared after the lecture on which the present essay is based was
delivered; references to it have been added where convenient to economize on
extensive bibliography.

price index which includes the price of services, then in a normally advancing economy one would tend to observe an inflation according to this index, even though consumer goods prices were stable or even falling slightly, simply because the price of labour tends to rise relatively to the price of commodities as the economy progresses. This bias of general price indexes is relevant to the common practice of using implicit price deflators for the gross national product as indexes of price movements. A similar problem is posed by the question whether prices should be measured inclusive or exclusive of taxes; the difficulty here is that if the government increases taxes on commodities or labour in order to deflate the economy, this will tend to put up prices inclusive of taxes and will therefore appear to contribute to the inflation, at least temporarily, if prices inclusive of taxes are taken to measure inflationary behaviour. However, the problems arising from the fact that different price indexes behave somewhat differently will not be too serious if there is really a significant inflation going on, though the choice of price index will affect the measurement of the rate of inflation.

Not only are there difficulties connected with the choice among index numbers, but index numbers by their method of construction contain biases which may be important in the assessment of whether there is an inflation or not, and the measurement of the degree of inflation, if the inflation is of the mild kind. In particular, most price indexes do not take adequate account of improvements in the quality of goods, nor do they do very well with introducing and incorporating the behaviour of the prices of new goods. Now one important part of the process of economic growth comprises the gradual improvement of the technical quality of existing goods, so that a good of the same name and general description actually provides more service and satisfaction if produced at a later date than at an earlier one; and another important part of the growth process comprises the introduction of new products, products which command high prices when they are first introduced and then become mass-produced so that their prices fall. But price indexes typically do not correct quoted prices sufficiently for improvements in product quality, nor do they typically begin to include new products until after they have become mass-produced, so that the initial phase of falling prices is not reflected in the index. For both these reasons price indexes may, if one is not cautious in using them, create the impression of inflation when in fact no genuine inflation is present; for the shortcomings of the typical index may give an upward bias to price measurements of as much as a two or three per cent increase per year. For example, the Stigler Committee on Price Statistics in the United States[1] found that the appearance of inflation over the period since 1950, at the rate of about two per cent per year, might be entirely accounted for by the inadequacy of the consumer price index in taking into account changes in the quality of goods and the introduction of new goods. But it is not necessarily true that all countries' indexes are upward-biased to this extent—in fact, a similar study of the Canadian consumer price index failed to reveal any substantial upward bias.[2]

There is finally the difficulty that in some countries, particularly in the major European countries during and after the war and evidently in many underdeveloped countries at the present time, strong efforts have been made to suppress inflation by price and wage fixing; moreover, some of the more cunning governments have attempted to prevent the appearance of inflation in their price indexes by subsidizing those commodities which are particularly important components of the indexes while at the same time rationing them.

These are the difficulties raised by the definition of inflation I have adopted, according to which inflation is identified with a sustained rise in prices. There are other definitions of inflation, most of which attempt to go beyond the description of inflation to the causes of it. For example, quite frequently, particularly in popular discussion, inflation is defined as consisting in an increase in the quantity of money, or in an increase in the quantity of money at a faster rate than real national output is expanding; frequently also inflation is defined alternatively in terms of a sustained governmental budget deficit; and again inflation is often defined as a situation of chronic excess demand

---

[1] George Stigler, et al., *The Price Statistics of the Federal Government*, National Bureau for Economic Research, New York, 1961.

[2] A. Asimakopulos, 'The Reliability of Price Indexes as Measures of Price Trends', Staff Study, Royal Commission on Banking and Finance, Toronto 1962 (mimeographed).

for goods and services. These definitions have in common that they attempt to define inflation in terms of what is thought or alleged to cause it; and this, in my judgment, is a serious error of theoretical approach to inflation, inasmuch as the conditions to which these definitions call attention could exist without there being any inflation in the sense of a sustained rise in prices.

The error is particularly serious when it appears in discussions of economic policy, since definition of inflation in terms of the policies held to be responsible for it induces opposition to those policies regardless of whether their application would be inflationary or not, and thus stands in the way of intelligent use of those policies when the problem is not inflation but deflation. In the early 1930s, for example, there was a great deal of opposition to monetary expansion as a policy for overcoming mass unemployment, on the grounds derived from post World War I experience that such a policy would be gravely inflationary. As it proved, what expansion of the money supply there was in the 1930s was not inflationary but, to use the word that was coined precisely to circumvent the opposition just mentioned, reflationary—that is, it served to increase national income without inducing a significant rise in prices. Similarly, there was in the United States prior to the tax cut of 1964 a great deal of opposition to the proposal to reduce taxes as a means of stimulating economic activity and employment, on the grounds that this would mean a larger budget deficit and that a budget deficit is inherently inflationary. Causal definitions of inflation, therefore, tend to impede thought rather than facilitate it, and should accordingly be avoided as far as possible and used only with great care.

In my survey of inflation theory I propose to discuss six topics, each of which, obviously, I shall have to deal with fairly briefly. I shall first present an historical sketch of the problem of inflation and the views concerning it, because I believe that in this particular area of economics and economic policy economists are more the slaves of ideas derived from past experience than in most areas, and I find it useful to try to keep in mind the historical background of current discussions in order to maintain a proper scientific perspective. There is always a great temptation in economics, particularly in economics concerned with public policy, for the economist simply to accept some popular definition of the problem and to try to work with that conception, when what the economist should be doing is to examine whether the conception of the problem held by government, the general public, newspaper editorial writers, and so forth is really a relevant and fruitful one, or a misconception that distracts attention from the fundamental economics of the situation. Next I shall sketch out the two major approaches to the analysis of inflation that have been developed, the Keynesian approach and the quantity theory approach. The quantity theory approach is probably most familiarly known under the general description of the theory of the inflation tax. Then I shall comment on the debate that raged a few years ago, but which seems to have died down considerably in recent years (since say 1962), the debate over cost-push versus demand-pull inflation. This debate originated in the economic situation of the United States in the latter 1950s, which was characterized by rising prices coupled with a lower level of employment and activity than had been customary and which raised the question whether inflation was due to the autonomous upward movement of costs or whether it could be explained by the pull of demand. In this connection I shall also deal with a particular piece of analytical apparatus that has had considerable influence on the practical analysis of the inflation problem, the so-called Phillips curve. Then I shall summarize some empirical findings on inflation, and finally discuss the policy issues involved in the choice among price stability and other economic objectives.

II. A BRIEF HISTORICAL SKETCH OF
INFLATION PROBLEMS AND THEORY

In understanding current arguments about and views on inflation, it is I think necessary to attach a great deal of importance to the impact on public opinion of the inflations that took place during World War I and continued after that war in the continental European countries, and particularly to the impact of the German hyperinflation in the early 1920s. That experience came after a long period of stable or declining prices, and had tremendous political implications; and one of its results was to build into popular and professional ideas about economic problems a series of ideas about inflation that are not necessarily generally valid.

In the first place, in both the United Kingdom and the United States the war was financed by inflationary policies which involved rising prices, rising wages, and rising rates of interest. One of the main apparent features of this inflation was what is commonly known as the wage-price spiral—the process of wages rising because prices rise and of prices rising because wages rise, in a continuous sequence; and one of the main prevailing ideas about that sequence was the idea that wages always lag behind prices—in other words that inflation has the effect of cheating the working force out of real income, to the benefit of the recipients of profit income. This idea about the inflationary sequence has been an important one ever since then; nevertheless, it turns out on closer analysis that in most inflations one does not find this lag of wages behind prices—one cannot detect a significant shift of the distribution of income away from the wage earners. Earl Hamilton's major study of the influence of the inflow of gold into Spain in the great Spanish inflation[1] appeared to find such a wage-price lag; but recent research has shown that Hamilton's statistics were biased and that one cannot in fact find such a lag in the classical Spanish case;[2] and one certainly cannot detect it in the statistics of other inflations (so long as these are open inflations).[3]

A second contribution of the World War I inflation and the German hyper-inflation to ideas on inflation was the idea that the cause of inflation is necessarily budget deficits and the resort to the printing press to finance government expenditure. A third idea, which derived particularly from the German hyper-inflation, was that inflation inevitably leads to the destruction of the rentier class, the people living on interest and the rent of property, and also tends to wipe out the middle class who

[1] E. J. Hamilton, *American Treasure and the Price Revolution in Spain, 1501–1650*, Cambridge 1934; *Money, Prices and Wages in Valencia, Aragon, and Navarre, 1351–1500*, Cambridge 1936; *War and Prices in Spain, 1651–1800*, Cambridge 1947.

[2] R. A. Kessel and A. A. Alchian, 'The Meaning and Validity of the Inflation-Induced Lag of Wages behind Prices', *American Economic Review*, Vol. L, no. 1, March 1960, pp. 43–66.

[3] Cf. Kessel and Alchian, op. cit; A. J. Brown, *The Great Inflation, 1939–1951*, London, 1955; Bronfenbrenner and Holzman, op. cit., pp. 647–8.

live on salaries and other kinds of fixed incomes. Finally, the World War I experience greatly reinforced the quantity theory approach to monetary problems. This is not only evident in prevailing views of what caused the inflation, that is resort to the printing presses, but was also manifest, for example, in the development of the purchasing power parity theory of exchange rates.

All of these ideas about inflation, which were derived from the World War I experience, were driven into the thinking of politicians, newspaper editorial writers, the general public, and professional economists by the tremendous emotional shock of the eruption of inflation after a long historical period of a relatively stable value of money. And these ideas, as I have already mentioned, had a strong influence on thinking about the great depression in the 1930s, inasmuch as the fear of inflation and of any policies that might provoke it, such as budget deficits and monetary expansion, was a formidable barrier to the adoption of intelligent policy to overcome the depression. For example, when the pound sterling was eventually forced off gold the reaction of financial opinion was to expect an immediate rise in prices sufficient to offset the devaluation, the idea being that currency depreciation must inevitably be accompanied by an equivalent inflation of prices in domestic currency. There was also great opposition in Britain to the idea of deficit budgeting, and in fact the National government, at the same time as it went off the gold standard, introduced a severe increase in taxes and a reduction in various government expenditures to demonstrate its financial orthodoxy, a policy obviously not designed to help solve the depression. The subsequent policy of cheap money was adopted only with considerable worry about its inflationary effects, one of the main arguments for it being that it would assist the government to balance the budget by reducing the interest charges on the debt inherited from World War I. In the United States, Roosevelt was elected on a promise to restore budgetary balance; and his revaluation of gold rested on the extremely naïve idea that raising the dollar price of gold would automatically raise the prices of commodities back to their predepression levels, and so cure the depression. In this and other ways the World War I inflationary experience created a climate of opinion that inhibited intelligent policy-making in the 1930s, when the problem for economic policy was not inflation but severe deflation.

This conflict between orthodox ideas on policy derived from the early 1920s and the realities of the situation of the 1930s had a great deal to do with the success of the Keynesian revolution. The conflict created an impasse in policy-making, a conflict which centred on monetary and fiscal policy, and the new theories of Keynes offered an intellectually respectable detour around the impasse to a solution of the urgent problem of mass underemployment.

The experience of World War I also had a strong influence on the policies followed in financing World War II, policies which were derived in part from the lessons of the earlier experience and in part from the ascendant ideas of the Keynesians. (Keynes himself played an important part in the designing of wartime finance in England, in his role as an adviser to the Treasury.) There was, in the first place, considerable popular opposition to inflationary financing of the war in a predominantly free enterprise environment, derived from the experience of World War I and particularly from the idea that inflation inevitably involves a reduction in the real incomes of the wage earners to the benefit of the entrepreneurial and managerial classes. A great deal of the pressure for the type of wartime economic policy that was adopted came from the fear that inflationary financing would deprive the wage earners of the gains they had made in the interwar period, and that it would promote an undesirable redistribution of income in favour of the 'profiteers', the villains of the popular mythology of the World War I inflation; it was this pressure that underlay the early introduction of wage and price controls. Another aspect of World War I finance that influenced financial policy in World War II was the experience of rising interest rates under inflation, which had created considerable difficulty for war finance in World War I: rising interest rates had made it difficult to float government loans, because the market would expect interest rates to rise and hence would be unwilling to subscribe to new issues, and this in turn would force the interest rates on government debt up still further, reinforcing the expectation of rising rates. The result of paying attention to the lessons of World War I, together with the Keynesian insistence that 'interest is a purely monetary phenomenon', was a method of war financing that primarily involved heavy reliance on physical controls (rationing and allocation) and on controls of prices and wages as a means of obtaining command of the real resources the governments needed without bidding up their prices, and on the financial side relied on deficit financing to meet the requirements that were not met by taxation, using a combination of cheap money and a system of issuing government debt more or less on demand, to keep interest rates steady. The central principle of wartime financing was that the physical controls would prevent cheap money from leading to an inflationary bidding-up of prices, confining its influence to depressing interest rates, and that the prevention of rising interest rates would in turn encourage subscriptions to issues of government debt. In fact, the result was some downward movement of interest rates, because the stabilization of rates removed the uncertainty that underlay the wide margin between short-term and long-term rates that developed in the 1930s; and the downward movement helped sell the government debt because the expectations factor worked in the opposite direction to what it had done in World War I. The Keynesian contribution to wartime economic policy consisted in the development of the technique of analysing the problem of obtaining resources for the war effort in terms of the so-called inflationary gap (as it was called in the United States—in the United Kingdom, such analysis concentrated on the 'manpower budget'). This technique involved forecasting total production and the prospective demands on it, the difference constituting the prospective excess of demand over supply, as a basis for devising policies to trim the demand to fit the supply.

The methods of financing World War II did succeed in preventing substantial inflation during the war, but they did so at the expense of piling up trouble for the postwar period, trouble which was accentuated by the continuation in the post-war period of the cheap money policies adopted during the war. A large part of the motivation for both the wartime policy and its continuance after the war was the belief that there was likely to be a catastrophic recession after the war, which could be mitigated by giving the public plenty of liquid wealth to sustain its postwar expenditures. This belief reflected both the success of the Keynesian Revolution and the 'secular stagnation' theories that developed from it in the United States, and the tendency of economists to be unduly influenced by their contemporary environment of opinion. Most wars have been followed by inflations, not by depressions, and World War II was no exception; moreover, the piling up of liquid assets in the hands of the public during the war and the postwar continuance of wartime cheap money policies made it exceptionally easy to finance inflationary demands on limited productive resources. In some European countries the wartime piling up of liquidity was offset by monetary reforms; but in other countries, particularly the United States and the United Kingdom, monetary reforms were not attempted.

In this general situation of postwar inflation, it was natural for economists to turn their attention to the analysis of inflation; and it was also natural that they should attempt to apply the Keynesian model of income determination to this analysis. What, in fact, they tended to do was to apply the Keynesian model and the algebraic techniques associated with it to the analysis of the inflationary process, in the course of so doing elaborating on the model in various ways suggested by the contemporary arguments about inflation. In general, these models were based on the simplest saving-investment version of the Keynesian analytical system, and paid little or no attention to the monetary elements of that system. They assumed, in effect—which was indeed fairly realistic in the circumstances of contemporary policy—that demand could always be financed, and concentrated on other determinants of demand than the quantity of money, rates of interest, or the availability of funds.

The inflation of the immediate postwar period can be described fairly definitely as one of excess demands based on the availability of finance at low rates of interest. But the inflation continued past what was then called the conversion period into the middle and latter 1950s.[1] In the latter 1950s, in the United States, unemployment was higher than it had been in the

---

[1] This statement should be qualified by reference to the findings of the Stigler Committee referred to in the previous section.

immediate postwar period and yet prices still seemed to be rising; at the same time, the wartime fears of postwar recession had belatedly been replaced by serious concern about the problem of inflation. The result was a prolonged debate over whether it was appropriate to use monetary restriction to combat inflation, a debate which centred on the question of the causes of the contemporary inflation. On one side of this debate was the 'cost-push' school of thought, which maintained that there was no excess demand, but that prices were rising because in particular markets wages were being pushed up by trade union bargaining power, or prices were being pushed up by the administrative action of oligopolistic firms with market power. On the other side was the 'demand-pull' school which maintained that the cause of the inflation was excessive demand. Later, in the United States, there developed a third school of thought, associated with the name of Charles Schultze, which advanced the 'sectoral demand-shift' theory of inflation. This was a combination of the demand-pull and cost-push theories, the central notion being neither that wages and prices were being pushed up without economic reason, by autonomous forces, nor that they were being pushed up by a general excess of demand, but instead that in a growing economy demand keeps shifting from one sector to another and that prices rise readily in the sector to which demand has been shifted, but do not fall as readily in the sector from which demand has shifted, so that there is a general process of escalation of prices based neither on 'cost-push' nor on the pull of excess demand.

This debate reflects the revival of the monetary explanation of inflation that emerged gradually from the experience of the late 1940s and early 1950s, an explanation which concentrates on the proposition that inflation is fundamentally a monetary phenomenon and that to stop inflation it is necessary to take action to limit the expansion of the quantity of money. The latter 1950s were distinguished by a change in the general climate of opinion among economists, in that much more emphasis came to be placed on monetary factors and on monetary policy than had been the case since the early 1930s. At the same time, a whole new set of policy considerations came into the picture. The experience of the 1920s had estab-lished price stability as a goal of economic policy. In the 1930s, full employment became established as a primary policy goal, and this was formalized by legislation passed during and after the war by the United States and various other countries. With the Cold War and the emphasis that has come to be placed on promoting the economic growth of the under-developed countries, economic growth has gradually been elevated to an objective of economic policy in advanced countries, along with price stability and high employment. At the same time, the defects of the Bretton Woods system, particularly the failure of the postwar international monetary arrangements to provide for an adequate international reserve money, have led to the balance of payments appearing as a difficult policy problem, first for the European countries, of course, but more recently for the United States; consequently, the objective of balance-of-payments stability or balance-of-payments equilibrium has been raised to the position of a major policy objective as well. Thus recent discussions of economic policy problems have been concerned with the relative importance of these various objectives and the possibility of conflict among them; and this raises the question of how inflation and policies to prevent it are related to the pursuit of the other objectives of economic policy.

III.   THE KEYNESIAN ANALYSIS OF INFLATION

As mentioned in the introductory section of this essay, there are two major approaches to inflation to be found in the postwar literature; broadly speaking, these can be said to follow one another in time. The early postwar literature on inflation was almost exclusively Keynesian, and it has only been towards the latter part of the period that the quantity theory approach has attracted a substantial number of adherents. The Keynesian theory was dismissed by many of its critics in the 1930s and the early 1940s as simply a theory of depression; it was maintained that the Keynesian theory was an *ad hoc* theory developed to explain the great depression of the 1930s and that its scope was confined to the explanation of that depression. But with the successful use of the Keynesian analytical method in the planning of war finance, that opinion changed drastically, and it was recognized that Keynesian theory actually was extremely

adaptable to the analysis of the problem of inflation.[1] The
adaptability of the Keynesian analysis to inflationary problems,
in my judgment, stemmed from two of its major features,
though I do not want to imply that those who adapted it to
the problem of inflation were fully conscious of these features.

In the first place, the savings-investment equilibrium condition provided a direct approach to the question of inflation
in terms of the demand for and supply of goods; this, of course,
is the main attraction of the Keynesian theory—it does go
right to what seems fairly common-sensical and understandable,
the aggregate demand for goods and what determines it. The
Keynesian savings-investment equilibrium condition is fairly
simple to understand and to operate with, and it can be converted very easily from an analysis of what determines the level
of output to an analysis of what determines the level of prices.
For underemployment conditions, the Keynesian theory says
that the level of output will adjust to the level at which the
savings forthcoming from that output in real terms will be
equal to the amount of investment going on. In conditions of
full employment, on the other hand, the variable whose adjustment brings about equilibrium between savings and investment
is not the level of real output or of employment, but the level
of money income, more specifically of the money price level
of full employment output. If the levels of money prices or
wages can be related by some mechanism to the amount of
saving or investment measured in real terms, the savings-
investment equilibrium condition provides an apparatus for
analysing the effects of inflationary shocks on the level of
wages and prices. This is the first reason, I think, why the
Keynesian analysis proved so attractive for the analysis of
inflation: that the savings-investment equilibrium condition
is simple to understand, and can be very easily adapted to
conditons in which money prices and wages rather than real
output are the variables that bring about equilibrium.

The second feature, which I think is even more important,
is that the analysis of the *General Theory* rests on the assump-

[1] The savings-investment equilibrium condition can also be used to determine
the distribution of income in a fully-employed competitive economy; see for
example Nicholas Kaldor, 'Alternative Theories of Distribution', *Review of
Economic Studies*, Vol. 23, no. 2, 1956, pp. 83–100.

tion that money wages are determined exogenously and are to be taken as given; it does not include a theory of what determines money wages. This treatment of money wages means that in applying the theory to full employment conditions one is at liberty to adopt any treatment of the determination of money wages one likes. In practice, this meant that writers on inflation were free to use the assumption that wages are determined period by period by negotiations that take into account previous changes in the cost of living, or the assumption that wages are determined by the interaction of the demand for and supply of labour, or the assumption that wages are determined by a struggle for shares in the national income. Similarly, they could assume that prices are determined by reference to past costs, firms adding a profit margin to their costs and raising their prices as costs rise, or that prices are determined by the interaction of demand and supply, or again that price determination represents a struggle among social groups. In other words, since the *General Theory* did not specify a theory of money wages, it was possible to get a great deal of variety into models that used essentially the same apparatus.

I have already referred to the wartime development of Keynesian inflation theory, and specifically to the inflationary gap analysis that was characteristic of discussions of war finance, especially in the United States. An important contribution to this line of analysis in the immediate postwar period was the work of Bent Hansen, the Danish economist, initially made available to English readers by Ralph Turvey and Hans Brems.[1] Hansen's work consisted primarily of elaborate and essentially sterile exercises with the formal apparatus of the Swedish approach to monetary theory; but he did, in contrast to the Keynesian concentration on the demand for goods, introduce the important distinction between the goods market and the factor market and develop an analysis of inflation in terms of the goods gap and the factor gap. Turvey and Brems provided a dynamic version of this analysis.

The most important work that was done in the immediate postwar period consisted in the construction of dynamic models

[1] Bent Hansen, *A Study in the Theory of Inflation*, London, 1951; Ralph Turvey and Hans Brems, 'The Factor and Goods Markets', *Economica*, Vol. 18, no. 69, February 1951, pp. 57–68.

of inflation. Essentially this involved constructing first or second order difference equations suited to the problem, and analysing the various types of dynamic behaviour such equations can generate; and the process derived its interest mostly from the fact that at that time few economists were conversant with the mathematics necessary to convert the Keynesian theory from a static theory of the determination of real output to a dynamic theory of the determination of money national income or prices. The simplest way of doing this was to assume that the Keynesian propensity to consume holds for money income and consumption expenditure, so that a rise in prices would increase real saving from a given level of real income, yielding an inflation model based on 'money illusion'.[1] A more sophisticated approach was to work, not in terms of aggregate consumption and 'investment', but in terms of the distribution of income between wages and profits, on the assumption that the propensity to save out of profits is higher than the propensity to save out of wages.[2] In such a model the inflationary process starts with a reduction in the total output available for division, or an increase in the share of output demanded by one of the participants in production; the struggle of each group to preserve its absolute share then leads to increases in wages and prices that either come to an end at a higher level of prices or proceed indefinitely, depending on whether or not one or both groups is prepared to accept a reduction of its real income through the inflationary process. A more elaborate and realistic version of this model introduces a rentier group with a fixed money income that cannot avoid being robbed by inflation; in this variant the inflationary process reaches a limit if the rentier group can be robbed of enough real income to satisfy the other claimants to income.[3] A still more elaborate model could be constructed, using the distinction between the goods and the factor markets and introducing the possibility that prices and

[1] For a pioneering example, see Arthur Smithies, 'Behaviour of National Money Income under Inflationary Conditions', *Quarterly Journal of Economics*, Vol. 56, no. 4, November 1942, pp. 113–29.

[2] An example of this approach is Franklyn D. Holzman, 'Income Determination in Open Inflation', *Review of Economics and Statistics*, Vol. 32, no. 2, May 1950, pp. 150–8.

[3] See for example C. G. F. Simkin, 'Notes on the Theory of Inflation', *Review of Economic Studies*, Vol. 20, no. 52, 1952–53, pp. 143–51.

wages might be either demand-determined or cost-determined. Such a model was constructed by Turvey, and used to provide a fourfold classification of inflations.[1]

Despite the variety of their construction, all of these models were basically the same. At the formal level they involved a first- or second-order difference equation relating the price level or change in the price level in one period to the price level or change in the price level in the previous period or two periods, the parameters of the mathematical relationship incorporating the precise behaviour assumed in the theoretical model. The second-order equation tended to be preferred, partly I suspect because that equation yields more complex dynamic behaviour possibilities, and in particular may result in an oscillatory path of prices over time.

As a simple example, consider the inflation model $p_t = ab\,p_{t-1} + C$, where p_t is the price level at the time t and a, b, C are constants, C serving to introduce an exogenous disturbance to start off the inflationary process. This model can be arrived at in a variety of ways: ab can be a single constant representing the marginal propensity to spend out of money income operating with a one-period lag; or a can represent the determination of wages in period t by the cost of living in period $t-1$, and b the fixing of current prices by a mark-up on current wage costs; or a can represent the determination of wages in period t by demand in period $t-1$, and b the determination of prices this period by the spending of wages this period; and so on.

This type of model is capable of dealing with two questions: the speed with which inflation proceeds, and whether or not inflation will automatically come to an end at a stable higher level of prices. In the simple model just presented, prices will converge on an equilibrium level or rise indefinitely according as ab is less or greater than unity; and the speed of inflation at any time will depend on the length of the period and the magnitude of ab, in the non-converging case approaching the limit inflation rate of $ab-1$ per period. Convergence of prices on a new equilibrium level requires that, whatever the inflationary mechanism is, it does not result in full compensation of all sectors of the economy for past rises in prices; in

[1] Ralph Turvey, 'Some Aspects of the Theory of Inflation in a Closed Economy', *Economic Journal*, Vol. 61, no. 243, September 1951, pp. 532–43.

other words, it results in a permanent reduction of the absorption of goods by one or more of the income-receiving sectors of the economy, via the exploitation of money illusion or the redistribution of real income.

The analytical essence of these models is the redistribution of real income so as to increase real saving, this redistribution resulting from the inflationary process itself. A major criticism that can be brought against them is that, to obtain their results, they assume what is essentially arbitrary behaviour, particularly when they assume that wages or prices are determined by previous changes in the cost of living or of production according to an institutionally-given constant. Such assumptions do not make much economic sense when applied to a sustained inflationary process in which people can be assumed to be capable of learning from experience and appreciating what is going on about them. That is, while one could reasonably assume that over short periods wage-earners, for example, believe that the value of money is stable and demand only sufficient wage increases to compensate for past increases in the cost of living, once the inflationary process gets under way the assumption that wage and price adjustments respond only to past changes and that the response is not affected by changing expectations about the future based on understanding of the interaction of wages and prices becomes increasingly arbitrary. The models can, however, be saved from this criticism by assuming that the coefficients of reaction to past wage and price changes incorporate a (rather crude) process of formation of expectations about future developments from past experience.

A more fundamental criticism is that the relationships of the models are assumed to be independent of the monetary environment, spending being related only to income: no attention is paid to the problem of financing a rising level of spending, or to the effects of a rising money income on the demand for money and thus on interest rates and spending. In other words, the models assume either an unlimited supply of idle balances or the continuance of a permissive monetary policy. While both assumptions could be defended as reasonable for the period in which the models were developed, they are obviously not defensible as generally realistic; and recognition of the necessity of one or the other to the analysis underlines both the arbitrariness of the behaviour assumptions of the models, and the extent to which the models ignore the influence of monetary factors and monetary policy on inflation.

To conclude the discussion of Keynesian inflation models, I should add that relatively little attempt at empirical verification and testing of these models was undertaken until the American debate over cost-push versus demand-pull in the late 1950s. The most elaborate earlier effort of which I am aware was a major study by Dow and Dicks-Mireaux of the postwar inflationary experience of the United Kingdom. It is obviously easy enough to set up a cost-push model of the wage-price spiral, and use it to analyse the movement of wages and prices in an inflationary sequence; the difficulty is to sort out from the simultaneous upward movement of wages and prices the causal relationships among movements of the two. Dow and Dicks-Mireaux found that the data were consistent with the causal relationships they posited to begin with; but they made no serious effort to test their theory against other theories, and, as I shall argue later, it is extremely difficult to devise any such test; consequently, their work amounted only to one possible description of the inflationary process they analysed.[1]

As already mentioned, the Keynesian analysis of inflation concentrates on the redistribution of income in the inflationary process; this provides an alternative type of test of the Keynesian models. For the war period, one can without much trouble verify that there were substantial redistributions of income away from those who had started the period with assets the income on which was fixed in money terms; but this redistribution can be attributed largely to the method of financing the war through cheap money combined with price controls and rationing. For the postwar inflation period, there is little

---

[1] J. C. R. Dow, 'Analysis of the Generation of Price Inflation', *Oxford Economic Papers*, Vol. 8, no. 3, September 1956, pp. 252–301; J. C. R. Dow and L. A. Dicks-Mireaux, 'The Determinants of Wage Inflation: United Kingdom, 1946–56', *Journal of the Royal Statistical Society*, Vol. 122, no. 2, 1959, pp. 145–74. For further references and discussion, see Bronfenbrenner and Holzman, op. cit., p. 683. The comments below relate to the earlier phases of these authors' work; subsequently they shifted their emphasis from 'cost-push' towards 'demand-pull' factors in inflation.

indication of any substantial redistribution of income attributable to the inflationary process.[1] It is possible to detect some
redistribution among particular groups; but for this type of
model to be proved useful for the analysis of inflation, it would
be necessary to establish that the inflationary mechanism works
by redistributing income among major income-receiving groups.
This in turn would require that some of such groups be unable
or unwilling to protect their real incomes from the impact of
inflation; in fact, on the contrary, such protection is available
to all groups in a freely competitive system, through negotiation
of contracts to take account of expected inflation, and is
increasingly resorted to as the fact of inflation is recognized.
Consequently the Keynesian approach to inflation in terms of
income redistribution seems less satisfactory than the alternative quantity theory approach to which I now turn, an approach
which concentrates on the effects of inflation on wealth rather
than on real income and its distribution.

IV.   THE QUANTITY THEORY APPROACH TO
INFLATION

The quantity theory approach to inflation differs essentially
from that of the Keynesian models just discussed in the basic
assumptions from which it starts: instead of assuming that
wage changes provoke price changes and conversely through
institutionally given (and therefore arbitrary) reaction coefficients it assumes that in an inflation the economy becomes
accustomed to the expectation of continued inflation, so that the
processes of determining wages and prices are fundamentally real
processes and not arbitrary processes determined exogenously.
The basic postulate of the quantity theory models of inflation
is that there is a stable demand function for money in real
terms, into which the rate of inflation enters as a cost of holding
real balances, which cost influences the quantity of real balances
held. Given this function, the rate of increase of the nominal

[1] G. L. Bach and Albert Ando, 'The Redistributional Effects of Inflation'
Review of Economics and Statistics, Vol. 39, no. 1, February 1957, pp. 1–13;
see also Bronfenbrenner and Holzman, op. cit., pp. 647–9. The latter assert
that postwar inflation has unambiguously eroded the shares of interest, rent,
and dividends, though they do not provide a specific reference and note with
respect to dividends that low pay-out ratios increased capital gains.

stock of money determines the rate of inflation, the public eventually coming to expect that rate of inflation and adjusting its stock of real balances (or ratio of real balances to real income) to it. In order to maintain its real balances constant in the face of inflation, the public must accumulate money balances at a rate equal to the rate of inflation; this accumulation of money balances in order to preserve real balances is achieved at the cost of sacrificing the consumption of current real income in order to maintain real balances intact, the release of current real income constituting the equivalent of a 'tax' on the holders of real balances; the tax on real balances, in turn, accrues as revenue to the beneficiaries of the inflationary increase in the money supply.[1]

The basic analytical apparatus of this approach to inflation is represented in the accompanying diagram (Figure 1), in which the rate of inflation is measured on the vertical axis, and the ratio of money stock to money income (or of real balances to real income) is measured on the horizontal axis, the demand for real balances as a function of the (actual and expected) rate of inflation being represented by the demand-for-money curve DD'. With price stability, the ratio of real balances to real income is OD'. With the rate of inflation established and expected to continue at OP, the demand for real balances relative to income falls to OM, the cost of holding real balances under inflationary conditions reducing the quantity demanded by MD'. The area of $OPP'M$ represents the proportion of real income that holders of real balances are obliged by the inflation to accumulate in the form of money balances in order to keep their real balances intact—the inflation tax expressed as a proportion of real income.

The quantity theory approach to inflation, which views inflation as imposing a tax on holdings of real balances, has some definite implications that are in contrast with those of the Keynesian approach discussed in the previous section.

[1] M. Friedman (ed.), *Studies in the Quantity Theory of Money*, Chicago, 1956, esp. M. Friedman, 'The Quantity Theory of Money—A Restatement', and Philip J. Cagan, 'The Monetary Dynamics of Hyperinflation'; Martin J. Bailey, 'The Welfare Cost of Inflationary Finance', *Journal of Political Economy*, Vol. 64, no. 2, April 1956, pp. 93–110; R. A. Kessel and A. A. Alchian, 'Effects of Inflation', *Journal of Political Economy*, Vol. 70, no. 6, December 1962, pp. 521–37.

In the first place, the redistribution of income involved in inflation is not primarily a redistribution among income groups, but a redistribution from the holders of cash balances to, in the first instance at least, the controllers of the money supply; in other words it is a redistribution from the community at large in its capacity as a holder and user of money to the monetary authority, not from one group of participants in the distribution of the national income to another. In the second

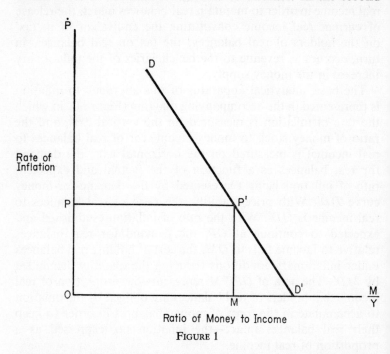

Ratio of Money to Income

FIGURE 1

place, the rate of inflation is determined, once inflation becomes established, by the rate of increase of the money supply rather than by the institutional factors governing the responses of wages and prices to one another—the institutional factors are assumed, or predicted, to adapt themselves to the rate of inflation. In the initial phase of inflation, however, the rate of inflation is likely to be less than the rate of increase of the money supply owing to the persistence of belief in the stability of prices, and thereafter for a period the rate of inflation is likely to exceed the rate of increase of the money supply owing to the effects of growing belief in the continuance of inflation in reducing the demand for real balances.

In the third place, the cost of inflation appears, not as a socially undesirable redistribution of income—since the owners of wealth, once they become accustomed to the fact of inflation, will incorporate the rate of inflation in the money rate of interest on loans fixed in money terms—but as the waste of resources involved in the effort of the public to economize on the use of money by substituting real resources for it. Such substitution, which may take such forms as shortening the intervals between wage payments, holding stocks of goods instead of money, and so forth, will be carried to the point where the alternative rate of return on the real resources substituted for the use of money is equal to the rate of inflation. In Figure 1, the cost of inflation to the economy is measurable by the area $P'MD'$, and can be approximated by the formula

$1/2 \ \dot{P} \ \dfrac{M}{Y} \ \eta$, where $\dot{P}$ is the rate of inflation, $\dfrac{M}{Y}$ is the ratio

of money to income held at the given rate of inflation, and η is the inflation-elasticity of the ratio of money to income. (In a more elaborate analysis, it would be necessary to recognize that the fact that interest is not paid on cash balances implies a social loss from the substitution of real resources for money in the absence of inflation, a loss aggravated by the effect of inflation in discouraging the use of money.) Finally, the notion of inflation as a tax, and of the cost of inflation as a sort of 'collection cost' of this tax, implies certain analogies between inflation and the more explicit taxes levied by the government, including the concept of the optimum rate of inflation from the point of view of the government, that is, the rate of inflation that maximizes the proportion of national income put at the government's disposal by inflation; these analogies have been developed by Martin J. Bailey in an important article on the welfare cost of inflationary finance.[1]

The quantity theory approach to the theory of inflation has been subjected to a substantial amount of empirical testing, both in A. J. Brown's study of *The Great Inflation, 1939–51*, and by members of the University of Chicago Money and

[1] Martin J. Bailey, op. cit.

Banking Workshop. The most striking evidence in its favour is Philip Cagan's study of six hyper-inflations, which discovered a remarkably stable demand function for money of the type depicted in Figure 1 underlying the behaviour of the six economies undergoing hyper-inflation. Brown's study, which assembles a great deal of information without analysing it with the same rigour as Cagan, confirms the quantity theory approach in a number of ways; for example, Brown finds no clear evidence of the wage lag of World War I popular belief and many of the Keynesian models, and shows that inflations do not necessarily tend to 'gallop away', countries having experienced inflations of up to one hundred per cent per annum and more without the inflation accelerating into hyper-inflation. So far as substantial inflations are concerned, the evidence therefore seems to favour the quantity theory approach over the Keynesian approach. For the mild type of inflation typical of the United States and other advanced countries in recent years, however, the approach has not proved nearly so useful. The theory implies the existence of a stable demand function for money in which the expected rate of inflation appears as one of the arguments; but while many researchers have established the existence of satisfactorily stable demand functions for money for such countries, the expected rate of price change has not appeared as a significant determinant of the quantity of money demanded. This might be accounted for on the hypothesis that the public only becomes sensitive to inflation after a certain threshold rate of price increase has been passed, or that recognition that the situation has been characteristically inflationary comes only with a very long lag. Whatever the reason, the theory has not succeeded in providing as convincing an explanation and method of analysis of mild as of strong inflations. Neither the Keynesian nor the quantity theory approach to inflation, of course, is very well adapted to dealing with the problems of suppressed inflation.

V. COST-PUSH VERSUS DEMAND-PULL INFLATION

As mentioned in the brief historical sketch of inflationary experience provided in an earlier section, the issue of whether inflation is the consequence of the upward push of costs or the upward pull of demand on prices became a lively issue in the late 1950s in the United States as a consequence of the co-existence of an apparent upward trend of prices with a higher average level of unemployment than had characterized the immediately preceding period. It is necessary, however, to resist the temptation to think of this problem as a specifically American problem developed in that period, for the issue began to be debated in the United Kingdom and other European countries very soon after the War. The importance of the debate stems largely from the difference between the recommendations for anti-inflationary policy to which the two views of the cause of inflation lead, the demand-pull explanation leading to the recommendation of monetary restraint and fiscal orthodoxy and the cost-push explanation leading to the rejection of macro-economic measures of this sort in favour of policies directed at the processes of price formation and wage determination. The difference in policy recommendations is not entirely a difference between right-wing conservative and left-wing radical solutions, since fiscal policy can be directed to radical objectives, while on the other hand the alternative policies recommended have covered a very wide range. In fact, these recommendations have ranged from direct wage and price fixing, or the establishment of national wage or income policies to be implemented by voluntary co-operation of business and labour with 'guide lines' laid down by government, through trust-busting or union-busting policies, to policies designed generally to improve the mobility of labour and the efficiency of competition in the economy, such as were recommended by the American Commission on Money and Credit.[1] Nevertheless, the two schools of thought did differ fundamentally over policy, the one school recommending measures involving a higher level of unemployment in order to stop inflation, the other preferring measures that sought to restrain inflation without sacrificing employment (both schools were united in the belief that inflation ought to be stopped, a conviction that became increasingly strong in the United States in that period). In the debate, the economic issues became so closely bound up with the political issues that for

---

[1] *Money and Credit: Their Influence on Jobs, Prices and Growth*, Report of the Commission on Money and Credit, Englewood Cliffs, 1961.

some writers at least it is difficult to determine whether the economic analysis preceded the policy recommendations or vice versa.

The issue of cost-push versus demand-pull was in my judgment largely a spurious one, for three reasons. The first, which I have already developed in criticism of the Keynesian inflation models, relates to the failure of the disputants to investigate the monetary assumptions on which the rival theories were based. Neither cost-push nor demand-pull inflation models can generate a sustained inflation unless it is assumed either that the demand for money can be compressed indefinitely without adverse effects on demand and employment, which runs contrary to the theory and fact of monetary behaviour, or that the monetary authority permissively provides the additional money required to circulate the national income at ever-increasing prices, in which case the behaviour of the monetary authority becomes the crucial factor in the inflation (and, in addition, the question arises for the cost-push theory as to what determines the pace of inflation). The two theories are therefore not independent and self-contained theories of inflation, but rather theories concerning the mechanism of inflation in a monetary environment that permits it. The real issue between them, therefore, was an issue of policy; whether inflation could be stopped by attacking the mechanism of cost and price determination or whether it could only be stopped by attacking aggregate demand.

In the second place, the argument was in large part based on differences between the two theories in their definitions of full employment. To elaborate on this, consider the curve shown in Figure 2, which expresses the proposition that the rate of price change in the economy is a function of the percentage of unemployment, prices being stable at the unemployment rate B. Now if 'full employment' is defined as existing when the demand for goods is just sufficient to prevent prices from either rising or falling—that is, defined by the point B— it follows as a mere tautology that inflation must be associated with excess demand for goods and labour or 'over-full' employment. If, on the other hand, full employment is defined independently by reference to the level of unemployment at which unfilled vacancies would just equal the number of men seeking work, or some equivalent concept of what percentage of unemployment is technically necessary to the efficient functioning of the labour market, or is identified with the percentage of unemployment regarded as normal in some past period or as politically desirable in the present, the result is extremely likely to be a concept corresponding to some such point as A. Between points A and B inflation can co-exist with less than

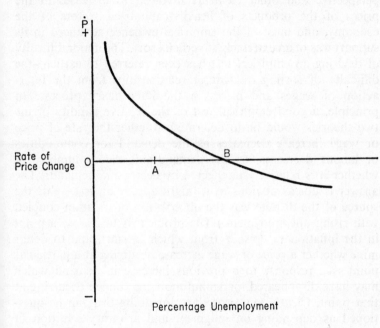

FIGURE 2

full employment on this definition, and such inflation can only be explained by reference to forces that push prices up in spite of the absence of excess demand as reflected in 'over-full' employment. Again the real issue between the two theories appears as a policy issue, in this context the issue of whether the actual level of unemployment is to be regarded as too great or too small, the former description implying the need for anti-inflationary policies other than policies entailing a further increase in unemployment.

In the third place, it is extremely difficult if not impossible

E

to devise a test capable of determining whether a particular
inflation is of the demand-pull or cost-push variety. Much of
the case for the cost-push interpretation of the US inflation of
the late 1950s rested on a very casual contrast of the period
with the earlier postwar period when unemployment was
substantially lower and bottlenecks were apparent in important
sectors of the economy, and a very naïve view of the time-
perspective and other elements involved in increases in the
prices of the products of heavily-capitalized sectors of the
economy, and most of the empirical evidence advanced in its
support was of an extremely superficial sort. The major difficulty
of devising an empirical test has been referred to earlier—the
difficulty of sorting out causal relationships from the interaction of wages and prices in the inflationary process. In
principle, a good empirical test of the relative validity of the
two theories would be to determine whether the rate of price
or wage increase decreases as the demand for commodities
or labour decreases, as the demand-pull theory implies, or
whether it is relatively unaffected by decreasing demand. (The
answer is not as obvious as it might appear at first sight: the
source of the dispute was the observation of inflation coupled
with rising unemployment.) The problem is to choose a point
in the inflationary episode from which to start, and to determine whether a price or wage increase occurring at a particular
point is a response to a previous increase in demand which
may have disappeared, or an autonomous change occurring at
that point. Clearly any procedure for doing this can be questioned as depending on judgment and arbitrary selection of
evidence. The most fruitful line of attack is through a statistical
cross-section study of a number of labour or commodity
markets, though this method also raises difficult problems of
interpretation; incidentally, the studies conducted on these lines
have tended to come out with results contrary to the cost-push
hypothesis.[1]

Before leaving the cost-push versus demand-pull debate, it
is appropriate to comment briefly on the alternative theory of
inflation that was put forward at the time and enjoyed widespread but brief popularity, the 'sectoral demand-shift' theory

---

[1] For a survey of the quantitative tests of inflation models and some discussion
of the difficulties, see Bronfenbrenner and Holzman, op. cit., part IV, pp. 630–9.

of inflation propounded by Charles L. Schultze.[1] This theory sought to reconcile the apparently observed absence of general excess demand with the demand-pull explanation while rejecting the cost-push theory, by introducing the notion that in a dynamic economy progress involves continual shifts of demand from sector to sector, and the proposition that such shifts raise prices in the sectors towards which demand shifts, but do not lead to price reductions in the sectors from which demand shifts away owing to the downward rigidity of wages and prices in a modern industrial society, so that on balance prices would display an upward trend despite the absence of general excess demand. This theory—aside from the fact that empirical evidence failed to confirm the proposition that sectoral price increases are explained by upward shifts of demand—suffered from the same defects as the two rival theories it sought to challenge—failure to investigate the monetary preconditions for inflation, and imprecision respecting the definitions of full employment and general excess demand.

While the debate over cost-push versus demand-pull was raging in the United States, a new and very interesting approach to the problem of inflation and anti-inflationary policy was developed by A. W. Phillips.[2] This approach by-passed the argument over the causes of inflation, and instead concentrated on the dynamics of the market for labour. The Keynesian literature on the policy problems of inflation had long included the general notion that the rate of wage increase is in part at least a function of the rate of unemployment, such that wages (and therefore prices) tend to rise faster the lower the rate of unemployment. Phillips' contribution was to develop an empirical relationship, apparently stable over a long period of British economic history, incorporating the idea, in the form of a functional relationship between the rate of wage increase and the percentage of unemployment—what has since come to be called 'the Phillips curve'. Such a relationship is not at

[1] Charles L. Schultze, *Recent Inflation in the United States* (Study Paper no. 1 for Joint Economic Committee, Study of Employment, Growth, and Price Levels) Washington, 1959; for critical discussion and references, see Bronfenbrenner and Holzman, pp. 612–13.

[2] A. W. Phillips, 'The Relation Between Unemployment and the Rate of Change of Money Wage Rates in the United Kingdom, 1862–1957', *Economica*, Vol. 25, no. 100, November 1958, pp. 283–99.

first sight apparent in the statistics, which seem to suggest that at low levels of unemployment the rate of wage increase is high and varies erratically, whereas at higher levels of unemployment the rate of wage increase is low but does not vary much with the level of unemployment (some critics of the Phillips curve still maintain, with some justification, that this is really all the figures show). Phillips was able to explain the data for both high and low unemployment rates by a single relationship, however, by assuming that the relationship is curvilinear— similar to that shown in Figure 2—rather than linear. From this relationship, and an assumption about the rate of increase of productivity, it is possible to determine the level of unemployment necessary to achieve price stability—a level which Phillips puts at about $2\frac{1}{2}$ per cent for the United Kingdom and 7 to 8 per cent for the United States.[1]

The central contribution of Phillips' approach is to substitute an empirical relationship between the rate of inflation and the percentage of unemployment for the vague literary and judgmental arguments about how much reduction in employment would be necessary to halt inflation that had previously dominated the debate about economic policy—a method of determining relevant fact that allowed one side to continue to imply that a trivial reduction in employment, or a very temporary larger reduction, would completely stop inflation, and the other side to continue to assert that an intolerably high level of unemployment would be necessary even to make a dent in the inflation. As against this, there are some serious doubts about the applicability of the Phillips curve to the formulation of economic policy. On the one hand, the curve represents only a statistical description of the mechanics of adjustment in the labour market, resting on a simple model of economic dynamics with little general and well-tested monetary and value theory behind it. On the other hand, it describes the behaviour of the labour market in a combination of periods of economic fluctuation and varying rates of inflation, conditions which presumably influenced the behaviour of the labour market itself, so that it may reasonably be doubted whether the curve would continue to hold its shape if an

---

[1] A. W. Phillips, 'Employment, Inflation and Growth', *Economica*, Vol. 29, no. 113, February 1962, pp. 1–17.

attempt were made by economic policy to pin the economy down to a point on it.

The Phillips curve has been elaborated on subsequently, particularly as a result of the research done for the Commission on Money and Credit, through the development of the concept of 'trade-offs' among policy objectives. Earlier I referred to the lengthening of the list of economic policy objectives in recent years, and the consequent possibility of conflicts among objectives. Conflict among objectives means that the economic policy-makers must sacrifice or 'trade-off' a lesser achievement of one objective against a greater attainment of another. The Phillips curve expresses empirically the terms on which unemployment and price stability can be traded off against one another. It is an obvious extension of the Phillips curve approach to attempt to determine statistically the trade-offs between these objectives and, say, the rate of economic growth; such a study was conducted for the Commission on Money and Credit by Lawrence Klein, and in a less rigorous fashion by the Scitovskys.[1] So far, the Phillips curve appears to be far the most reliable of such relationships, and even the existence of that relationship has been doubted by researchers working on the US data.[2] The question of policy objectives and potential conflict among them is dealt with further in the final section.

VI. SOME EMPIRICAL FINDINGS ON INFLATION

This section is devoted to a brief discussion of empirical findings on inflation that have a bearing on current arguments about inflation. The arguments I refer to are not so much arguments

[1] L. R. Klein and R. Bodkin, 'Empirical Aspects of Trade-Offs among Three Goals: High-Level Employment, Price Stability, and Economic Growth', and Tibor and Anne Scitovsky, 'Welfare Aspects of Economic Growth, High-Level Employment and Price Stability', *Inflation, Growth and Employment* (Englewood Cliffs, 1963). For discussion of these papers, see M. Bronfenbrenner, 'A Sample Survey of the Commission on Money and Credit Research Papers', and Harry G. Johnson, 'Objectives, Monetary Standards, and Potentialities', *Review of Economics and Statistics*, Vol. 45, no. 1, Part, 2, Supplement, February 1963, pp. 111–28, and 137–46.

[2] For example, R. J. Bhatia, 'Unemployment and the Rate of Change in Money Earnings in the United States, 1900–1958,' *Economica*, Vol. 28, no. 111, August 1961, pp. 285–96.

among economists as arguments that one finds brought against inflation in the speeches of politicians, the pronouncements of central banks—which are a way of conducting politics by other means—and newspaper editorials. For brevity, the discussion is framed in the form of answers to a series of questions about inflation.

(i) Does inflation necessarily accelerate into hyper-inflation?

The answer is no. There is a fairly close relationship, at least in some inflations, between the rate of increase of the money supply and the rate of increase of prices. The acceleration into hyper-inflation only occurs if the expansion of the money supply accelerates, and that does not necessarily happen. Nor is there a low critical limit to the rate of inflation, beyond which the economy soars into hyper-inflation: Brown's evidence, as well as other evidence on Latin-American inflations, shows that various countries have experienced really substantial rates of inflation without the inflation getting out of hand.[1]

(ii) Does inflation necessarily lead to monetary collapse?

The answer is no, provided that the price system is uncontrolled and prices are allowed to rise freely. The strongest evidence on this point comes from the Chinese postwar hyper-inflation, during which money continued to circulate despite the extremely rapid rise in prices.[2] Cagan's evidence suggests the same conclusion. Where monetary breakdowns do occur is where rapid inflation is combined with general price control, so that money ceases to be usable for making transactions because the nominal value fixed by price controls comes to be far above the real value determined by the plethora of money and the shortage of goods. This is the explanation, for example, of the breakdown of the German currency after World War II and the adoption of the use of cigarettes as a medium of exchange. If prices are free to rise money remains usable because its real value is adjusted to the inflation.

(iii) Does inflation redistribute income away from the savers, the middle class, etc., on a socially intolerable scale?

[1] A. J. Brown, op. cit., chap. 8.
[2] Colin D. Campbell and Gordon C. Tullock, 'Hyperinflation in China, 1927–49', *Journal of Political Economy*, Vol. 62, no. 3, June 1954, pp. 236–45.

The answer again is no. Most of the evidence we have on mild inflations indicates that it is difficult to detect such large-scale redistributions of income over any substantial period.[1] Over a short period, when an inflation has occurred that was not expected (as typically happens in war), there may be substantial redistribution of income and wealth away from those groups that have made their occupational choices and their savings and investment decisions in the expectation of the continuance of stable prices. But in the longer run, when the expectation of inflation becomes built into the economy's behaviour patterns, the nominal reward for saving (money interest rates) comes to contain an allowance for expected future inflation, and employment contracts and wage and salary relativities are readjusted to conform with the underlying demand and supply situation. For example, school and college teachers in the United States were for a long time sufferers from inflation; but their salaries have now been for the most part adjusted to the growing scarcity of teachers. It can be argued on the contrary that once inflation has come to be expected, it is the termination of inflation by monetary restriction that will cause socially intolerable redistributions of income and wealth, because borrowers who borrowed at high interest rates on the expectation that rising prices would make the real interest rate substantially less than the nominal interest rate will then find themselves obliged to pay higher real rates of interest than they had counted on. (This was one of Keynes' main arguments against Britain's return to the gold standard at the old parity after World War I.)[2]

(iv) Does inflation cause economic inefficiency?

Not too much work has been done on this question; but the evidence seems to indicate that inflation does not reduce economic efficiency, at least when the inflation is mild and reasonably steady and prices and wages are not controlled.[3] In fact, a good case can be made out, and supported by some

[1] See Bronfenbrenner and Holzman, op cit., Part VI, for references and discussion.

[2] J. M. Keynes, *The Economic Consequences of Mr. Churchill*, London, 1925.

[3] See Harold Wolozin, 'Inflation and the Price Mechanism', *Journal of Political Economy*, Vol. 67, no. 5, October 1959, pp. 463–75, for evidence that inflation does not appear to reduce the efficiency of the price system, as reflected in relative price adjustments.

empirical evidence produced in the US and the UK, that inflation of this kind tends to increase efficiency by increasing the
mobility of labour from low-productivity to high-productivity
regions and occupations.[1] On the other hand, inflation that
proceeds erratically, the rate of inflation varying sharply from
one year to the next, and that is accompanied by policies of
price control over important consumption goods and services
designed to shield the real consumption of some groups of the
population from the effects of inflation—in other words, the
type of inflation characteristic of the underdeveloped countries
—indubitably causes serious inefficiencies of allocation of
current resources and of investment.[2]

(v) Does inflation hamper economic growth?

This is a difficult question, because both cross-sectional
differences among countries and historical differences in a
given country with respect to the rate of inflation are usually
associated with other differences of circumstances, so that an
observed relation between inflation and slow growth is not
sufficient to establish an adverse causal connection between
inflation and slow growth. In fact, there is frequent evidence
(especially for underdeveloped countries) that the causal connection runs the other way, from slow growth to inflationary
policies. For what such evidence is worth, it tends to show
that if the inflation is mild (between zero and six per cent,
according to the findings of the Commission on Money and
Credit),[3] the rate of inflation does not affect the rate of growth,
but that either rapid inflation or deflation is associated with
slower rates of growth. This evidence, though frequently
interpreted by central banks as an argument for price stability,
seems to argue for mild inflation as the best environment for
economic growth.[4]

[1] For example, it is shown by Donald Dewey, 'Labour Turnover as an Index
of Unemployment in the United States, 1919–58', *Journal of Industrial Economics*,
Vol. 8, no. 3, June 1960, pp. 265–87, that turnover (a measure of mobility)
varies inversely with unemployment. Unpublished work by R. G. Lipsey for
the UK also supports the statement in the text.

[2] This point has been frequently made with reference to Latin-American
inflations. See for example Tom E. Davis, 'Eight Decades of Inflation in Chile,
1879–1959: A Political Interpretation,' *Journal of Political Economy*, Vol. 71,
no. 4, August 1963, pp. 389–97.

[3] Op. cit., p. 44.

[4] See Harry G. Johnson, op. cit., for this point.

In summary, for countries with an advanced economic structure, high incomes, and a fairly free and competitive economic system, most of the assertions usually made in policy arguments about inflation turn out not to be confirmed by the empirical evidence. It is necessary to point out, however, that this is not necessarily true of underdeveloped countries that rely on sharply inflationary policies to promote development, coupled with policies of price control designed to protect the real consumption standards of the labouring or the urban classes. In other words, it seems necessary in the analysis of inflation to distinguish between advanced and underdeveloped countries, between mild and fierce inflations, and between competitive and controlled economies.

VII. POLICY ISSUES CONCERNING INFLATION

This final section discusses some recent policy issues respecting inflation. Policy to deal with inflation is a subject on which a great deal has been written and argued by eminent authorities without adding substantially to knowledge, and in some cases subtracting from it. I have already described how the objectives of economic policy have been broadened from the simple objective of price stability characteristic of the 1920s to a list that includes in addition high employment, balance-of-payments equilibrium, and economic growth. The presence of balance-of-payments equilibrium on the list reflects the inadequacy of the present international monetary system. The inclusion of economic growth in the list—at least in the economists' list—reflects in my judgment an unfortunate propensity of those concerned with political economy not to think very hard about things before they write or speak about them. The growth objective, unlike the others, is a very difficult one to render precise enough for analysis—not only is the rate of growth a statistic whose significance economic science lacks adequate tools to evaluate, but our knowledge of the sources of growth and the policies required to promote it is only in its infant stage, and riddled with confusions. In any case, the notion of 'growth' as an objective of policy is used in an extremely loose fashion. In North America, at least, when people refer to the desirability of economic growth frequently

what they really mean is that they are in favour of less unemployment, this preference involving growth only in the sense
that in the process of moving up to a higher level of employment the economy's measured rate of growth will be transi-
tionally higher than if the unemployment percentage remained
constant; whereas if growth is to be an objective distinct from
high employment, the rate of growth should be defined in
relation to a normal level of unemployment and the argument
for growth should relate to policies for achieving a higher rate
of growth with that normal level of unemployment.

For brevity, it is most convenient to present recent policy
issues concerning inflation in terms of an 'orthodox view' and
its limitations, the orthodox view representing what is to be
found in official and central bank pronouncements and such
documents as the Report of the Commission on Money and
Credit. This orthodox view, which has been asserted particularly strongly by central bankers, is that there is no inconsistency between the objectives of policy, and that in fact
price stability is the key to the other objectives. Price stability,
it is alleged, will ensure high employment by promoting confidence; in the same way it will promote economic growth,
and it is even argued that only price stability will permit
'sustainable' economic growth; and finally, price stability will
ensure competitiveness in the international economy and
hence preserve balance-of-payments equilibrium.

I find this collection of assertions extremely questionable,
both theoretically and empirically. In particular, the assertion
that price stability will take care of the balance of payments
seems to me to be absolute nonsense: a country produces a
particular collection of goods for export and exchanges this
collection for another collection it imports, and there is no
reason in economic theory or experience for believing that
stability of the price of one batch of goods in terms of another
or of money will preserve equilibrium in a changing world.
The movement of a country's price level required to maintain
balance-of-payments equilibrium at fixed exchange rates
depends on both the real trends in the world economy and
on monetary developments in other countries. For example,
if the rest of the world is inflating, a particular country can only
stabilize its price level by deflating as the rest of the world

inflates, and running a larger and larger trade surplus; conversely, if the rest of the world is deflating, maintenance of price stability will make the country less and less internationally competitive and oblige it to inflate and run an increasingly large trade deficit. Thus the use of the need to keep the balance of payments in balance as an argument for price stability seems to me purely a propaganda argument for according priority to price stability over other objectives of policy.

So far as the argument from price stability to high employment is concerned, the argument of the preceding section is highly relevant. Given the existence of the Phillips curve (or at least of a relationship of some kind between unemployment percentage and rate of wage increase), and the empirical trade-off between price stability and unemployment, it is of course always possible to define full employment implicitly as that level of unemployment which is consistent with price stability, and so to conclude that full employment and price stability are not at all inconsistent. But there is nothing sacred or commandingly desirable about the percentage of unemployment at which prices are stable, unless one starts from the postulate that price stability has crash priority over other objectives—especially if it is recognized that the choice between more rapidly rising prices and higher unemployment is a choice respecting the distribution of economic welfare between owners of monetary and financial assets and owners of human labour, the former group losing something (though it may only be psychic satisfaction) by inflation and the latter demonstrably losing substantially from unemployment.

So far as the argument from price stability to economic growth is concerned, this is initially beset by the confusions already noted concerning the meaning of 'growth'. The empirical evidence does not indicate that price stability is the key to rapid economic growth—different countries have succeeded in growing rapidly with rising, falling or stable prices at different periods of time. Nor does theory suggest that price stability maximizes growth: rather it suggests that the trend of prices will within limits have little influence on growth, since the economy will become accustomed to and expect the continuance of any established trend. What may impede growth, however, are unanticipated changes in the rate of change of prices, associated with changes in economic policy; but such changes include both inflationary and deflationary policy changes.

In opposition to the orthodox view on price stability and the objectives of economic policy just discussed, many economists have advanced arguments on behalf of inflation as a means of achieving a greater degree of fulfilment of the other objectives of policy. The argument for inflation as a means of securing full employment is an obvious one, though such a policy would soon encounter balance-of-payments problems in a country on a fixed exchange rate, and it might be ineffective in a country where labour is relatively immobile. Another argument with considerable validity is that a strong demand for labour increases mobility and therefore the efficiency of resource allocation and indirectly the rate of growth. Some other arguments for inflation as a means of increasing the rate of economic growth are much less convincing, because they rely on the questionable assumption that one group in the economy is capable of realizing that inflation is going on while other groups are not. I refer in particular to the argument, expounded by Nicholas Kaldor[1] among others, that inflation is good for growth because it increases the real rate of return on investment. This argument assumes that the rate of interest at which entrepreneurs can borrow is unaffected by the expectation of inflation, implying that though borrowers are aware of inflation lenders are not. (Equally inconsistent is the counter-argument, put forward by adherents of the orthodox view, that inflation impedes growth because savers are deterred from saving by the expectation that inflation will rob them of their savings—this argument is doubly inconsistent, because the expectation of robbery by inflation might lead savers to save more rather than less.)[2] If the argument is formulated correctly in terms of the inflation tax approach, it appears that whether inflation promotes growth depends on how the proceeds of the inflation

[1] Nicholas Kaldor, 'Economic Growth and the Problem of Inflation', *Economica*, Vol. 26, nos. 103 and 104, August and November 1959, pp. 212–26 and 287–98.

[2] See, for example, Norman Buchanan and Howard S. Ellis, *Approaches to Economic Development*, New York, 1955, ch. 14, esp. p. 311, and Howard S. Ellis, 'Monetary Policy as an Instrument of Progress', in UNESCO, *International Science Bulletin*, Vol. VI, no. 2, 1954, pp. 269–74, esp. p. 270.

tax are spent: if they are spent on investment growth will probably be promoted, whereas if they are spent on consumption growth will probably be retarded.

Let me conclude with some comments on the general issues involved in the contemporary discussion of the objectives of policy and the possibility of conflicts among them. The most important difficulties in the discussion stem from the complexity of economic growth as an objective of policy. The other objectives are capable of qualification in a meaningful way, and of evaluation in terms of accepted techniques of analysis. The rate of growth is not susceptible of comparable treatment because it is not a magnitude but the rate of change of a magnitude, and economics has barely begun to develop theories concerning the determinants and the welfare implications of rates of change of economic variables. It is, for example, a simple matter to show that a lower percentage of unemployment normally implies a higher level of output and a higher absolute level of saving. But it does not necessarily follow that the increase in saving will be sufficient to yield a higher rate of growth, because the increase in output that is responsible for it also raises the denominator of the growth rate; in fact, an analysis on the lines of the Harrod–Domar equation tends to result in the conclusion that the growth rate will fall rather than rise, while an analysis is on neo-classical lines leads to the conclusion that in the long run the growth rate will be determined by the exogenous influences of the rate of technical change and the rate of population growth.[1]

For the same reason, it is very difficult to formulate satisfactorily the problem of choosing the policy combination yielding the optimum mixture of growth, price stability, and employment: the rate of growth is not a concept comparable to the rate of inflation and the rate of unemployment, so that it is difficult to pin down what is involved in trading off growth against other objectives. For intelligent policy-making, in principle it is necessary first to be able to quantify the Phillips curve relations among objectives, and second to be able to attach weights or values to the numbers along the axes. For the trade-off between unemployment and price stability this

[1] Harry G. Johnson, op. cit.; J. E. Meade, *A Neo-Classical Theory of Economic Growth*, London 1961.

can be done, though so far the only attempt to do it is to be found in a study conducted by G. L. Reuber for the Canadian Royal Commission on Banking and Finance.[1] That study estimates the value of the output lost through unemployment, and uses the inflation tax approach to estimate the resource waste entailed in inflation, arriving at a combination of inflation and unemployment that minimizes the loss to the economy from incomplete fulfilment of its objectives. But non-fulfilment of these objectives entails in each case a loss of current real income, which can be compared, whereas the growth objective cannot be readily reduced to measurement in terms of current real income. Unless one believes that growth is costless, evaluation of the difference in economic gain or loss between different growth rates involves comparing the future benefits of faster growth with the additional present sacrifices required to achieve it—and in this area the tools available to the economist are notoriously weak and difficult to manage.

[1] G. L. Reuber, *The Objectives of Monetary Policy*, Staff Study, Royal Commission on Banking and Finance, Toronto 1962, mimeographed. The part of this study referred to here is available in G. L. Reuber, 'The Objectives of Canadian Monetary Policy, 1949–61: Empirical "Trade-Offs" and the Reaction Function of the Authorities', *Journal of Political Economy*, Vol. LXXII, no. 2, April 1964, pp. 109–32.

CHAPTER IV

MONEY IN A NEO-CLASSICAL ONE-SECTOR GROWTH MODEL*

The neo-classical one-sector growth model has become a standard piece of equipment in the economic theorist's tool kit. Nevertheless, most of the available expositions of it are needlessly complicated and mathematical, and tend to obscure the simplicity of the central analytical propositions. Moreover, these expositions are for the most part confined to the case of a non-monetary economy. The purpose of this essay is to present a geometrical exposition of the one-sector growth model for the simplest possible case,[1] and to apply it to the analysis of the role of money in such a model. Section I presents the simple model. Section II indicates how relaxations of the assumptions of that model with respect to savings behaviour, the durability of capital, and technical change can be accommodated; Section III is a digression on the application of the

---

* This essay draws on and elaborates the analysis of my 'The Neo-Classical One-Sector Growth Model: A Geometrical Exposition and Extension to a Monetary Economy', *Economica*, Vol. XXXIII, No. 131, August 1966, pp. 265–87. Unfortunately, as James Tobin has pointed out to me, that article contained a crucial error in the treatment of the Keynesian savings assumption, which is corrected in the present version. I am indebted to Tobin also for helpful comments on this version.

[1] The simple model, and the use of it to establish the golden rule conditions, are due to A. L. Marty. See his 'The Neo-Classical Theorem' (*American Economic Review*, Vol. LIV, no. 6, December 1964, pp. 1026–9). For other geometrical expositions of growth theory, see R. M. Solow, 'A Contribution to the Theory of Economic Growth', *Quarterly Journal of Economics*, Vol. 70, no. 1, February 1956, pp. 65–94; T. W. Swan, 'Economic Growth and Capital Accumulation', *Economic Record*, Vol. 32, no. 63, November 1956, pp. 334–61; John Buttrick, 'A Note on Growth Theory', *Economic Development and Cultural Change*, Vol. 9, no. 1, Part 1, October 1960, pp. 75–82; W. M. Corden, 'A Brief Review of Some Theories of Economic Growth', *Malayan Economic Review*, Vol. 6, no. 1, April 1962, pp. 1–12; J. E. Meade, *A Neo-Classical Theory of Economic Growth* (London: Allen & Unwin, 1961); F. H. Hahn and R. C. O. Matthews, 'The Theory of Economic Growth: A Survey', *The Economic Journal*, Vol. LXXIV, no. 296, December 1964, pp. 779–902.

model to various problems in the theory of economic development. Section IV applies the model to growth in a monetary economy, on alternative assumptions about the savings behaviour of the economy, with special reference to the questions of the neutrality of money in a growing economy and the capacity of monetary policy to influence economic growth.

I.　THE SIMPLE MODEL

The simplest possible growth model assumes that production requires the use of two factors of production, labour and capital, which are employed in a production function that is subject to constant returns to scale and diminishing returns to increases in the ratio of one factor to the other; that capital is physically the same product as consumption goods, and that when output is used to add to capital stock, it lasts forever; that labour grows at a constant percentage rate (n); and that saving (equals investment) is a constant fraction of income.

On these assumptions—particularly that of constant returns to scale, which enables output per factor and the marginal products of factors to be expressed as functions of the ratios of factors—the economics of growth can be summarized in the diagram of Figure 1. The abscissa of the Figure represents capital per worker (k) and the ordinate represents output (y) and other income magnitudes per worker. $O . y$ graphs output per worker as a function of capital per worker, and $O . sy$ graphs savings per head as a function (via income per head) of capital per worker. The line $O . kn$, with slope n (the rate of growth of population) graphs the investment required to supply the new additions to the labour force with the same capital per head as the existing labour force.

The first proposition to be established is that the economy will converge in the long run on a rate of growth equal to the rate of growth of the labour force, n. To prove this, it is sufficient to establish that the economy will converge on an equilibrium stock of capital per head and therefore output per head, since if output per head is constant, total output must grow at the same rate as the number of heads. As the diagram shows, there will be such an equilibrium stock of capital per head (capital–labour ratio in the economy), such that saving per

head is just sufficient to equip the new workers with the same
stock of capital per man as the pre-existing workers possess.
This equilibrium stock (Ok_e) is indicated by the intersection
of $O . sy$ with $O . kn$ at T. To prove that the economy's growth
must converge on T, suppose that the economy began with the
stock of capital per head represented by k_m less than the
equilibrium stock k_e; with this stock, output would be k_mP
and savings k_mQ, whereas k_mR would be sufficient to equip the

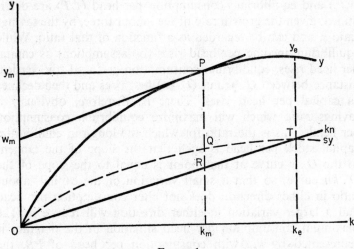

FIGURE 1

additional workers with the same capital per man as existing
workers, so that QR would be available to increase capital
per head. Thus capital per head would increase above Ok_m[1]
and would continue to do so until it reached Ok_e. Similarly, if
capital per head were above Ok_e, saving would be insufficient
to equip the additional labourers with the same capital per
head as existing labourers command, and capital per head
would fall over time to Ok_e. T and k_e thus represent a stable
equilibrium. Both the existence and the stability of this equilibrium derive from two assumptions implicit in the diagram;
that there are sufficiently diminishing returns in production,

[1] The increase in capital per head would be something less than QR, approxi-
mately $QR/1 + n$.

and that at some output per head saving is more than sufficient to equip new workers with the capital per head available to existing workers. It should be noted that at T, $n = s \cdot \dfrac{y}{k}$, that is, the growth rate is equal to the savings ratio divided by the capital–output ratio. This is the familiar Harrod–Domar growth equation; but in this model the capital–output ratio adjusts to the growth rate, and not the other way around.

In the analysis just presented, equilibrium income per head ($y_e k_e$) and equilibrium consumption per head ($y_e T$) are determined, given the growth rate of the labour force, by the savings ratio s, and can be regarded as a function of that ratio. While equilibrium income per head rises (by assumption) as capital per head rises, equilibrium consumption per head (the vertical distance between $O \cdot y$ and $O \cdot kn$) first rises and then declines as capital per head rises. There is, therefore, obviously a savings ratio which will maximize equilibrium consumption per head. This is the ratio for which the long-run equilibrium capital stock per head is such that the slope of the tangent to the $O \cdot y$ curve at that point is equal to the slope of the $O \cdot kn$ curve, so that a small variation of the capital–labour ratio in either direction does not alter consumption per head and a larger variation in either direction will reduce it. The maximum consumption per head situation in the diagram is represented by k_m, with consumption per head of PR, the savings ratio required to achieve it being Rk_m/Pk_m.

The behaviour requirements for achieving maximum consumption per head may be defined in two alternative ways, each economically illuminating. First, the slope of $O \cdot kn$ is n, the equilibrium rate of growth of the economy; and the slope of $O \cdot y$ at P is the marginal (gross and net) product of capital (owing to the assumption that capital lasts forever) and also the own-rate-of-return on capital (since units of output and capital are identical and exchange one for one on the market). Hence the condition for maximum consumption per head can be expressed as equality of the rate of return on capital with the growth rate. Second, the savings per head required to maintain the maximum consumption per head are measured by Rk_m, the savings ratio required being Rk_m/Pk_m; the income earned by the capital stock per head is $y_m w_m$ (the quantity of capital per head $Ok_m = y_m P$ multiplied by the marginal product of capital, the slope of the tangent at P, $w_m P$) and the share of capital in output is $y_m w_m / Oy_m$. Since (by the parallelism of $w_m P$ and $O . kn$ required for maximization of consumption) $y_m w_m = Rk_m$, the condition for maximum consumption can be expressed as equality of savings with the income of capital or of the savings ratio with the share of capital in income. This condition, it may be noted, will be automatically fulfilled if, as is assumed by a number of writers on growth theory, capitalists save all their income and workers consume all theirs.

The condition for maximum consumption per head, expressed in the second form, has been designated as 'the golden rule of accumulation'. This designation, however, is misleading, to the extent that it implies that some quality of optimality attaches to maximum consumption per head at all points of time. There is no reason to assume that maximum consumption per head would represent maximization of welfare in terms of social utility or consumers' preferences, and certainly no reason to assume that a society not on the golden rule growth path should set itself the objective of moving itself onto that path, or that a society on the golden rule path should stay on it, since to do either would involve rearranging its pattern of consumption and saving over time, with effects on welfare falling outside the compass of the analysis. The conditions for maximum consumption per head apply only to alternative equilibrium growth paths of the economy, and are deduced entirely from consideration of supply factors—the exogenously given rate of growth of the labour force, and the production function, which determines the functional relation between output per head and capital per head. Utility and welfare considerations do not enter into the problem. The analysis is therefore most properly conceived as establishing the technical limits on the possibility of raising consumption per head by increasing capital per head in an expanding economy.

In conclusion to this section, it should be noted that there is nothing in the foregoing analysis to prevent the savings ratio from being such that the economy overshoots the capital–labour ratio that maximizes consumption per head—in fact, this possibility rather than its more commonly assumed converse is illustrated in Figure 1. Nor is there anything to preclude a savings ratio implying, on the equilibrium growth path, a rate of return on capital that is negative, or less than some minimum demanded by capitalist investors. The problems raised by this possibility presuppose a monetary economy, and are investigated in a subsequent section.

II. RELAXATION OF THE ASSUMPTIONS

A. *The Savings Assumption*

The assumption that a constant proportion of income is saved is completely arbitrary and theoretically indefensible, an analytical relic of naïve Keynesianism deriving no logical support from utility maximization theory. Nor can it be defended on the empirical argument of consistency with the observed secular constancy of the ratio of saving to income, since that observation pertains to an economy characterized by population growth and technical progress and is equally consistent with less naïve theories of saving. Consequently, little of theoretical advantage can be gained by complicating the model by assuming that aggregate saving is the sum of saving from capital income and saving from labour income, each being related to the total income of the relevant factor by a different but still fixed saving ratio, the saving ratio from the income of capital being assumed to be higher than that from labour income.[1] The model can, however, readily be extended in this direction if so desired.

The modifications required relate only to the construction of the savings-capital per head relationship ($O . sy$ in Figure 1) and take advantage of the fact that the distribution of income between the factors is uniquely related to the capital–labour ratio through the form of the production function. This relationship can be expressed in terms either of the elasticity of substitution between the factors in production, or of the elasticity of output per unit of labour with respect to the capital–labour ratio.

As is well known, if the elasticity of substitution is greater than unity, the share of capital will rise as the capital–labour ratio rises; and, consequently, so will the ratio of savings to

---

[1] Note that this assumption is not equivalent to assuming that the society is composed of workers and capitalists, the two classes having different savings ratios; that assumption raises the problem that as workers save and accumulate capital they merge into the capitalist class.

income on the assumption of a higher savings ratio out of capital income than out of labour income. Conversely, if the elasticity of substitution is less than unity, the capital share and the saving ratio will fall as the capital–labour ratio rises; and if the elasticity of substitution is unity, the relative factor shares and the savings ratio will be constant. The first two of these possibilities will affect the relation between the curves representing saving per head and output per head, but the general lines of the analysis will not be affected (though the analysis will indicate the possibility of fulfilling the golden rule conditions by an appropriate transfer of income between the two factors).[1]

Alternatively, the share of capital can be identified with the elasticity of the curve depicting output as a function of capital per head at the point corresponding to each particular capital–labour ratio.[2] If the elasticity of the curve is constant, capital's share and the savings ratio are constant; if the elasticity increases as the capital–labour ratio rises, capital's share and the savings ratio rise with the capital–labour ratio, and conversely. Again, the general results are the same.

A step towards a more traditional theory of saving could be made by assuming that the savings ratio rises with income per head, and may either fall or rise as the rate of return on capital falls. On the first of the latter two alternatives, the savings ratio might either rise or fall with income per head, on the latter it would necessarily rise; in either case the possibility of unstable and multiple equilibrium would be present. The impression of orthodoxy would, however, be somewhat spurious, as the posited

---

[1] It might appear that fluctuations in the elasticity of substitution as capital per head increased might, by producing fluctuations in the savings ratio, lead to multiple equilibrium. Robert Solow has shown me that this is not so, since regardless of the behaviour of the elasticity of substitution savings per unit of capital must fall as capital increases. Let $y = f(k)$; then the savings ratio $s = s_w \dfrac{(f-kf')}{y} + s_p \dfrac{kf'}{y}$, where s_w and s_p are the savings ratios from wages and rent of capital; and $\dfrac{sy}{k} = s_w \dfrac{f}{k} + (s_p - s_w)f'$. This must decline as k increases because an increase in k reduces both the average product $\left(\dfrac{f}{k}\right)$ and the marginal product (f') of capital

[2] The marginal product of capital is $y_m w_m / y_m P$; the average product is $Pk_m / Ok_m = Oy_m / y_m P$; the elasticity of output with respect to capital (marginal product divided by average product) is therefore $y_m w_m / Oy_m$, previously identified with the share of capital in output.

relationships between saving and its determinants implicitly assume a process of maximizing utility over time that is not specified by the model.

An approach more in keeping with the context of equilibrium growth would be to assume that saving is motivated by a desire to achieve a preferred ratio of wealth to income. This approach can be formulated in diagrammatic terms in two alternative

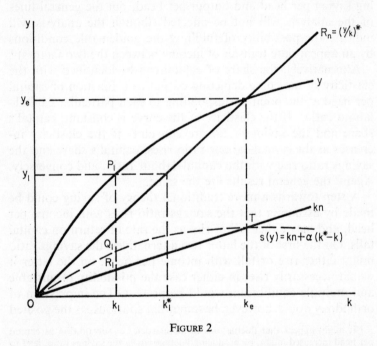

FIGURE 2

but fundamentally equivalent ways, depending on whether one wishes to emphasize the desired ratio to income of wealth in the narrow sense of the value of material capital, or of wealth in the broad sense of the capitalized value of the productive services of both non-human and human wealth. Both exploit the fact that wealth in either sense is uniquely correlated with the level of output.

The first approach is illustrated in Figure 2. In the Figure, P_1 represents the initial situation, with capital–labour ratio Ok_1 and output per head of Oy_1, the initial ratio of output and income to non-human capital being represented by the slope of OP_1 and the non-human-wealth-to-income ratio by its reciprocal (slope with reference to the vertical axis). The desired ratio of non-human wealth to income is represented by the slope of OR_n with reference to the vertical axis. To achieve this ratio, the average individual is assumed to save from current income a fraction α of the difference between his desired and his actual non-human capital stock $(Ok_1{}^* - Ok_1)$ over and above what must be saved to maintain the current non-human-capital-to-income ratio (R_1k_1); specifically his savings (Q_1k_1) are equal to $k_1n + \alpha(k_1{}^* - k_1)$. His savings behaviour at other levels of income is derived in the same way to yield the savings curve $O \cdot s(y) = \alpha(k^* - k) + kn$, the economy reaching growth equilibrium when the desired ratio of non-human capital to income is reached at the capital–labour ratio Ok_e and the output per head $k_e y_e$. In that equilibrium, the economy will be above or below the maximum-consumption-per-head level of capital, according as the rate of return on capital at the desired ratio of non-human capital to income is below or above the rate of population growth n.

The second approach is illustrated in Figure 3, where P_1 is again the initial situation, and the slope of OR_t with reference to the vertical axis represents the desired ratio of total (human and non-human) wealth to income. Non-human wealth is Ok_1. The value of total wealth $(O \cdot K_1)$ is found by drawing OM parallel to w_1P_1 to intersect y_1P_1 produced, P_1M_1 being the value of labour income capitalized at the rate of return on capital ruling at P_1; the desired value of total wealth is $OK_1{}^*$. The individual is assumed to save a fraction β of the difference between his actual and his desired total wealth, over and above the amount (R_1k_1) he must save to maintain the current wealth-to-income ratio; his savings function is $O \cdot s(y) = \beta(K^* - K) + kn$. These savings can only be invested in non-human capital; but accumulation of non-human capital raises the value of human capital in two ways, increasing the real wage and reducing the rate of interest at which it is capitalized. The economy reaches its equilibrium growth path when the actual ratio of total wealth to income is equal to the desired ratio: in the diagram, with income $y_e k_e$, capital–labour ratio Ok_e, and wealth-to-income ratio OK_e. Note that in this case the equilibrium output, non-human capital stock, and total wealth per head are defined by equality of the slope of Oy with the slope of OR_t, that is, by equality of the rate of return on non-human capital and the (average and marginal) desired ratio of income to total wealth.[1] In equilibrium, the economy will be above or below the level of capital per head yielding maximum consumption per head, according as the reciprocal

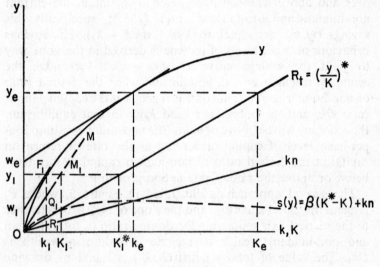

FIGURE 3

of the desired ratio of wealth to income (the desired ratio of income to wealth) is below or above the rate of population growth n.

The foregoing analyses have assumed for simplicity that the desired ratio of non-human or total wealth to income is fixed, independent of the level of income and wealth; there is no difficulty in extending the analysis to allow this desired ratio to vary with the level of income and wealth. A priori, one might be inclined to assume that the ratio rises as wealth and income rise.

[1] This implies that the economy must come into equilibrium growth with a positive rate of return on capital, which is not necessarily the case with the Keynesian constant propensity to save assumption or the postulate that saving is motivated by a desired ratio of material capital to income.

B. *Depreciation*

Relaxation of the assumption that capital once accumulated lasts forever raises no serious difficulties. It does, however, require drawing a distinction between gross and net output, gross and net saving and investment, and the gross and net marginal product of capital, the difference in each case corresponding to depreciation.

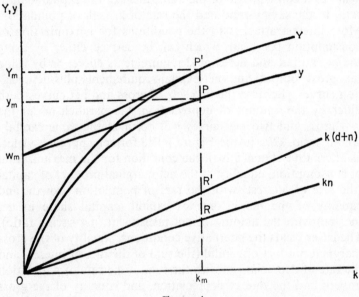

FIGURE 4

The simplest assumption is that capital depreciates by 'evaporation', a certain fraction (d) of the existing stock disappearing at each moment of time. Thus replacement requirements are a constant fraction of the stock. This model is represented in Figure 4, where $O \cdot kn$ as before represents the net saving required to equip the additional labour resulting from the growth of the labour force with the same capital per head as existing workers, $O \cdot k(d + n)$ represents the gross saving required to make good depreciation of the existing stock and equip new workers with the same capital as existing workers, OY represents gross output as a function of the capital–labour ratio, and Oy $(= OY - dK)$ represents net output after allowance for depreciation. The savings curve $O . sy$ (not shown in the diagram) may be drawn either gross or net.

Since depreciation is rigidly tied to the current stock of capital, it is evident that the same demonstration of the convergence of the growth rate of the economy on the rate of growth of population will apply in this case as in the previous case; and that in equilibrium the Harrod–Domar equation will hold, again as a consequence of the adjustment of the capital–output ratio to the saving ratio and the rate of growth of population. More interest attaches to the conditions for maximization of consumption per head, which can be derived either by using the net output and net capital requirements curve, or by using the gross output and net-capital-requirements-plus-depreciation curves. (Because the two sets of gross and net curves both differ by the amount of depreciation, the parallelisms of the two gross and two net curves will occur at the same capital–labour ratio, Ok_m in the Figure.) The former approach yields, as alternative statements of the condition for the maximization of consumption, equality of the net marginal product of capital (the rate of interest) with the rate of population growth, and equality of the net income of capital (capital share in net income) with the amount of net investment (net saving ratio). The latter yields the alternative conditions, equality of the gross marginal product of capital (the sum of the rate of interest and the rate of depreciation) with the sum of the rate of population growth and the rate of depreciation, and equality of the gross income of capital (share of capital in gross output) with the amount of gross investment (share of gross investment in gross output). Since depreciation appears on both sides of these two equalities, it nets out to yield the same conditions as previously stated.

An alternative assumption about depreciation is the 'one-hoss-shay' assumption, according to which capital equipment lasts with unchanging efficiency for a fixed period of time and then collapses into worthlessness. On this assumption, the ratio of depreciation to the existing stock is a variable and not a constant, since it depends not only on the fixed life of capital equipment but on the rate of growth of the economy. (The faster the rate of growth, the smaller is the amount of capital installed in the part that is now collapsing, relative to the size of the current stock.) Since, however, the capital requirements curve is drawn for the rate of growth of population, which is exogenously determined, this feature of depreciation requires only the incorporation in that curve of the value for d (the ratio of depreciation to existing stock) appropriate to the value of n. The demonstration of the convergence of the growth rate on the rate of growth of population becomes heuristic rather than rigorous (though it can be established mathematically). Its intuitive plausibility is reinforced by the consideration that if gross saving is assumed to be a fixed proportion of gross income, the proportion of it required to make good the collapse of capital installed in the past will increase as the rate of growth falls towards the long-run equilibrium level, and vice-versa; whereas if net saving is assumed to be a fixed proportion of net income, net income, and therefore the amount of net saving, relative to gross output will fall as the rate of growth falls towards the equilibrium level (because the proportion of the capital stock collapsing will rise), and vice versa. The use of a gross or net savings curve to demonstrate convergence, however, implicitly compresses the implications of the growth history of the economy for contemporary replacement requirements into the form of the saving curve, and ignores some possible complexities in the dynamic process of convergence on the equilibrium growth rate.

Diagrammatically, the conditions for maximization of consumption per head are the same as in the previous case: equality of the net rate of return on capital with the rate of population growth or of the gross rate of return on capital with the sum of the rate of population growth and the rate of depreciation, and equality of the share of capital with the savings ratio, either gross or net. These statements, however, conceal a complication that is of economic importance, concerned with the meaning of depreciation. In the previous case, depreciation by assumption corresponded exactly with the reduction in the contemporary productive capacity of the existing capital stock and the associated loss in its value. In the present case, depreciation represents the disappearance of capital constructed in the past, and is not directly connected with the loss of value of capital equipment as it ages, a loss which is associated not with a reduction in its current productivity but with a shortening of the period over which it will be productive. In other words, depreciation in this model is the real loss of capital through wearing out of parts of the capital stock, not the depreciation allowance that business firms would charge to permit the replacement of the present stock when it wears out. Similarly, yet income is conceived as gross income less replacement cost of worn-out equipment, not as gross income less replacement allowances for the existing stock. The 'golden rule' conditions must be interpreted in accordance with these concepts of depreciation and net income; they would appear much more complex if framed in terms of accounting concepts of depreciation and net income and the corresponding definition of the rate of return on capital.

C. *Technical Change*

The model assumes only one exogenous source of economic growth to which the economy adjusts, the rate of population increase, and does not allow for the possibility of growth through exogenous technical change. Customarily, in growth theory, it is assumed that technical change occurs at a constant rate, but that it may be neutral, biased towards labour-saving or biased towards capital-saving, 'neutrality of innovation' being capable of definition in two major ways. One is Hicksian neutrality, defined as innovation that raises the marginal productivity of both factors in the same proportion. The other is Harrodian neutrality, defined as innovation that, at a constant rate of return on capital, would keep the capital-to-output ratio constant and raise output per man at the same rate as technical progress occurs.

The diagrammatic model can easily be extended to take account of technical progress of the Harrod-neutral type, since such progress can be equated to an increase in the effective supply of labour (the quantity of labour measured in 'efficiency units') at a rate equal to the rate of technical progress. All that is required is to relabel the abscissa of Figure 1 as the ratio of capital to efficiency-units of labour, and to redefine n as the sum of the natural rate of growth of the labour force (p) and the rate of growth of efficiency-units supplied per man associated with Harrod-neutral technical progress (t). The diagram can then be used to demonstrate the convergence of the rate of growth of the economy on the equilibrium rate $(p + t)$, determined by the exogenously-given rates of population growth and technical progress. The conditions for maximum consumption per head are alternatively that the rate of return on capital should be equal to the sum of the rates of population growth and (Harrod-neutral) technical change, and that the proportion of income saved should be equal to the share of capital in national income, as before. Cases of biased technical progress (biased by reference to the standard of Harrod-neutrality) cannot be readily analysed diagrammatically, however; nor can cases of technical progress defined in terms of the Hicksian concept of neutrality (except in the case of a Cobb–Douglas production function, where Hicks-neutrality and Harrod-neutrality are the same thing).

III. APPLICATIONS TO DEVELOPMENT THEORY

The model developed in section 1 can be readily applied to illustrate some propositions in the theory of economic development.

One such proposition is the possibility of a 'low-level equilibrium trap', and the associated conclusion that what is needed to start a country on the path of self-sustaining economic growth is some sort of 'big push' or 'minimum critical effort', designed to raise capital and income per head above some initial level beyond which the economy will grow automatically, in the sense of steadily raising capital and income per head.

Two alternative possibilities of a low-level equilibrium trap are illustrated in Figures 5 and 6. In Figure 5 it is assumed that at low levels of income per head the savings ratio is low, whereas after some critical level of capital and income per head the savings ratio begins to rise, approaching a new higher level as the economy becomes richer; the rate of population increase is assumed constant, independent of the level of income per head. In Figure 6 the savings ratio is assumed either to be constant (the dashed curve $O . sy$) or, more realistically perhaps, to vary inversely with the rate of population growth (the initially long-, then short-, dashed function $O . s(y)$); the rate of population growth is assumed to be a function of income per head, being zero for low income levels, then rising rapidly as

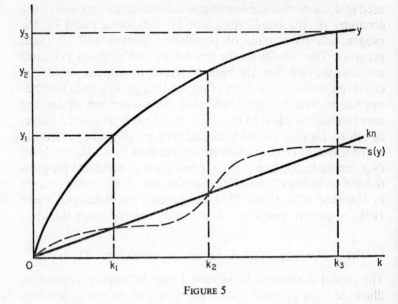

FIGURE 5

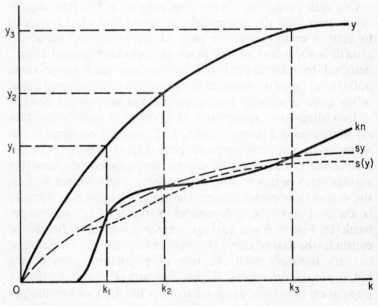

FIGURE 6

income per head rises, then gradually falling to a constant rate at high levels of income. In both cases, there is a stable low-level equilibrium, with income per head and capital per head constant respectively at Oy_1 and Ok_1; an unstable intermediate-level equilibrium with income and capital per head constant respectively at Oy_2 and Ok_2, from which any chance divergence would cause the economy either to grow in income and wealth towards y_3, k_3 or retrogress towards y_1, k_1; and a high-level stable equilibrium with income and capital per head respectively constant at Oy_3 and Ok_3, which may be interpreted in the present context as the stage of full development. Starting at y_1, k_1, a small once-for-all injection of additional capital per head would produce only a temporary rise in income per head, the economy being unwilling to save enough from the higher income to prevent the capital per head available to future generations from declining as income grew. In order to move the economy onto a path of self-sustaining economic growth, enough additional capital must be provided to raise the capital–labour ratio above Ok_2. Similarly, a slight rise in the savings ratio would not suffice to move the economy out of the neighbourhood of its present income per head; in order to start it on a self-sustaining growth path, the savings ratio must be raised sufficiently so that it lies completely above the capital requirements curve at the left-hand side of the diagram.[1]

The diagrammatic apparatus can also be used to explain the seriousness of the handicap to development of rapid population growth, and the growing importance currently being attached to programmes of birth control. Figure 7 depicts two economies, equipped with the same aggregate production function and saving the same proportion of national income, but differing widely in their rates of population increase (n_1 and n_2). The growth of country 1, the country with the low rate of population increase, converges on the income level Oy_1 and capital stock Ok_1 per head, while the growth of country 2, the country with the high rate of natural increase, converges on the lower levels of income and capital per head Oy_2 and Ok_2. More significantly, the maximum consumption

[1] A third possibility of a low-level equilibrium trap could be constructed by assuming a constant savings ratio but allowing increasing returns to increases in the capital-labour ratio for low levels of capital-intensity.

per head obtainable (on a sustained basis) by country 2 is Ow_{m2}, whereas country 1 can obtain the substantially higher consumption per head Ow_{m1}. Moreover, as the diagram is drawn country 2 must raise its savings ratio to achieve the maximum consumption per head available to it, while country 1 must actually reduce its saving ratio. In general, however, the relation between the savings ratios in the two countries required to maximize their respective levels of consumption per head at all points of time depends on the characteristics of the

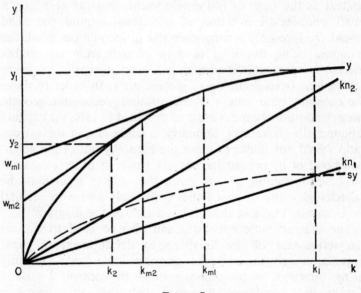

FIGURE 7

aggregate production function: by the golden rule, the required savings ratios are equal to the shares of capital in national income, and as previously explained this share rises or falls with income and capital per head according as the elasticity of substitution between capital and labour is greater or less than unity (alternatively, as the elasticity of output per head with respect to capital per head rises or falls as capital per head increases). Whatever is required of the shares of income saved in the two countries, however, it remains true that the maximum obtainable level of consumption per head must be lower in the country with the higher rate of population increase. It is also evident that its rate of population increase may be great enough to confine that country to a poverty level of consumption per head, whatever it does with its savings ratio and whatever donations of foreign aid it receives—unless foreign aid is provided on a permanent basis and its amount increases at the rate at which the country's population is growing.

IV. EXTENSIONS TO A MONETARY ECONOMY*

A. *Assumptions and Problems*

The model of economic growth developed in preceding sections is a 'real' model, in which the only asset available for holding by the public is material capital; this section extends the model to take account of the existence of money. To do so, it is assumed that money exists in the form of non-interest-bearing currency[1] (fiat money) issued by a government or issuing agency ('the monetary authority'), additions to the money supply being effected by the printing of additional currency and the distribution of it to the public.[2] The public is assumed to regard

---

* This section owes a great deal to James Tobin's two classic articles on the subject, 'A Dynamic Aggregative Model' (*Journal of Political Economy*, Vol. 63, no. 2, April 1955, pp. 103–15), and 'Money and Economic Growth' (*Econometrica*, Vol. 33, no. 4, October 1965, pp. 671–84). I am also grateful to Tobin for having convinced me that my analysis of the Keynesian model published in the *Economica* article referred to in the initial footnote was incorrect; this error led me into producing an analysis that was not only wrong but more cumbersome than the correct analysis, so that I am quite happy to scrap it. The analysis of section (b) below duplicates the relevant results of Tobin's second article; to my mind, the approach employed here is somewhat simpler to grasp than Tobin's, which starts from and then modifies a model in which the influence of price-level expectations is excluded by the assumption that the real value of money is fixed.

Section (c) below adds to the Tobin model the utility yield of real balances as an item of real income influencing saving. I am indebted to Alvin Marty and Milton Friedman for pointing out that this item should be included in the analysis.

[1] This assumption could be relaxed, and 'money' allowed to bear interest at some fixed rate. It should be noted that while the analysis is presented in terms of monetary policy, it can—on the commonly-adopted assumption that government debt is treated by the public as a net addition to wealth—equally well be interpreted as an analysis of the influence of fiscal policy on growth; this is the approach of Tobin, op cit.

[2] It must be assumed that this is done in some random fashion; if distribution were proportional to existing balances held, individuals would have an incentive

F

money as net wealth; in technical terms, the model is an 'outside money' model. It should be emphasized that the assumptions that money is non-interest-bearing and that it is treated as net wealth are crucial to the analysis.

Following the classical tradition of monetary theory, it is assumed that wages and prices are perfectly flexible, in the specific sense that the real value of the public's holdings of money is instantaneously adjusted to the desired level of real cash balances. The desired level of real cash balances per person is assumed to be a function, first, of the level of per capita income or per capita wealth, either non-human or total non-monetary wealth (in the present model this is a matter of indifference, since in the absence of technical change income per head, capital per head, and the capitalized value of human labour services are uniquely correlated); second, of the rate of return on material capital; and third, of the expected rate of return on money balances. For simplicity, it is assumed that, *ceteris paribus*, the desired level of real cash balances bears a fixed ratio to whichever scale variable, income or the two definitions of wealth, is assumed to determined monetary and saving behaviour, so that this ratio is a function of the two rate of return variables. The rate of return on capital, on the assumption that capital is the same stuff as output and lasts forever, is the marginal product of capital. The expected rate of return on money balances is the negative of the expected rate of change of prices, being negative when prices are expected to rise, zero when prices are expected to remain constant, and positive when prices are expected to fall. It is assumed that the expected rate of change of prices is equal to the actual rate of change of prices; the actual rate of change of prices, in its turn, is determined by the rate of growth of real output, and the rate of growth of the money supply provided by the monetary authority. Whatever the monetary authority does with the supply of money, the desired level of real balances will be secured by an appropriate movement of the price level; but the required price level change will determine the rate of return on real balances, and hence influence desired real balances and through them the growth of the economy. Further, the increase

to increase their cash balances in order to increase their shares of new money. I am indebted to discussion with Miguel Sidrauski for this point.

in real balances secured in this way will influence the accumulation of real capital, the mechanism depending on the theory of saving employed.

Three alternative assumptions about saving will be explored, two being variants of the Keynesian assumption of a constant ratio of saving to income and the third being that saving behaviour is governed by a desired ratio of wealth to real output. The two variants respectively ignore and take account of the utility yield of real balances as an item of real income influencing saving. The analysis based on the first assumption includes some remarks on the Keynesian problem of a possible minimum to the rate of return at which real investment will be undertaken.

The main emphasis of the analysis is placed on two related problems: the 'neutrality' of money in the context of economic growth, and the possibility of using monetary policy to influence the growth of the economy. In all three models, money is by assumption 'neutral' in the comparative-statics sense that a once-for-all change in the quantity of money, superimposed on a trend rate of growth of the money supply maintained by the monetary authority, would produce a once-for-all change in the price level with no real effects on the economy. In the context of growth theory, however, the question arises whether money is 'neutral' in the more relevant sense that a difference in the rate of change of the money supply maintained by the monetary authority would make no difference to the speed with which the economy approaches its equilibrium growth path, and, most fundamentally, that a difference in the rate of change of the money supply would make no difference to the output and consumption per head characteristic of the equilibrium growth path. If money is not neutral in the former sense, monetary policy can accelerate or retard the economy's approach to long-run equilibrium growth, and if it is not neutral in the latter sense, monetary policy can influence the characteristics of equilibrium growth.

For analytical simplicity, the monetary authority is assumed, not to fix the rate of growth of the money supply, but to govern the rate of increase of the money supply so as to achieve a target rate of price inflation or deflation, a higher rate of inflation or a lower rate of deflation requiring a higher rate of monetary expansion *ceteris paribus*. This assumption implies that, if the economy starts below its long-run equilibrium ratio of capital to output, the money supply is expanded at a declining rate as capital accumulates, the rate of expansion converging on the rate of growth of population plus the monetary authority's target rate of price change (which may be negative). Also, the policy question of whether the monetary authority can influence the characteristics of the equilibrium growth path is cast in terms of whether it can shift the economy towards the golden rule path. Though, as previously argued, there is no real justification for regarding such an objective as desirable, this formulation of the problem seems consistent with the spirit of growth theory.

B. *The Keynesian Constant Savings Ratio Model*[1]

On the assumption that aggregate saving is a constant proportion of aggregate income, the growth of real balances as the economy grows, whether by increasing capital per worker or by growth in the number of workers at a constant ratio of capital to labour only, appears as an addition to current real output in the reckoning of the current income from which savings are made, and therefore raises the ratio of saving to output. However, the growth of real balances also absorbs saving, since the additional real balances must be held, so that the net effect is a reduction in the ratio of savings invested in the creation of material capital to output, as compared with the ratio that would obtain in a pure barter economy. Given the rate of growth of aggregate output, the absolute increase of real balances will be greater, and therefore the reduction in the ratio of real capital investment to output will be greater, the greater is the desired ratio of real balances to output.[2] Actually, the rate of growth of aggregate output cannot be taken as given, but will be interdependent with the ratio of real investment to output; but it is intuitively evident and can be proved that, allowing for this relationship, the ratio of real

---

[1] Contrary to the contention of my *Economica* article, it makes no difference whether aggregate saving is assumed to be a constant proportion of aggregate income, or *per capita* saving a constant proportion of *per capita* income.

[2] Alternatively, it could be assumed that the ratio relates real balances to 'disposable income', the sum of output and receipts of real balances.

investment to output will vary inversely with the ratio of real balances to output.[1]

Since the rate of return on real capital is fixed by the capital to labour ratio (or the level of output per head) the desired ratio of real balances to output will vary inversely with the rate of increase of prices maintained by the monetary authority. Thus the ratio of material capital investment to output will vary directly with the rate of increase of prices maintained by the monetary authority. This in turn implies that the more expansionary is monetary policy, the faster will the economy grow (starting from any level of output per head below the equilibrium level for a barter economy), and the higher will be the level of capital per head at which the economy arrives on its long-run equilibrium growth path.

The mechanics of the model are illustrated in Figure 8. In the Figure, $O \cdot y$, $O \cdot kn$, and $O \cdot sy$ have the same meanings as on previous diagrams. $O \cdot y'$ is disposable income *per capita*; it is the sum (*per capita*) of output and the current increment of real balances, the latter being determined by output, the ratio of real balances to output (earned income) b, and the current rate of growth g. Total saving is $O \cdot sy'$ and the saving available for investment in real capital is $O \cdot s'(y)$

$$= O \cdot sy\left[1 - \left(\frac{1}{s} - 1\right) gb\right].$$ It should be noted that g is itself a

function of $s'(y)$, so that one cannot simply shift the $O \cdot y'$ curve to represent the effects of varying the level of b; however, the proof previously mentioned ensures that this heuristic procedure gives the correct answer. Moreover, the prime concern of the analysis is with the equilibrium at the point T at which $O \cdot s'(y)$ crosses the capital requirements curve $O \cdot kn$, and here the rate of growth of output must be $g = n$.[2] The

---

[1] Output per head is $y = f(k)$. Let disposable income per head be $y' = y(1+bg)$ where b is the ratio of real balances to output demanded and g is the growth rate. Saving will be sy', from which must be deducted savings devoted to increasing real balances bgy, leaving real savings $s'(y) = sy\left[1 - bg\left(\frac{1}{s} - 1\right)\right]$.

Now $g = \dfrac{f'}{y}s'(y) = f's - f'bg(1-s) = \dfrac{f's}{1+f'b(1-s)}$.

Hence $s'(y) = sy\left[1 - \dfrac{bf'(1-s)}{1+bf'(1-s)}\right]$, and it is evident that $\dfrac{\partial s'(y)}{\partial b} < 0$.

[2] The dynamics of the process of adjustment to the long-run equilibrium

relation between $O . y'$ and $O . y$ is governed by the following conflicting factors. As y rises, the rate of return on real capital must fall, tending to raise the desired ratio of real balances to income and the ratio of y' to y; on the other hand, an increase in y means a decline in the growth rate, for a constant savings ratio, since it implies a higher capital to output ratio and therefore a smaller proportionate 'deepening' of capital per unit of output; and this implies a reduction in the ratio to

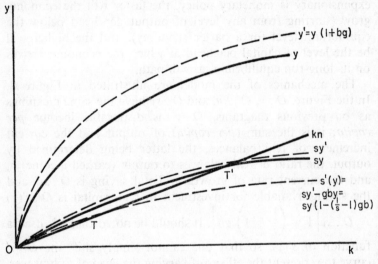

FIGURE 8

income of the additional real balances required by growth, and therefore of y' to y. The magnitude of b, the desired ratio of real balances to income, will (*ceteris paribus*) be greater the smaller the target rate of price increase or greater the target rate of price decrease maintained by the monetary authority. Hence the intersection at T of $O . s'(y)$ with $O . kn$ must be farther to the right of the diagram, the lower the target rate of price deflation or higher the target rate of price inflation set by the monetary authority. An upper limit is set by the point T'',

growth path, in both this and the models presented subsequently, are complex and raise awkward problems which cannot be readily handled diagrammatically.

which would imply a rate of inflation great enough to reduce the desired real balance ratio to negligibility.[1]

In this model, therefore, money is neutral neither in the sense that the rate of convergence on the equilibrium growth path is independent of the rate of monetary expansion, nor in the more fundamental sense that the characteristics of the equilibrium path are independent of monetary policy. It follows that within limits monetary policy in this model can be used to move the economy towards fulfilment of the golden rule conditions. If the economy's saving behaviour causes it to overshoot the golden rule ratio of real investment (accumulation of material capital) to output, this can be counteracted by contraction of the money supply to generate a deflationary price trend. There may be a limit on the application of such a deflationary policy, however; if material capital is desired only for its yield, while money yields utility services, there would be a presumption that investment in real capital would cease if the rate of return on money accruing from deflation exceeded the rate of return on real investment. (In a more general portfolio-balance model, with risk attaching to both assets and risk-aversion, there would be no such presumption.) If, on the other hand, the economy's saving behaviour causes it to fall short of the golden rule ratio of real investment to output, it can be nudged towards that position by an increase in the rate of expansion of the money supply. The extreme limit of such a policy would be a rate of inflation that reduced the ratio of real balances to income to negligibility and raised the ratio of real investment to output to the economy's savings ratio; this ratio might still fall short of that ratio required by the golden rule for maximizing consumption per head.

In this model, as in neo-classical growth models generally, it is assumed that the real savings produced by the savings ratio get invested in capital goods, regardless of the rate of return earned thereon. Keynesian economists frequently assume that investors demand a certain minimum rate of return on real investment, and that rather than take less they will accumulate saving in the form of cash. In this model, the results of such behaviour would

---

[1] This assumes that the public is precluded from issuing monetary debt to the monetary authority, an assumption that would be less reasonable in a fiscal policy model.

be an increase in the real value of cash balances through deflation, until real balances had risen to the level per head required to reduce the ratio of real savings to output to that required for the economy to grow at its long-run equilibrium rate, with an equilibrium capital–labour ratio such as to yield the required minimum rate of return on real investment. This result could be achieved alternatively without deflation by sufficient expansion of the money supply. The assumed investor behaviour, however, is arbitrary, in that it rests on the implicit Keynesian assumption that the (actual and expected) rate of return on money balances is precisely zero; if, instead, it is assumed that the (actual and expected) return on money balances varies inversely with the rate of inflation, and that investors demand a minimum premium of the rate of return on real investment over the rate of return on cash balances, it follows that the long-run growth equilibrium of the economy would involve a rate of return on real investment equal to the required premium, plus the equilibrium growth rate of population, minus the rate of growth of the money supply (the difference between the last two being the rate of return on the money supply); and the monetary authority could, subject to the limits discussed in the previous paragraph, offset the demands of investors for a premium by operating on the rate of growth of the money supply.

To conclude the discussion of this model, it should be noted that the analysis can readily be extended to include Harrod-neutral technical progress, by redefining labour in efficiency-units.

C. *The Utility Yield on Real Balances*

The model analysed in the preceding section treats income as the sum of current output and the receipts of additional real balances associated with the process of economic growth. The assumption of a demand for real balances, however, implies that such balances yield a flow of 'convenience services' or utility, which is at once a component of real consumption and real income, and should be included in the definition of the income that determines savings behaviour.

Consideration of the influence of this element of income by itself leads to conclusions about the influence of monetary policy on growth opposite to those indicated by the previous analysis of the influence of receipts of real balances. For while receipts of real balances are income that has to be saved, thereby (with a constant overall savings ratio) reducing the proportion of output available for investment in material capital, the services of real balances are income that has to be consumed, thereby (again with a constant overall saving ratio) reducing the proportion of physical output consumed and raising the ratio of real investment to output. Since, for any given level of output per head (and corresponding rate of return on real capital), the desired ratio of real balances to output will vary inversely with the rate of increase of prices maintained by the monetary authority, the ratio of real saving to output will be higher the less expansionary or the more contractionary is monetary policy (ignoring for the time being the influence of monetary policy on saving through its influence on additional receipts of real balances). Consequently, the less expansionary (or more contractionary) is monetary policy (defined by the target rate of price change), the faster will the economy grow, starting from any level of output per head below the long run equilibrium level, and the higher will be the long-run equilibrium level of output per head itself. This proposition, however, is subject to the possible restriction previously mentioned, that under certain conditions real investment might cease, if the rate of price deflation yielded a rate of return on real balances greater than that on real investment. (If the notion of the superior liquidity of money over real capital is admissible in a model of this kind, the maximum return on real balances allowable would in these circumstances be less than the return on real capital by the amount of the liquidity premium.) It follows that, so far as the influence of monetary policy through the service yield of cash balances is concerned, money is non-neutral in the two senses of being able to influence both the current rate of growth and the characteristics of the long-run equilibrium growth path.

Since the rate of real saving (the ratio of material investment to output) is influenced by monetary policy through the influence of the latter on the magnitudes relative to income of both receipts of additional real balances and the utility of real balances held, and these influences though opposite in direction are differently determined and can be expected not to cancel out, money remains non-neutral in both the senses just mentioned when the utility yield on real balances is taken into account. However, recognition of this element in the problem has the consequence that the direction of the influence of monetary policy on the growth equilibrium of the economy is no longer unambiguous. A more inflationary policy may raise or lower the current growth rate of output and the long-run equilibrium level of output per head, depending on whether the growth-stimulating (long-run equilibrium output-raising) effect of lower real-balance receipts outweighs the growth-inhibiting (long-run equilibrium output-reducing) effect of a lower utility yield on real balances.

A more subtle and important point is that it is no longer correct to discuss the problem in terms of moving the economy towards the golden rule situation as previously defined. When account is taken of the utility yield of real balances, the golden rule situation has to be defined in terms of two criteria: choice of a saving ratio that satisfies the golden rule conditions, to maximize consumption of commodities per head; and pursuit of a monetary policy of deflation at a rate equal to the golden rule rate of return on real capital, to maximize the utility yield on real balances. (Since this rate of return is equal to the rate of growth of the economy, the latter requirement would be fulfilled by the maintenance of a constant nominal stock of money.)

Given the existence of a saving ratio different from that indicated by the golden rule, the problem is to select a monetary policy that will maximize long-run equilibrium consumption per head of commodities and real balance services together; and since a policy may well have opposite effects on the quantity of consumable commodities available and the utility yield of real balances, it would be incorrect to assume that policy should aim to maximize the available quantity of consumable commodities, that is, to push the economy towards the golden rule situation with respect to the output of commodities alone. Specifically, assume that the influence of monetary policy via additional receipts of real balances dominates its influence via the utility yield, so that a more inflationary policy would increase the material investment ratio, and that the economy's saving ratio would make it fall short of the golden rule position even under barter economy conditions. An inflationary policy would raise output and consumption of commodities per head, but it might reduce the utility yield of real balances more than it increased commodity consumption. The proper policy to follow to maximize long-run equilibrium total consumption per head obviously depends on the outcome of the interaction of the relevant parameters.

To construct a geometrical version of this model, it is necessary to hypothesize a quantifiable measure of the utility yield

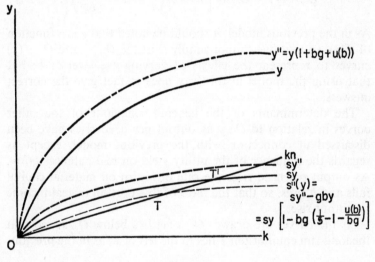

FIGURE 9

on real balances. For this purpose it is assumed that the utility yield as a proportion of income per head is an increasing function of the ratio of real balances to income, represented by $u(b)$, where $\dfrac{du}{db} > O$ and $\dfrac{d^2u}{db^2} < O$ until $u(b)$ attains a maximum representing satiation with real balances.[1]

[1] The logic of national income accounting suggests that the utility yield per unit of real balances be reckoned at the alternative opportunity cost of holding such balances, which is the difference between the yields on material capital and real balances, $r + \dfrac{\dot{p}}{p}$, where r is the rate of return on material capital and $\dfrac{\dot{p}}{p}$ is the rate of inflation. (The return on money, $-\dfrac{\dot{p}}{p}$, is already reckoned in the real

The mechanics of this model are illustrated in Figure 9. In the Figure, $O \cdot y$, $O \cdot kn$, and $O \cdot sy$ have the same meanings as before. $O \cdot y''$ is the revised concept of disposable income *per capita*; it is the sum *per capita* of current output y, the current increment of real balances bgy determined as in the previous model, and the imputed value of real balance services, $u(b)y$. Total saving is $O \cdot sy''$; the saving available for investment in material capital is

$$O \cdot s''(y) = O \cdot sy \left[1 - bg\left(\frac{1}{s} - 1 - \frac{u(b)}{bg}\right) \right].$$

As in the previous model, it should be noted that g is a function of $s''(y)$, so that one cannot simply shift the $O \cdot y''$ and $O \cdot s''(y)$ curves to represent the effects of varying the level of b; but that using the model in this way does in fact give the correct answers.

The determinants of the general behaviour of the other curves in relation to $O \cdot y$ as output per head rises have been discussed in connection with the previous model, except as regards the influence of the utility yield on real balances $u(b)y$. As output per head rises the rate of return on material capital falls and b rises, so that the ratio of this portion of real income to output rises.

As the curves are drawn, $O \cdot s''(y)$ lies below $O \cdot sy$, so that the long-run equilibrium T lies to the left of T' as in the previous

balance receipts portion of disposable income.) This procedure, however, produces economically nonsensical results. The imputed yield as a proportion of income is $\left(r + \frac{\dot{p}}{p} \right)b$, where b varies inversely with $\left(r + \frac{\dot{p}}{p} \right)$; if the demand for real balances is inelastic with respect to their cost, the formula implies that real income from this source will be higher the lower is the ratio of real balances to ouput; and in any case it implies that if the demand for real balances is satiated $\left(-\frac{\dot{p}}{p} = r, \text{ so that real balances cost nothing to hold} \right)$, total disposable income *per capita* is lower, *ceteris paribus*, than if it is not. It seems preferable to adopt a procedure that reflects effects on economic welfare rather than on conventional accounting magnitudes.

The approach adopted here corresponds to measuring the real income derived from holding real balances by integrating the area under the demand curve subtended by the quantity of cash balance services consumed. The usual difficulties with this approximation are disregarded on the grounds that the marginal utility of consumption of commodities may reasonably be assumed constant for the purposes of this model.

model. This relationship of the curves and equilibrium positions, however, is not necessary, but involves the implicit assumption that the influence of the utility yield of real balances on the saving ratio is outweighed by the influence of additional real balances; algebraically, that $\left(\dfrac{1}{s} - 1\right)$ is greater than $\dfrac{u(b)}{bg}$. If the converse were true, $O \cdot s''(y)$ would lie above $O \cdot sy$, and T would lie to the right of T'. This is an important possible alternative, for two reasons.[1]

First, it means that—confining attention to the assumption that the $O \cdot y$ curve does not bend down towards the horizontal axis—capital per head and output per head may be higher in a monetary economy than in a non-monetary economy with the same saving ratio. The neglect of the utility yield of real balances in the Keynesian case previously analysed produced the erroneous implication that, given the saving ratio, material capital and output per head in long-run equilibrium will always be lower in a monetary than in a non-monetary economy.[2]

Second, depending on whether the $O \cdot s''(y)$ curve lies below or above the $O \cdot sy$ curve, a more inflationary policy, which will have the effect of reducing the desired ratio of real balances to output b, will raise or lower the $O \cdot s''(y)$ curve, increase or decrease the speed with which the economy approaches its long-run equilibrium growth path, and increase or reduce the long-run equilibrium levels of capital per head and output per head. Thus, as previously pointed out, while money will be non-neutral with respect to growth in the two senses of influencing the rate of growth in other than long-run equilibrium growth situations, and of influencing the characteristics of the long-run growth path, these influences will not be unidirectional as in the previous model but will depend on circumstances.

There is unfortunately no obvious simple way to extend the

---

[1] One should also note that, since $\dfrac{u(b)}{b}$ and g will both fall as the capital to labour ratio increases, and the relation of $O \cdot s''(y)$ to $O \cdot sy$ depends on the relative magnitudes of $\dfrac{u(b)}{bg}$ and $\left(\dfrac{1}{s} - 1\right)$, $O \cdot s''(y)$ may cross $O \cdot sy$ one or more times.

[2] James Tobin has pointed out to me that comparison of a barter and a monetary economy in this fashion is probably unfair, since it leaves unanswered the question of how the barter economy performs the functions of money in a monetary economy.

diagrammatic technique so as to add consumption of the services of real balances to consumption of commodities and thus permit analysis of the influence of monetary policy on total consumption in long-run growth equilibrium.

D. *The Desired Wealth to Income Ratio Model*

As pointed out previously, the Keynesian assumption that a constant proportion of income is saved makes little theoretical sense. The consequences of the alternative theory that saving is motivated by the desire to achieve and maintain a certain ratio of wealth to real output are illustrated in Figure 10. The

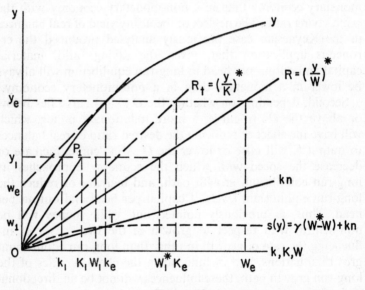

FIGURE 10

desired ratio of total wealth to output is represented by the reciprocal of the slope of $O . R$. With real equilibrium at P_1, material capital is Ok_1, human capital is k_1K_1, and real monetary wealth is K_1W_1, total wealth being OW_1. The real value of the stock of money is equal to the desired value of cash balances, which in turn is related to total non-monetary wealth or (more complexly) to total wealth through a desired cash-balance ratio which depends on the rate of return on material capital and the rate of return on cash balances, the latter depending on the rate of growth of output and of the money supply. The ratio of real investment to output is assumed to be determined in part by the desire to maintain the current wealth-to-output ratio, and in part by the desire to increase the wealth-to-income ratio towards the desired level represented by $O.R.$ In long-run equilibrium, output is Oy_e, material capital per head Ok_e, the value of human capital per head k_eK_e, and real monetary wealth per head K_eW_e. In contrast to the real model previously discussed, the rate of return on capital must be higher than the desired ratio of income to wealth. Moreover, this rate of return will be lower, and the level of output per head prevailing in long-run growth equilibrium will be higher, the lower the ratio of monetary to total wealth desired under long-run equilibrium growth conditions.

Since under these conditions the rate of growth of output must be equal to the rate of growth of population, the rate of return on cash balances and consequently the desired ratio of monetary to total wealth will be a decreasing function of the rate of increase of the money supply, so that total non-monetary capital per head will be an increasing function, and the rate of return on capital a decreasing function, of the rate of increase of the money supply.

This formulation of the argument, however, is somewhat misleading, since it neglects the influence of the rate of return on real capital on the desired money-to-wealth ratio. A clearer picture of the relationship, perhaps, is conveyed by considering the effect of an increase in the desired money to wealth ratio, starting from the initial level of non-monetary wealth K_e: this increase would be provided by a once-over change in the price level, after which prices would continue to change at the previous rate. The community would then find that its total wealth-to-income ratio was higher than desired, and it would start to decumulate wealth, including non-monetary wealth. The result of decumulation would be to raise the rate of return on material capital, and so tend to reduce the desired ratio of money to total wealth, thereby mitigating the decline in wealth that would otherwise be necessary to restore equilibrium. Alternatively, one might construct a locus OW, representing total actual wealth for the varying levels of output per head, on the assumption that monetary policy aims at a target rate of change of prices, the intersection of OW with OR indicating the characteristics of the equilibrium growth path, and OW lying further to the right the lower the target rate of price increase (higher the target rate of price decrease). This construction would, however, entail the complexity of compressing into the shape of OW the growth history of the economy, except at the intersection point.

In this model, as in the Keynesian models previously considered, money is not neutral in the long-run equilibrium sense that the characteristics of the economy on the equilibrium growth path will be independent of the rate of change of the money supply. On the contrary, the monetary authority can increase or decrease output and capital per head in growth equilibrium, by increasing or decreasing the rate of expansion of the money supply. It can thus move the economy towards the fulfilment of the golden rule conditions, within limits set by the desired wealth to income ratio and the condition that the rate of deflation cannot exceed the rate of return on material capital. As indicated earlier, however, the services of cash balances should be included in the definitions of income and consumption; the long-run monetary policy suggested by golden rule considerations would therefore be that which maximized the excess of disposable income (including the value of the services derived from real balance holdings) over the capital requirements of population growth, subject to the two restrictions just mentioned.

E. *Concluding Remarks: Savings Behaviour and Inside Money*

The basic reasons for the non-neutrality of money in the models explored in previous sub-sections, in the fundamental sense that monetary policy influences the characteristics of the equilibrium growth path, is that these models relate savings behaviour to other variables than the rate of return on investment. If, in line with the more traditional approach to saving as an intertemporal exchange of consumption goods, saving behaviour were represented as a willingness to accumulate assets until the rate of return on them reached a minimum set by the social rate of time preference, the long-run neutrality of money would be re-established.[1] This would, however, involve treating the rate of time preference as independent of the stock of wealth and its composition, which is an extremely questionable assumption, especially for a monetary economy in which wealth can be stored in the form of either real capital or real balances, each with its own rate of return.

The models explored have all been 'outside money' models, in which real balances constitute an addition to material wealth in the form of capital goods. If on the contrary it were assumed that money is of the 'inside' variety, created against private debts—the question of what happens to the banking profits earned by lending at interest while borrowing interest-free is temporarily ignored—real balances would not constitute a net addition to material wealth, but instead an indirect means of holding material wealth. In that case, monetary policy would not be able to influence growth through its influence (via the desired money to income ratio) on the magnitude of the supplement to earned income received in the form of additional real balances, and therefore on the material savings ratio. Instead, the influence of monetary policy on growth would be confined to the influence of the target rate of inflation or deflation on the utility yield of real balances.

The existence of this influence, however, results from carrying over from the outside money model the assumption that money bears no interest, so that monetary policy exercises a leverage over the real rate of return on money balances. There is no real justification for making this assumption.[2] The non-payment of interest on demand deposits, which constitute a substantially more important means of payment than currency in most advanced countries, is a consequence of legal restriction rather than natural law—and to an important extent it is evaded by the cancellation of service charges against hypothetical interest earnings. If it were not for this legal restriction, the merits of which are extremely doubtful,[3] and for the imposi-

---

[1] This approach is adopted in a University of Chicago Ph.D. thesis by Miguel Sidrauski.   [2] I am indebted for this point to discussion with R. A. Mundell.

[3] See, for example, George J. Benston, 'Interest Payments on Demand Deposits and Bank Investment Behavior', *Journal of Political Economy*, Vol. LXXII, no. 5, October 1964, pp. 431–49. The case for allowing the payment of interest on demand deposits has been made cogently on numerous occasions by my colleague Milton Friedman.

tion of legal reserve requirements on banks, which in effect impose a special tax on the commercial banks equal to the interest they forgo on assets held involuntarily in the form of non-interest-bearing central bank liabilities, competition in the commercial banking business would result in holders of demand deposits being offered a rate of interest equal to the rate of return on real capital, less the costs of the financial inter-mediation that allows deposit-holders to hold their wealth in the more convenient form of deposits rather than real capital. In that case, the cost of holding money rather than material capital would be equal to the social cost of creating it, and money would be neutral with respect to economic growth.[1]

This conclusion leads to the final observation, that what is basically responsible for the non-neutrality of money in the models analysed is the assumption that money is a non-interest-bearing asset (or, more generally, an asset with a return fixed in nominal terms, which return has for convenience been equated to zero in this analysis). This assumption stems in part from the current institutional arrangements for the provision of the supply of money, the wisdom of which is questioned in the preceding paragraph, but more importantly from the convenience to the classical tradition of monetary analysis of the outside money concept, so useful in demonstrating the neutrality of money under static equilibrium conditions. For the construction of models of growth incorporating money, it might be preferable to employ an assumption about money that, instead of ensuring non-neutrality by accepting existing monetary institutional arrangements as defining money, en-sured neutrality by re-defining institutional arrangements for supplying money. Specifically, neutrality would be assured by assuming that monetary arrangements guarantee holders of money a rate of return on their real balances equal to the rate of return available on real investment.

[1] In these conditions, there would be nothing to choose between a policy of maintaining price stability and a policy of deflating at a rate equal to the rate of interest. The recognition that modern money is mostly inside money may be partly responsible for the decline in popularity of the classical monetary theorist's recommendation of the latter policy. If money were all inside money and com-petition prevailed there would be an argument for price-level stability on the grounds that this would conveniently make real and nominal rates of interest equal.

CHAPTER V

NOTES ON THE THEORY OF TRANSACTIONS DEMAND FOR CASH*

I. INTRODUCTION

One of the great contributions to the advancement of monetary theory made by Keynes in his *General Theory of Employment, Interest and Money* was his attempt to replace the mechanical treatment of velocity as a technological and institutional constant, characteristic of the 'classical' theory he attacked, by a theory of demand for money as an asset alternative to other interest-bearing but less liquid assets. Keynes's own theory of demand for money, however, was an awkward compromise between the preceding treatment of velocity as a constant, and a fully generalized asset theory of demand for money. For he divided the demand for money into two parts—M_1, the transactions and precautionary demand for money, and M_2, the speculative demand for money—and treated the first part in a conventional fashion as bearing an institutionally-determined proportionality relationship to income, confining the analysis of the demand for money as an asset to the speculative demand for money. It was left to subsequent writers, writing in the 1950's,[1] to integrate the theory of transactions demand into a generalized capital-theory approach to demand for money, by treating cash demanded as a form of inventory held for the services it yielded, and its quantity as depending

* *The Indian Journal of Economics*, Vol. XLIV, Part I, no. 172, July 1963, pp. 1–11.

[1] William J. Baumol, 'The Transactions Demand for Cash: An Inventory Theoretic Approach', *Quarterly Journal of Economics*, Vol. LXVI, no. 4, November 1952, pp. 545–56. James Tobin, 'The Interest-Elasticity of Transactions Demand for Cash', *Review of Economics and Statistics*, Vol. XXXVIII, no. 3, August 1956, pp. 241–7.

on other economic variables and responding to changes in them.

The inventory approach to transactions demand is a signicant contribution, both as a means of integrating the theory of transactions demand for cash with the increasingly popular capital-theory approach to monetary theory, and because it permits the demand for cash to be deduced from alternative opportunity cost considerations without the need to introduce uncertainty of expectations or a vaguely-specified 'utility' attached to the holding of money *per se*. Nevertheless, the inventory approach is one unfamiliar to the general tradition of monetary theory, and involves some complexities frequently puzzling to the student. The following notes on the approach and the chief conclusions to which it leads may therefore prove useful. They begin with a simplified and unrealistic case, designed to illuminate the core of the approach, and proceed to the normal and more complicated case; the Appendix illustrates the theory by a concrete example based on the charging practices of the British clearing banks. The notes make no pretence to originality, with the exception of the diagrammatic technique employed, which may be helpful to those versed in such techniques.

II

Assume that at the beginning of each period the individual receives a certain sum T in the form of assets of some kind (e.g. deposits) bearing interest at the rate i per period, and that the payments he has to make with those transactions assets come due in an even flow over the period. To meet these payments, he withdraws cash lots at intervals over the period, each withdrawal costing a fixed sum b and a charge per unit of cash withdrawn of $\frac{1}{2}k$ per unit. The problem is to arrange the withdrawals so as to maximize the yield obtained (or minimize the loss incurred) on the individual's total transactions assets over the period between their receipt and expenditure.

It is intuitively obvious that the optimum arrangement will entail withdrawals of equal amounts of money (i.e. withdrawals spaced at equal intervals over the transactions period). To prove it, assume that the individual can make only two withdrawals, one at the beginning and one at some other time during the period. If he withdraws a proportion x of the original sum, this will meet his cash needs for a fraction x of the period, during which he earns interest on the residual proportion $1 - x$ in the amount of $i \, x \, (1 - x)T$; and his earnings will be maximized for $x = \frac{1}{2}$ (i.e. equal withdrawals, equally spaced). Since the same argument applies for the period of expenditure financed by any two successive withdrawals whatever the number of withdrawals, it follows that the optimum arrangement entails equally-spaced withdrawals of equal amounts of cash. The problem is, therefore, to determine the optimum size (C) or number $(n = T/C)$ of withdrawals.

The individual can be thought of as holding an average transactions balance during the period of $t = \frac{1}{2}T$, divided between an average cash holding $c = \frac{1}{2}C$ and an average holding of non-cash assets (deposits) $d = t - c$. The cost of providing the cash balance is $bn + kt = b \cdot \dfrac{t}{c} + kt$; the earnings received on the non-cash assets are $id = i(t - c)$; and the net yield (or net loss) on the total of transactions is $y = (i - k)t - ic - b\dfrac{t}{c}$. This is maximized (minimized) when

$$\frac{dy}{dc} = \frac{bt}{c^2} - i = 0,$$

that is, when $c = \sqrt{\dfrac{bt}{i}}$, the net yield (or loss) then being

$y = (i - k)t - 2\,ic = (i - k)t - 2\sqrt{ibt}$ (note that if $b \geqslant \frac{1}{4}it$, the individual will cash his assets immediately).

The optimum cash balance $(c = \sqrt{bt/i})$ varies inversely with the square root of the rate of interest and directly with the square root of the average transactions balance; its elasticity with respect to the rate of interest is $-\frac{1}{2}$ and with respect to the average transactions balance $+\frac{1}{2}$. $\left(\dfrac{\delta c}{\delta i} = -\dfrac{1}{2i}\sqrt{\dfrac{bt}{i}} = -\dfrac{\frac{1}{2}c}{i};\right.$

$\left.\dfrac{\delta c}{\delta t} = \dfrac{1}{2t}\sqrt{\dfrac{bt}{i}} = \dfrac{\frac{1}{2}c}{t}\right)$. Similarly, the ratio of the cash to the transactions balance $\left(\dfrac{c}{t} = \sqrt{\dfrac{b}{it}}\right)$ varies inversely with the square roots of the rate of interest and the average transactions balance; its elasticity with respect to each is $-\frac{1}{2}$. $\left(\dfrac{\delta(c/t)}{\delta i} = -\dfrac{1}{2i} \sqrt{\dfrac{b}{it}}\right.$

$= -\frac{1}{2} \dfrac{c/t}{i}; \dfrac{\delta(c/t)}{\delta t} = -\dfrac{1}{2t} \sqrt{\dfrac{b}{it}} = \left. -\frac{1}{2} \dfrac{c/t}{t}\right).$

Correspondingly, the net yield increases (loss decreases) more than proportionally as the rate of interest and the average transactions balance increase,

$$\left(\frac{\delta y}{\delta i} = t - c > \frac{y}{i}; \frac{\delta y}{\delta t} = i - k - \frac{b}{c} > \frac{y}{t}\right).$$

The formula for the optimum cash balance has one interesting property worth commenting on. Provided that the rate of expenditure is the same, the optimum cash balance is independent of the frequency and the regularity with which payments are received, since a shortening or lengthening of the period whose expenditure is financed reduces or increases both the average transactions balance t and the return on funds invested over the period i in the same proportion. Thus any change in the frequency or regularity of receipts would affect the average non-cash assets d only, leaving the average cash balance unchanged.

The determination of the optimum cash balance, and the effects on it of changes in the interest rate and the amount of the transactions balance, can be illustrated geometrically by reference to Figure 1. In the diagram, the average cash balance is measured along the abscissa and the cost incurred and yield obtained by maintaining it at different levels is measured along the ordinate. YY represents the interest earned on the average deposit-holding, which declines from a maximum of it when the average cash balance is zero to nothing when the transactions balance is held entirely in cash (i.e. the whole sum is immediately withdrawn). EE represents the cost of the withdrawals required to maintain the cash balance. It consists of two parts; a fixed sum kt (represented by FF) corresponding to the part of the withdrawal charge which depends on the amount withdrawn and hence is the same in the aggregate regardless of the number of withdrawals; and a variable part (the vertical distance between EE and FF equal to $\dfrac{bt}{c}$), corresponding to the fixed charge per withdrawal, which is smaller the fewer the withdrawals and larger the average cash balance.

The net yield obtained (net cost incurred) by maintaining an average cash balance of a given size is the vertical difference between YY and EE; and the net yield is maximized (cost

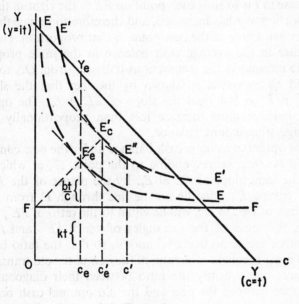

FIGURE 1

minimized) when the slopes of EE and YY are equalized—in Figure 1, when the cash balance is Oc_e, with net yield $Y_e - E_e$.

An increase in the rate of interest will increase the slope of YY; the tangency point E_e which defines Oc_e, the optimum average cash balance, will be shifted to the left, and the optimum average cash balance will be reduced. Conversely, a reduction in the rate of interest will increase the optimum average cash balance.

An increase in the average transactions balance will shift all three curves; but since the slope of YY depends only on the rate of interest and will therefore be unchanged, and FF represents a fixed-cost element which does not affect the slope of EE, the problem of the effect of such an increase reduces to its effect on the point E_e (and the corresponding average cash balance Oc_e) at which the slope of EE is equal to that of YY. This problem can be approached by considering the effect of an increase in the transactions balance in shifting EE with reference to F as origin—say to $E'E'$.

As a preliminary, it may be observed that the effect of an increase in t is to shift each point on EE to the right in the same proportion as t has increased, and therefore to reduce the slope of the new curve at the new point in that proportion. Hence an increase in the average cash balance in the same proportion as the increase in the transactions balance—from Oc_e to Oc'— would be excessive, as shown by the fact that the slope of $E'E'$ at E'' is less than the slope of EE at E_e. The optimum cash balance must increase less than proportionally to the average transactions balance.

The optimum average cash balance under the new conditions would be Oc'_e, corresponding to the point E'_e at which $E'E'$ has the same slope as EE at E_e. By the nature of the EE and $E'E'$ curves, E'_e must lie on the line through E_e from F; and the ratio of Oc'_e to Oc_e will be equal to the ratio of FE'_e to FE_e. Now, the areas of the rectangles of which FE'_e and FE_e are diagonals are respectively bt' and bt, so that the ratio between these areas is equal to the ratio of the new to the old transactions balance; consequently the ratio between their diagonals, and therefore between the new and the old optimal cash balances, must be equal to the square root of that ratio. Consequently, the optimum average cash balance increases with the square root of the average transactions balance.

III

Now assume that instead of being paid in interest-bearing assets the individual is paid in cash, and that to acquire interest-bearing assets he must pay a fixed sum B plus a charge per unit of assets acquired of $\frac{1}{2}K$ per unit. Clearly he will withhold part of his cash to meet expenditure at the beginning of the period, and invest only a part for subsequent withdrawal. The amounts of the withdrawals, and the average cash balance maintained during the period he is financing expenditure from his interest-bearing assets, will be as determined by the analysis of the previous section (since, as was there pointed out, the optimum cash balance is independent of the length of the period financed by the initial non-cash assets provided the rate of expenditure is the same). The individual's problem therefore is to choose the proportion a of his transactions money T to invest in interest-bearing assets to maximize his yield.

The net yield the individual derives from his transactions assets consists of two parts:

(*a*) The net yield earned on his non-cash assets during the first part of the period, in which he finances expenditure out of cash withheld from investment. The amount invested is $a . 2t$, which remains invested for a proportion $1 - a$ of the period and therefore earns interest at the rate $(1 - a)i$; so that the interest earned is $2a(1 - a)it$. Against this must be counted the cost of investment $B + Kat$, so that the net yield in this part of the period is

$$2a(1 - a)it - B - Kat.$$

(*b*) The net yield earned on the average transactions balance over the remainder of the period, as determined from the formula obtained in section I. The average transactions balance is at, and the rate of interest ai, so that the net yield in this part of the period is

$$a(ai - k)t - 2a\sqrt{ibt}.$$

The total net yield the individual derives from his transactions assets over the whole period is the sum of these two parts,

$$y = 2\,ait - a^2\,it - 2a\,\sqrt{ibt} - a\,(K + k)\,t - B.$$

This is maximized when

$$\frac{dy}{da} = 2\,it - 2\,ait - 2\,\sqrt{ibt} - (K + k)\,t = 0,$$

that is, when

$$(1 - a)t = \sqrt{\frac{bt}{i}} + \frac{\frac{1}{2}(K + k)t}{i} = c + \frac{\frac{1}{2}(K + k)t}{i},$$

$$\text{and } a = 1 - \frac{1}{2}\frac{K + k}{i} - \frac{c}{t}.$$

The maximum yield obtained by setting a at the optimum level is

$$y = \frac{t}{i}\left(i - \frac{K + k}{2} - \sqrt{\frac{ib}{t}}\right)^2 - B.$$

(Notice that a may easily be negative, implying that the individual will retain all of his initial transactions money in cash.)

The formula thus derived can be obtained more simply and directly by the following argument. Aside from the fixed deposit and withdrawal charges the individual must pay $\frac{1}{2}(K + k)$ per unit of cash invested and subsequently withdrawn; this cost must be covered by the interest earned on the money, so that the invested funds must remain invested for a period of at least $\frac{1}{2}\frac{(K + k)}{i}$. Accordingly, the individual must withhold cash sufficient to finance expenditure during this period, that is, cash amounting to $\frac{1}{2}\frac{K + k}{i}T$. If he withheld just this amount, he would subsequently have to withdraw a cash lot which had just earned its keep, and in doing so he would incur a withdrawal charge of b, thus suffering a loss which he could have avoided by not investing this cash lot in the first place. Thus he will withhold from investment cash amounting to $\frac{1}{2}\frac{K + k}{i}T + C$, giving an average balance over the first part of the period of

$$(1 - a)t = \frac{1}{2}\frac{K + k}{i}t + c.$$

The average cash balance held by the individual during the period is the weighted average of the average balances held during the two parts of the period—an average balance of $(1 - a)t$ held for $1 - a$ of the period, and an average balance c held for a of the period.

The optimum average cash balance is

$$(1 - a)\left(c + \tfrac{1}{2}\frac{K+k}{i}\,t\right) + ac$$

$$= c + \tfrac{1}{2}\frac{K+k}{i}\,t\left(\frac{c}{t} + \frac{1}{2}\frac{K+k}{c}\right)$$

$$= \sqrt{\frac{bt}{i}\left(1 + \tfrac{1}{2}\frac{K+k}{i}\right) + \left(\tfrac{1}{2}\frac{K+k}{i}\right)^2\,t}.$$

The optimum average cash balance varies inversely with the rate of interest, and directly with the average transactions balance, but the relationship is much more complex than in the previous case; it can be shown, however, that the optimum cash balance increases less than proportionally to the average transactions balance

$$\left[\frac{\delta c}{\delta t} = \tfrac{1}{2}\sqrt{\frac{b}{it}\left(1 + \tfrac{1}{2}\frac{K+k}{i}\right) + \left(\tfrac{1}{2}\frac{K+k}{i}\right)^2} < c/t,\right.$$

$$\text{whence}\quad \frac{t}{c}\cdot\frac{\delta c}{\delta t} < 1\Big].$$

Also, it is no longer true that the optimum average cash balance is independent of the period for which expenditure is financed by the initial receipt; instead, the optimum average cash balance increases as the period decreases, because the initial stage of the period during which a larger cash balance is held is constant, so that its weight increases as the period is shortened. However, if the costs of acquiring and cashing interest-bearing assets are fixed charges only, and not proportional to the amount deposited or withdrawn (i.e. $k = K = 0$), the conclusion of the previous section stands; the optimum cash balance would be independent of the frequency and the regularity with which payments were received, dependent only on the rate of expenditure, the rate of return on non-cash assets, and the fixed charge per withdrawal.

APPENDIX: A PRACTICAL
APPLICATION

Suppose that the individual's bank has the following charging scheme (modelled on actual banking practice)

(i) it charges £2 0s 0d per page of book entries; each page contains forty lines. Since the individual may be assumed to make only one deposit as compared with a number of withdrawals per period, this implies a fixed charge of 1s per withdrawal, no charge (effectively) for depositing, and no charges proportional to the amounts deposited or withdrawn on each occasion (in the formulae, $B = K = k = 0$, $b = £\frac{1}{20}$).

(ii) it allows credit for one page of entries against each £50 average balance; this amounts to an interest earning of 4% per annum, 1% per quarter, $\frac{1}{2}$% per month, or $\frac{1}{13}$% per week.

The problem is, what must the individual's income be, if the operation of his bank account is to cost him nothing, (a) if he is paid by a transfer to his bank account, (b) if he is paid in cash and deposits part of his pay for subsequent withdrawal?

Whether the individual is paid in cash or by transfer to his bank account, his optimum cash balance will be $c = \sqrt{\dfrac{bt}{i}}$, and his optimum cash withdrawal $C = \sqrt{\dfrac{2bT}{i}}$.

In case (a), where the individual is paid by transfer to his bank account, his net yield (loss if negative) on his account is $i(t - 2c)$. Thus if his account is to support itself, his optimum cash balance must be half or less of his transactions balance, and his optimum cash withdrawal less than half of his pay cheque. This implies that his pay cheque T must be greater than $\dfrac{8b}{i}$, where i is the rate of interest over the period which his pay cheque finances ($C = \sqrt{\dfrac{2bT}{i}} < \frac{1}{2}T$ implies $T > \dfrac{8b}{i}$). In concrete terms, if he is paid quarterly his pay cheque must exceed £40 a quarter, if he is paid monthly his pay cheque must exceed £120 a month, and if he is paid weekly his pay cheque must exceed £520 a week, if his account is to cost him no charges.

The same relationship may be put another way: if Y is the individual's annual income, f the frequency with which he is paid, and r the annual rate of interest, his pay cheque is $\dfrac{Y}{f}$ and the rate of interest earned during the period of expenditure financed by the cheque is $\dfrac{r}{f}$. For his bank charges to be zero, it is necessary that $\dfrac{Y}{f} > \dfrac{8bf}{r}$ or $Y > \dfrac{8b}{r} f^2$. In terms of the example, annual income must exceed £10 multiplied by the square of the frequency with which he is paid: if he is paid quarterly his annual income must exceed £160, monthly £1,440, weekly £27,040.

In case (b), where the individual is paid in cash, his net yield is $\dfrac{i}{t}(t - c)^2$. This would imply a gain from running a bank account (in the optimum manner) providing the optimum cash balance (withdrawal) is less than the average transactions balance (pay cheque). But the mathematical result here assumes that withdrawals (and their costs) are divisible, which is patently unrealistic; and for realism the amount deposited and withdrawn should be at least one optimum cash lot. This restriction requires that the optimum cash balance should be half or less of the transactions balance, so that this case gives the same numerical answer as the other.

In the charging system just discussed, an individual either pays bank charges or does not, but never earns a yield on his account. If the account earns more than it costs, the benefit goes to the bank. This suggests another problem, the relation between the size of the individual's pay cheque and the number of cheques he can draw without incurring a charge on his bank account (assuming each cheque is drawn for the same amount). Again, it is necessary to distinguish the two cases (a) where the individual is paid by transfer to his bank account, (b) where he is paid in cash and deposits part of the money in a bank account.

In the general case (a), the net yield of the account is $y = (i - k)t - ic - bn$, where $n = \dfrac{t}{c}$ is the number of withdrawals. Setting $y = 0$ gives the equation

$$bn^2 - (i - k)tn + it = 0, \text{ whence}$$

$$n = \frac{(i - k)t + \sqrt{(i - k)^2 t^2 - 4\,bit}}{2b}$$

Clearly the larger value of n is the solution sought. In the type of bank charging scheme described earlier, this becomes

$$n = \frac{iT}{4b}\left(1 + \sqrt{1 - \frac{8b}{iT}}\right),$$

whereas before T is the amount of the pay cheque and i the rate of interest over the period it finances. Alternatively,

$$N = \frac{rY}{4bf}\left(1 + \sqrt{1 - \frac{8bf^2}{rY}}\right)$$

where $N(= fn)$ is the number of cheques drawn per year, $Y(= fT)$ is annual receipts, f is the frequency of payment of annual receipts, and $r(= if)$ is the annual rate of interest. In the concrete example above, with $r = 4\%$ and $b = £\frac{1}{20}$, $n = \frac{1}{5}\frac{Y}{f}\left(1 + \sqrt{1 - 10\frac{f^2}{Y}}\right)$.

The relations between n and Y for the common frequencies of payment are as follows:

receipts	f	n as function of Y
quarterly	4	$n = \frac{1}{20}Y\left(1 + \sqrt{1 - \frac{160}{Y}}\right)$
monthly	12	$n = \frac{1}{60}Y\left(1 + \sqrt{1 - \frac{1440}{Y}}\right)$
weekly	52	$n = \frac{1}{260}Y\left(1 + \sqrt{1 - \frac{27040}{Y}}\right)$

(Note that for the number of cheques to be a real and not an imaginary number, the expression under the square root sign must be positive; and that by setting the expression at zero we obtain the minimum income necessary for the bank account to carry itself, as derived earlier in this section.)

In the general case (b), the net yield of the account is

$$2ait - a^2it - B - (K + k)at - a^2it/n - cn = 0$$

Setting this equal to zero gives the equation

$$bn^2 - (2ait - a^2it - B - (K + k)at)n + a^2it = 0$$

or with the general type of bank charging system described above

$$(B = K = k = 0)$$

$$bn^2 - ait(2 - a)n + a^2it = 0$$

On solution this gives (choosing the larger value of n, as before)

$$n = \frac{it}{2b} \cdot a \, [(2 - a) + \sqrt{(2 - a)^2 - 4b/it}]$$

Differentiating by a and setting the result equal to zero to find the value of a which maximizes n yields this value as $= 1 - \dfrac{b}{it}$. (As in the main argument, the value of a can be derived directly from the principle that funds deposited must remain invested long enough for the interest they earn to cover their withdrawal cost.) Assuming that a is positive,

$$n = 2 \left(\frac{it}{b} - 1\right) = \frac{iT}{b} - 2, \text{ and } N = \frac{rY}{bf} - 2.$$

In the concrete example of this section $N = \dfrac{4}{5} \dfrac{Y}{f} - 2$; thus if income is received quarterly, $N = \dfrac{1}{5} Y - 2$, if it is received monthly, $N = \dfrac{1}{15} Y - 2$, if weekly, $N = \dfrac{1}{65} Y - 2$.

PART TWO

MONETARY AND FISCAL POLICY
ISSUES IN NORTH AMERICA

CHAPTER VI

ALTERNATIVE GUIDING PRINCIPLES FOR THE USE OF MONETARY POLICY IN CANADA*

I. INTRODUCTION

This paper is directed to the specific question: what should monetary policy seek to do in the Canadian economy?

Monetary policy as traditionally conceived is concerned with short-run economic stabilization, the damping of the business cycle. This function has come to be expressed customarily in terms of the pursuit of the two objectives of price stability and high employment. In so far as prices and general economic activity tend to move upwards or downwards together, these two objectives do not conflict, but are essentially the same: a monetary policy directed at stabilizing either one of the price level or the level of unemployment would tend to stabilize both. The two objectives may, however, conflict if the level of unemployment considered desirable itself implies a rising trend of prices, or if the price level is rising for some reason other than an excessively low level of unemployment.[1] In recent years a third objective has been added to the list, the objective of economic growth; but for reasons that are too complex to be developed here, the objective of growth can in practice also be identified with the general goal of economic stabilization.[2]

* Prepared for the Royal Commission on Banking and Finance; first published as Essays in International Finance no. 44, International Finance Section, Princeton University, Princeton, New Jersey, November 1963.

[1] This statement is phrased to avoid a final judgment on the issue of cost-push versus demand-pull inflation, and also to allow for the influence, important in Canada, of foreign price trends on the trend of domestic prices.

[2] This is not to say that a government pursuing the objective of growth would necessarily conduct monetary policy on traditional lines; rather, the point is

In addition to the general objective of economic stabilization, expressed in the three goals of high employment, price stability and economic growth, monetary policy has in practice another objective, resulting from the role of the central bank as fiscal agent for the government, the objective of assisting the government to borrow in the financial markets on the most advantageous terms obtainable. This objective, which becomes paramount in wartime, may conflict and in the past has in fact seriously conflicted with the use of monetary control for purposes of economic stabilization. The problems raised by the conflict between the objectives of economic stabilization and cheap governmental financing, however, were most acute in the period before that with which the Commission is immediately concerned, and will accordingly be ignored for the most part in this paper.

More generally, this paper will ignore the possibilities of conflict between the objectives of monetary policy, important as they are to both the explanation of past policy and the formulation of future policy, and will instead be concerned with the use of monetary policy for the purpose of economic stabilization, defined in the very broad sense of damping cyclical fluctuations in the economy. The starting point of the argument is the assumption, presumed to be generally accepted, that the performance of monetary policy as an instrument for short-run economic stabilization in Canada in recent years has been definitely unsatisfactory.

It is not the purpose of this paper, however, to attempt to assign responsibility for the unsatisfactory record of Canadian economic policy with respect to economic stabilization in recent years. Instead, its purpose is to examine the merits and drawbacks of the alternative lines of action with respect to the guiding principles of future monetary policy that might be pursued by the Commission, in the light of the unsatisfactoriness of recent experience. For this purpose, it is sufficient to assume that the unsatisfactory record is the outcome of a combination of causal factors, which may include confusion

that the scope for monetary policy alone to stimulate growth seems limited to whatever contribution economic stabilization can make to growth. This point is implicit in the rather unsatisfying discussion of objectives contained in the Report of the Commission on Money and Credit.

in the minds of the government and the public with respect to the priorities of policy, insufficient co-ordination between the government and the Bank of Canada, errors on the part of the management of the Bank, and inadequate knowledge of the powers and limitations of monetary control of the economy on the part of all concerned.

Given the unsatisfactory nature of the record of the past, there are three main alternative positions that can be taken as to the conduct of monetary policy in the future. The first is to accept the record of the past as establishing that in practice monetary policy cannot achieve the degree of economic stabilization that has been expected of it, and to recommend that this fact be recognized by a corresponding writing-down of the standards for monetary performance to make them accord with what is achievable by monetary policy as operated in the past. The second is to take the record of the past as establishing that the performance of monetary policy with respect to economic stabilization could be improved by eliminating sources of error, and to recommend changes in the philosophy, institutional setting, and methods of monetary management that would help to improve performance. The third alternative is to take the record of the past as establishing that monetary policy should not be entrusted with major responsibility for short-run economic stabilization, but should instead be directed to providing a stable long-run monetary environment, the responsibility for short-run stabilization being transferred to other instruments of economic policy. Broadly speaking, the second alternative corresponds to the approach of the American Commission on Money and Credit, and the third to the approach of the British Radcliffe Committee.

The main part of this paper is devoted to discussion of the arguments for and against these three approaches, and exploration of their implications for the reform of the Canadian monetary system. As a prerequisite to examination of these approaches, however, it is necessary to make explicit certain assumptions about the nature of central banking, the way in which monetary policy operates, and the philosophy of economic policy, since these assumptions are important to the argument. In addition, it is relevant to point out that the arguments concerning the various alternatives depend crucially

on whether it is assumed that the country is on a fixed exchange
rate or a floating rate, since the choice of a fixed-rate system
imposes definite limitations on the freedom to use monetary
policy for economic stabilization. Finally, whatever the approach adopted, it is necessary to consider the merits of various
suggestions that have been made to give the monetary authority
special powers of selective control over certain types of credit
or certain kinds of credit institutions that are considered to play
an especially destabilizing role in economic fluctuations. Accordingly, the paper begins with a statement of fundamental assumptions, goes on to comment on the relevance of the choice between
fixed and floating exchange rates, discusses the three alternative
approaches to future monetary policy, considers the case for
and against various types of selective controls, and concludes
with a summary section containing the author's personal
judgments on some of the major issues.

II.　FUNDAMENTAL ASSUMPTIONS

In order to discuss alternative approaches to the future
conduct of monetary policy in a practically relevant way,
it is necessary to take a position on three fundamental matters,
all of which can be considered 'practical' questions, though
in different ways. These matters are the nature of a central
bank as an institution, the way in which monetary policy
affects the economy, and the philosophy of economic policy.

The importance of the institutional nature of a central bank
derives from the fact that monetary policy is entrusted to its
day-to-day management and influenced by its advice, rather
than being managed directly by the government as an integral
part of its general economic policy. The central bank is an
independent corporation, not a government department; its
personnel is selected by a different procedure than the Civil
Service; and its routine activities bring it into intimate contact
with one special sector of the economy, the financial system.
It is only to be expected, therefore, that it will develop its own
views on monetary policy, views that will be influenced in
general by the habits of thinking about economic affairs preva-
lent in the financial community, especially by that community's
concepts of 'soundness' and of 'financial morality', and in

particular by the financial community's assessments of the nature of contemporary national economic problems and the policies appropriate to deal with them, whether these assessments are grounded in thorough economic analysis or not. Further, since the central bank is a national institution part of whose work brings it into contact with its opposite numbers in other countries, the central bank's thinking on domestic policy problems will be influenced by the thinking of other central banks about their own and its policy problems. Finally, since the central bank in its day-to-day operations must establish and maintain working relationships with the financial system of the country, and since its effectiveness depends on its ability to manipulate that system, it will naturally seek to conduct its operations so as to avoid disrupting the functioning of the financial system.

In these respects, the central bank is not of course uniquely differentiated from government departments; departments of labour and agriculture, in particular, typically share the attitudes of their clients and in part serve to represent the interests of those clients to the government. The difference, however, lies in the fact that the central bank is at least partially independent, and is entrusted to formulate and carry out national policies that may be in direct conflict with the interests of the financial institutions with which it is normally in close contact.

The institutional nature of the central bank imposes two important limitations on the possibilities for improvement of the conduct of monetary policy, so long as monetary policy is entrusted to the management of a quasi-independent central bank. In the first place, there are narrow limits on the extent to which a central bank can be converted into an institution that controls the monetary system according to principles and methods of analysis that are radically different from those understood and accepted by the financial community. Secondly, the central bank itself will inevitably generate strong resistances to the pursuit of a monetary policy that threatens to disrupt established financial relationships or expectations.[1] In short,

---

[1] Cf. Bank of Canada Submission I, §E, 'Some Practical Considerations in Monetary Policy'. This section amounts to the assertion that it is better to endure economic fluctuations than to counter them by a monetary policy that disturbs the financial system.

if monetary policy continues to be entrusted to the management of a central bank—an assumption that is axiomatic—this itself imposes limits both on how far and in what ways the management of monetary policy can be improved, and on how vigorous monetary policy can be made to be. Recognition of these limits, however, may lead to any one of the three alternatives previously mentioned: it may be argued that, given the institutional character of a central bank, one should not expect monetary policy to achieve a very high standard of economic stabilization; or that there is still a wide gap between the attainable and the attained, that could be significantly narrowed by feasible changes in central-bank management and operating procedures; or that the central bank could contribute more efficiently to the prosperity and growth of the economy if it were relieved of the responsibility for short-run economic stabilization.

To discuss alternative approaches to the conduct of monetary policy fruitfully, it is necessary to take a position not only on what can reasonably be expected of a central bank, but also on what monetary control can be expected to achieve. This necessitates a general view of how monetary policy affects the economy. The view that seems to emerge from the research and thinking underlying the Reports of the Radcliffe Committee and the Commission on Money and Credit can be summarized very broadly as follows. Monetary policy has a direct and observable influence on interest rates and credit conditions, and through changes in these variables has an observable effect on the flows of credit through certain markets, and notably on the volume of bank loans and on the demand for mortgage financing of new residential construction. But what matters for short-run economic stabilization is not control over interest rates and credit conditions, or even over the volume of particular types of lending, but control over the volume of expenditures. And except in the case of housing, where the situation is complicated by the large-scale intervention of the government as a guarantor of mortgages the terms of which make their attractiveness to institutional lenders vary countercyclically, it is virtually impossible to establish that monetary policy has a reliable, speedy, and quantitatively significant influence on final expenditure.

This difficulty has led some experts to conclude that monetary policy has no influence on the economy. On the other hand, the weight of economic theorizing suggests that monetary policy ought to have some influence on economic activity; fragmentary evidence of such influence exists; and various well-known dramatic historical episodes testify that the influence of monetary factors can be significant, at least over the long run. Caution would therefore suggest the view that monetary policy does have an influence on economic activity, but that this influence varies with circumstances, with respect to both its magnitude and the time required for it to take effect. This view in turn suggests that the use of monetary policy for short-run stabilization is a difficult and hazardous enterprise.

This position, again, does not prejudge the issue between the three alternative approaches to the future conduct of policy. It can be argued with equal freedom that the central bank has done as well as could be expected, given the inherent difficulties of the task, and that there is no obvious way of improving its performance; or that the difficulties are a challenge to be overcome by more determined effort, requiring reform of the central bank to equip it better for an assault on the problems; or that the difficulties and risks of error are so great that the central bank would be better occupied with more modest responsibilities.

Finally, discussion of the alternatives requires a position to be taken on the general philosophy of control in a predominantly free-enterprise economy. Much of the discussion of monetary policy in the postwar period, and especially of 'selective' techniques of control extending beyond the traditional 'general' instruments of bank rate and open-market operations, has been concerned with questions of equity and consistency with the basic principles of a free-enterprise economy.[1] The position taken in this paper is the pragmatic one that the use of monetary policy, or for that matter any other 'general' policy instrument, for the purpose of economic stabilization necessarily involves frustrating the plans of some sectors or individuals in

---

[1] These questions have even been raised with regard to the traditional instruments; in the United States it has been argued that control of the rediscounting privilege gives the central bank an undesirable degree of arbitrary authority; and both there and elsewhere the advocacy of 'bills only' in open-market operations has been fundamentally a demand for fair competitive conditions for government-bond dealers.

the economy for the general good, and that in the economic world as it is this necessarily involves some inequity. Accordingly, the decision as to whether to supplement or substitute for traditional monetary policy by more selective methods of credit control should be taken on a balance of considerations of equity and effectiveness, rather than by reference to the pure principles of a competitive economy.

The Relevance of the Exchange-Rate System

As previously mentioned, it makes a considerable difference to the argument concerning the three alternative approaches to the future conduct of monetary policy whether the country is assumed to be on a fixed or a floating exchange rate. A discussion of the issues involved in the choice between the two alternative exchange-rate systems is beyond the scope of this paper: this section is confined to the implications of that choice for what it is possible for monetary policy to attempt or attain. These implications are, however, relevant to the discussion of which exchange-rate system is preferable.

The point of most importance is the familiar one that a country on a fixed exchange rate is obliged to conduct its economic policy so as to keep its balance of payments balanced. More precisely, a fixed exchange rate obliges a country to keep fluctuations in its balance of payments within the limits set by its available international reserves, supplemented by its international borrowing power. Given the importance of short-term capital movements in the contemporary world, and their volatility in responding to interest-rate differentials or speculative sentiments, a country on a fixed exchange rate is likely to be obliged to conduct its monetary policy primarily by reference to the effects of domestic interest rates on international capital movements, and this may well necessitate the pursuit of a monetary policy contrary to that indicated by the objective of domestic economic stabilization.[1] In addition, the need to

---

[1] In principle, the effect of international capital movements on the country's international reserve position could be overcome by operations in the forward-exchange market aimed at eliminating the covered interest differential between domestic and foreign capital markets. This technique was recommended to the Radcliffe Committee but rejected for what seem to be largely institutional reasons. The workability of the technique has been the subject of a continuing controversy among the experts; the United States monetary authorities claim

command international confidence, imposed by the presence of a large volume of internationally mobile short-term capital, may restrict the freedom of the monetary authority to use all the elbow-room potentially available to it, since confidence is inspired and maintained by conformity to what is regarded as orthodox financial behaviour by other central banks and the owners of internationally mobile capital. Finally, the adoption of a fixed exchange rate may aggravate the task of economic stabilization because it provides maximum scope for the transmission of expansionary and contractionary developments in foreign economies to the domestic economy.

A fixed exchange rate, in short, introduces the likelihood that a country will have to endure internal instability, either as an automatic result of the link with conditions in the rest of the world forged by the fixing of the exchange rate or as a consequence of pursuing the monetary policy required to balance the balance of payments by inducing appropriate movements of international short-term capital. A floating exchange rate, by contrast, provides more scope for the pursuit of an independent monetary policy. It does not of course insulate the economy from the influence of favourable or unfavourable developments in foreign markets, or from the impact of short- or long-term capital movements; but it does permit the economic authorities to attempt to prevent such developments from giving rise to fluctuations in the level of economic activity.[1]

The implications of the difference between the two exchange-rate systems for the choice between the three alternatives would seem to be as follows. First, since a fixed-rate system obliges monetary policy to be conducted primarily by reference to the state of the balance of payments, it necessarily lowers the standard of stabilization that can reasonably be expected

some success in using it in the past two years. Whether it could be an adequately effective insulator for Canadian monetary policy is a question beyond the scope of this paper; suffice it to remark that exploitation of the technique in support of a monetary policy aimed at short-run stabilization would involve a higher degree of sophistication in monetary policy than has been customary in the past, and possibly a greater chance of error.

[1] The extent to which a floating exchange rate provides this extra freedom of manœuvre depends on the degree to which wages and prices in the economy are 'sticky' so that relative domestic and foreign costs can be altered more easily by exchange-rate changes than by inflation or deflation of demand.

either from monetary policy as practised in the past or from an improved system of monetary management, by comparison with a floating-exchange-rate system. Second, in so far as adherence to a fixed-rate system obliges a country to practise orthodox central banking, both in order to command foreign confidence and because the fixed-rate system as currently operated involves a considerable amount of co-operation among central bankers, such adherence tilts the balance in favour of accepting the limitations of economic stabilization by traditional methods of central banking, rather than attempting to improve the performance of monetary policy by radical reform of the constitution and operating methods of the central bank, whereas adherence to a floating-rate system would tend to tilt the balance in the opposite direction. In addition, as already mentioned, adherence to a fixed-rate system greatly complicates the question of how, in fact, a better performance with respect to stabilization could be secured in practice. Thirdly, adherence to a fixed-rate system reinforces the argument for relieving monetary policy of the responsibility for economic stabilization, since it automatically imposes on monetary policy the prior responsibility of controlling international capital movements. But this additional responsibility undermines the case for directing monetary policy toward the creation of a stable long-run monetary environment, since if monetary policy is not directed at the control of international capital movements some other means has to be found to control either capital movements or the balance of trade, and the most direct means of doing this—exchange controls and trade controls (which include such devices as temporary tariff surcharges) —may well be either impossible to operate efficiently enough to be worth the effort, or, if efficient, more disruptive than the use of monetary policy for the same purpose. Under a floating-exchange-rate system, on the other hand, the problem of balancing the balance of payments does not exist;[1] the choice between the three alternatives is more definitely arguable in

[1] The balancing of the balance of payments may be secured by an inflow of foreign capital which is regarded as undesirable on some extraneous ground such as the dislike of American ownership of Canadian assets. The solution to this problem, if it is regarded as a problem, is clearly to increase Canadian savings and provide more incentive to Canadians to hold equities; both objectives would be served by a combination of surplus budgeting and easy money.

terms of strictly economic considerations; and the balance is tilted somewhat in favour of the third alternative by the fact that to some extent movements of the exchange rate will serve as an automatic stabilizer insulating the economy from changes in world markets.

III. ALTERNATIVE GUIDING PRINCIPLES FOR FUTURE POLICY

The preceding sections have outlined certain fundamental assumptions concerning the nature of central banking, the influence of monetary policy on the economy, and the philosophy of economic policy, and indicated the relevance of the choice between a fixed and a floating-exchange-rate system to the potentialities of monetary policy. The following sections discuss the three alternative approaches to the future conduct of monetary policy outlined in the introduction. In each case, the relevant section outlines the rationale of the approach under discussion, and describes briefly the kinds of recommendations for change in the conduct of monetary policy that adoption of the approach might suggest.

A. Lowering the Expected Standard of Performance of Monetary Stabilization Policy

There are several grounds for arguing that the unsatisfactory record of monetary stabilization in Canada in recent years represents about as good a performance as can reasonably be expected, and that the inference to be drawn from this experience is that expectations of performance have been set impossibly high and should be revised downward.

In the first place, it can be argued that the openness of the Canadian economy to the world economy, and particularly the dependence of the Canadian economy on the American industrial complex for markets for Canadian resource products and on the American capital market for capital for Canadian economic development, makes the Canadian economy respond sensitively to fluctuations in the rest of the world, and particularly in the United States, and narrowly restricts the possibilities of economic stabilization by domestic economic policy. On this argument, the unsatisfactory record of stabilization in Canada in recent years predominantly reflects the effects on the Canadian economy of the slowing down of American economic growth, and the balance-of-payments difficulties under which the United States has laboured in the same period; there is little that the Canadian policy-makers could do, or can be expected to be able to do in the future, to offset destabilizing influences emanating from the world economy. It can further be argued that over the long run Canadian prosperity and growth is best fostered by active participation in a liberal system of world trade and payments, and that the consequential exposure to economic fluctuations emanating from the world economy is a necessary price of long-run economic gains.

Secondly, it can be argued that the task of economic stabilization is inherently an extremely difficult one, and that there is no obvious way of effecting a significant improvement in its performance. The effects of monetary policy on the economy, in particular, are diffuse and far from predictable, and it is extremely doubtful how far monetary policy can successfully offset the effects of economic disturbances. Nor, it may be added, does the existing state of economic knowledge, whatever it may have to say about the theoretical possibility of efficient economic stabilization, hold out much prospect of significant improvement in the practical achievement of stabilization in the near future. At the present time, economic theory for the most part can contribute only a description of intricate economic relationships that must be better understood before stabilization policy can be made more efficient. That being so, the most that can be expected is a gradual improvement of performance as knowledge and experience accumulate.

Finally, it can be argued that the unsatisfactory performance of monetary policy in the past cannot be reasonably attributed to any easily remediable defects in the institutional arrangements for the conduct of monetary policy. A central bank, it can be argued, has been found by historical experience in the Western world to be the most appropriate institution for the conduct of monetary policy. Its partial independence of the government is essential to the role it has to play in relation to the domestic financial community and the international financial world. As a responsible institution, it can be trusted to seek the knowledge it needs to operate effectively, to exercise the best judgment of which it is capable in formulating monetary policy, and to learn from experience. Like any institution or individual entrusted with the exercise of judgment, it may make mistakes, either because the situations in which it must act are complicated, or because it is influenced by a transient climate of public opinion, or because the exercise of its powers and responsibilities affects its judgment. But the probability of mistakes is inherent in the process of entrusting decisions to the judgment of responsible institutions or individuals, and the risk of mistakes is the price that must be paid by a nation for attempting to improve its economic management by centralizing the control of economic decisions in the hands of responsible public servants. If on the average the record of economic management is not very satisfactory, the correct inference is that the possibilities of achieving economic improvement by entrusting important decisions to the judgment of responsible institutions are more limited than had been thought.

If these arguments are accepted, and the position is taken that the the unsatisfactory record of the past implies a need to write down expectations concerning the degree of economic stabilization attainable in the future, the main positive recommendation that emerges is that the public, the government, and the central bank should neither expect very much from monetary policy nor attach too much causal importance to it. This recommendation could be implemented in part by explicit incorporation in the Bank of Canada Act of the principle that the Minister of Finance, or the Government, is ultimately responsible for monetary policy, together with revisions of the wording of the Preamble to the Act designed to convey the sense that the objectives of policy listed are objectives of the Government's economic policy, and that the responsibility of the Bank is to conduct the day-to-day management of monetary policy so as to implement these objectives so far as is possible by monetary means. The purpose of both amendments would be to make the language of the Act reflect the view of the potentialities of monetary stabilization to which the arguments outlined above lead, while at the same time giving legal expression to the instrumental conception of the central bank on which the analysis of this paper is based.

The position that the degree of stabilization attainable by monetary policy is lower than has generally been regarded as satisfactory carries some other implications. If the standard of performance that can be expected of monetary policy is revised downward, there is still a choice open between accepting a lower standard for stabilization policy, and attempting to achieve some of the ultimate objectives of stabilization policy by other means. Three alternative forms of action along the latter line are conceivable and could be recommended. The first is to develop instruments of stabilization alternative to monetary policy of the traditional kind; such instruments could be either fiscal devices, or selective instruments of credit control— the latter are discussed in a subsequent section. The second is to develop or improve the means of compensating or offsetting the social consequences of instability, particularly of unemployment on the one hand and inflation on the other, and to recognize that if a socially undesirable degree of instability is regarded as economically unavoidable its effects could be mitigated by greater generosity toward the victims. The third alternative is to attempt to improve the capacity of the economy to absorb and adjust to instability with less damage; this would require more determined efforts to make management and labour more flexible and mobile than they are now.

B. *Improving the Performance of Monetary Stabilization Policy*

In order to argue that the performance of monetary stabilization policy could be substantially improved, it is not sufficient to point to the unsatisfactory record of the past and claim in the light of hindsight that the monetary authority should have been able to do better. Nor is it enough, to ensure improvement, to recommend that the Bank should become generally more alert, intelligent, and flexible. A serious argument must rest on a demonstration that monetary policy in the past has made errors that would, at least on a balance of probabilities, have been avoided had the system of monetary management been different, and different in certain definable ways.

Such a demonstration is extremely difficult; not only does it require a detailed examination of the past, and specifically of the state of opinion and the economic knowledge available at the time when various key decisions were taken, but it also requires a hazardous exercise in analysis of the might-have-been. What follows is not intended as an expression of the author's own views on these questions, but simply as an outline of a position to which an assessment of the evidence might lead and an exploration of its implications.

It can be argued that the performance of monetary stabilization in Canada in the recent past has fallen seriously short of an attainable standard for one or both of two major reasons, both of which reflect defects in the Canadian system of monetary control that could be remedied by changing the present arrangements for monetary management.

The first argument is that, either because the democratic governmental process failed to reflect accurately the preferences of the public, or because the ambiguity of the Bank of Canada Act with respect to the ultimate responsibility for monetary policy allowed the Governor of the Bank to impose his own preferences, the priorities according to which monetary policy was conducted were at variance with the priorities that public opinion would have approved, Specifically, monetary policy attached unduly heavy weight to the objective of preventing or restraining inflation, and unduly little weight to the objective of maintaining high employment.[1] Accordingly, it can be argued, the performance of monetary policy would have been better had the objectives of policy conformed to the preferences of the public; and performance in future could be substantially improved by ensuring that the objectives of policy pursued by the Bank do conform to the preferences of the public.

The specific recommendations to which a position based on this argument would lead depend crucially on whether it is maintained that failure in the past was the result of the Bank taking a different view on objectives than the Government, or of the democratic system failing to generate an accurate indication of the public's preferences.

---

[1] This argument is admittedly a difficult one to substantiate, since it depends on positing the existence of an ascertainable public opinion on the priorities of policy, and runs the danger of arguing from hindsight or of confusing personal preference with public opinion. Its plausibility must rest heavily on the facts that a large proportion of the country's academic economists disapproved of the Governor's monetary policy and expressed that disapproval publicly, and that the Government found it necessary eventually to remove the Governor of the Bank from his office.

If it is maintained that the failures of the past were due to the excessive exercise of independence by the Bank, the logical recommendation would be for reforms of the Bank's constitution designed to give the Government control over its actions. A minimal step in this direction would be to revise the Bank Act to assert explicitly that the Government is ultimately responsible for monetary policy, and that the Bank functions as the Government's monetary agent. This step, however, might accomplish little by itself. It would oblige the Bank to exert itself to discover the Government's policy intentions and priorities, at least in general terms, and to ensure that the Government regarded the monetary policy being pursued as consistent with its general economic objectives; but it would not oblige the Government to assume an active responsibility for the conduct of monetary policy, in the sense of laying down the lines to be pursued by monetary policy. To ensure that the Bank's conduct of monetary management did in practice conform to the Government's policies closely enough for the Government to be actively responsible for monetary policy, it would probably be necessary to oblige the Bank to look to the Government, not merely for general directions concerning the objectives to be pursued and the relative priorities attached to them, but for specific directions concerning the concrete monetary operations that the Government considered to be required by its general economic policy. A formal method of doing this would be to oblige the Government, acting through the Minister of Finance, regularly to communicate to the Governor of the Bank its views on what monetary policy should be. An alternative would be to strengthen the influence of the regular government departments primarily concerned with economic policy on the formulation of monetary policy, perhaps by setting up an interdepartmental committee to advise the Governor of the Bank.

If past policy failure is attributed to failure of the democratic governmental system to reflect public preferences with adequate accuracy, the problem of securing a substantially improved performance is much more difficult. There are two not necessarily mutually exclusive lines on which improvement could be sought. The first would aim at improving the expression of public opinion through Parliament. On this line of approach, the basic problem is the general one of securing effective democratic government by improving the quality of public understanding and discussion of issues so that public opinion is brought to bear on governmental decisions while they are being formulated, rather than left to be expressed in electoral approval or disapproval of the results of these decisions. This is a problem in public education—in the present context, of education of the public in the economics of policy choices—and it is doubtful how far such education can be promoted by changes in the institutional arrangements for the conduct of monetary policy. It is, however, arguable that the quality of public discussion and understanding of the issues involved in the use of monetary policy would be substantially improved if the Bank were obliged to publish regularly its own account of the actions it had taken, the purpose of these actions, and the results expected to follow from them, all in terms sufficiently concrete to permit informed discussion and appraisal.

The line of action just described assumes that Parliament is the proper body for the expression of public opinion and its translation into policy, and that it is the responsibility of the Bank to be guided by public opinion as represented by the Government in office. The alternative line of action rests on the different assumption—one that is more in keeping with the tradition of central banking—that elected governments are fallible and not entirely to be trusted, especially in matters of monetary management, and that it is the responsibility of central banks to formulate their own view of the public interest and pursue it, as the phrase goes, to the point of 'nagging' the Government. On this assumption, the failure of the past is attributable to inadequate or biased representation of public opinion in the management of the Bank, and the indicated line of reform would be to strengthen the representation of public opinion on the Bank's Board of Directors. Specifically, it can be argued that by the very nature of central banking financial opinion is likely to have an excessive influence on the Bank's thinking, and that this influence should be counterbalanced by functional representation of other sectors of the economy on the Board. In addition, it could be argued that since monetary policy affects the whole economy in a variety of complex ways, special representation should be given to professional economists, whose business it is to understand and study how the economy works.

The foregoing discussion is concerned with the contention that the past failures of monetary policy are in large part attributable to a failure of monetary policy to reflect the public's preferences with respect to the priorities of economic policy, a failure that could be remedied by improving the arrangements for monetary management. The second argument attributes past failure, not to the pursuit of objectives different from those preferred by public opinion, but to failure of the Bank to understand the economic relationships on which monetary policy was seeking to operate, or to make use of the available economic knowledge concerning those relationships, let alone attempt to improve on that knowledge. This attribution is much easier to support than the other, inasmuch as the economic analysis and assumptions employed in formulating the Bank's policy are on public record in the Annual Reports of the Bank and the speeches delivered by the Governor, and can be shown—in fact, have frequently been shown—to be illogical, inconsistent, inadequate, or factually wrong in a variety of respects crucial to efficient policy formation.

Given that the Bank in the past has displayed an alarming ignorance of elementary economic principles, not to speak of the results of scientific economic research, it can be argued that the performance of the Bank would have been much better had it possessed and applied an up-to-date knowledge of economics, and that its future performance could be substantially improved if it were made to realize the importance of economic science and research to its work, and obliged to base its policy actions on a thorough economic analysis of policy alternatives and consequences, and to improve its economic knowledge by a continuing large-scale research effort.

This prescription could be implemented by a variety of changes. The relevant recommendations could include the appointment of senior economists to the Board of Directors; a programme of exchanges between the Bank's staff of economists and economists in the universities; regular informal conferences of Bank officials and academic economists to discuss technical problems of monetary management or the bearing of general economic problems on monetary policy; regular publication of the results of the Bank's own research in a journal open to contributions from outside economists.

Many such changes could easily be effected by the Bank itself; that the Bank has not chosen to introduce them points to the main source of doubt concerning the probable effectiveness of this prescription, since it indicates that the Bank itself does not consider that more extensive and intensive use of economics and economists would help it to perform its duties. For the prescription to work, it would not necessarily suffice for the Bank to have to employ and argue with economists; the language of economics, like the language of the law, can be used to conceal the truth as well as to discover it, and the employment of an economist, like the employment of a lawyer, is not necessarily a guarantee of honest intentions. What the prescription aims at is to convert the Bank, as an institution, from the banker's habits of thought to those of the economist. Whether this could be done, and whether if it could be done the Bank could still function effectively in its relations with the financial system, are difficult questions whose answers depend on the institutional character of central banking. So far as the first question is concerned, it seems clear that the Bank's personnel would have to be persuaded of the value of the scientific approach to its problems. This would have to be achieved by experience; probably the most effective ways of making the bank undergo the experience would be to appoint senior professional economists to the Board of Directors, and to oblige the Bank to publish detailed economic analyses of its policy choices and their results, preferably with a commentary by independent economists. So far as the second question is concerned, avoidance of possibly serious disturbance of the traditional understanding between the Bank and the domestic and international financial communities might require an improvement in these groups' understanding of the economics of policy, highly desirable in itself but unattainable in practice. Nevertheless, the effort and risks involved in converting the Bank to a more economically oriented institution might well be considered worth undertaking, if the result promised to be a substantial improvement in the performance of monetary stabilization policy.

C. *Abandoning Short-Run Stabilization in Favour of a Stable Monetary Environment*

The preceding two subsections have been concerned with the alternative positions that past experience indicates that a lower standard of achievement should be expected of monetary stabilization policy, and that an appreciably better performance could be ensured in future by revising present arrangements for monetary management either to make the central bank's actions conform more closely to public preferences, or to make its operations more scientific, or both. This subsection is concerned with the third alternative, that the attempt to achieve short-run economic stabilization by monetary policy should be abandoned, and that instead monetary policy should be directed to creating a stable monetary environment in the economy.

There are three main arguments for the abandonment of short-run stabilization as a primary objective of monetary policy. The first starts from the observation that while in principle it should be possible to operate monetary stabilization policy efficiently, because monetary action can be taken swiftly and can be finely adjusted, in practice the use of monetary policy for stabilization purposes has been laggard and clumsy in its recognition of and reaction to both short-run changes in the contemporary economic situation and long-run changes in the economic environment. More specifically, monetary-policy changes have consistently lagged significantly behind changes in phase of the business cycle. What is more important, changes in the priorities among objectives expressed in monetary policy have lagged long behind changes in the economic environment or conjuncture: monetary policy in the period from the end of the war to the early '50's—a period of economic euphoria— was preoccupied with the danger of a deep recession, with the result that it contributed to inflation; it then became pre-occupied with the dangers of inflation, about the same time as the economic climate changed toward one of chronic depression, with the result that it contributed to unemployment and slow growth. Delay in the recognition of economic changes and adjustment to them, it can be argued, is inherent in the nature of policy-making institutions in a democratic society; but it is especially ingrained in the nature of the central bank, which lacks the mandate of an elected government to act speedily in emergencies. That being so, the central bank should not be entrusted with the responsibility for stabilization policy, since effective performance of that responsibility would require it to act with a speed and foresight, and a willingness to court unpopularity, that is contrary to its institutional nature and the political framework within which it must operate.

The foregoing argument derives from consideration of the position of the central bank in the system of government. The second argument derives from consideration of the institutional nature of the central bank and its position in the economy. The central bank, it can be argued, is primarily a banking institution, and its main business is with commercial banks and other financial institutions. Its organization and traditions are adapted to that role; they are not designed specifically for the purpose of control of the economy by manipulation of the money supply, and the degree to which they can be adapted to that purpose is severely limited. On the one hand, the position of the central bank in relation to the economy is not such as to encourage or force it to think continually of the requirements of the economy as a whole, but rather such as to concentrate its thinking on the requirements and interests of the financial sector. On the other hand, pursuit of a vigorous monetary policy directed at economic stabilization necessarily brings it into conflict with the interests of the financial institutions with which it normally works, a conflict it will naturally wish to evade or avoid. In short, reliance on monetary policy for short-run stabilization involves entrusting the job to an institution that is neither well equipped for nor single-mindedly enthusiastic about the responsibility. It can be argued that the prospective degree of stabilization attainable is not worth the difficulty of attaining it, and that it would be better to try to achieve economic stabilization by some other means.

The third argument is concerned with the economic possibility of stabilization by monetary means. As has been mentioned in an earlier section, economists have had little difficulty in verifying that monetary policy can influence interest rates and credit conditions, and great difficulty in detecting the influence of the latter, or of the quantity of money itself, on economic activity. Nevertheless, very few economists would be prepared to assert, and certainly none has ever attempted to prove, that monetary policy has no influence whatever on the economy. The most plausible view, on the basis of research to date, is that monetary policy has an influence on the economy that varies in magnitude and in timing and is by no means easily predictable. This in itself would suggest that the use of monetary policy for short-run stabilization might do more harm than good, the disturbance resulting from unintended or unanticipated effects of monetary-policy actions outweighing the intended beneficial effects. Further, recent theorizing on these matters suggests that one reason why the influence of monetary policy is difficult to detect is that enterprises and individuals make their plans on the basis of expectations about the normal state of the economy, including the normal state of credit conditions, and that these expectations adjust only slowly to changes in the way monetary policy is conducted. This line of thought readily leads to the conclusion that the vigorous pursuit of monetary stabilization policy may be not only not very effective in the short run but of decreasing effectiveness over time, since the economic decision-units at which monetary policy is directed will learn to manage their affairs so as to avoid being disturbed by changes in monetary policy; and to the further conclusion that vigorous use of monetary policy may impede the long-run growth of the economy, by adding to the uncertainties of economic decision-making and reinforcing speculative pressures that tend to keep long-term interest rates high.

All three of these arguments lead to the conclusion that the attempt to achieve economic stabilization by traditional monetary means should be abandoned, and that the objective of stabilization should be approached in some other way; none of them, however, excludes the possibility, explored in the next section, that a useful improvement in stabilization might be attainable by the use of selective credit controls. All three also imply, though with varying emphasis, that monetary policy ought to be directed toward the creation and maintenance of a stable long-run monetary environment for the economy. The first argument would suggest that since the monetary authority is likely to be a bad judge of what the current state of the economy requires in the way of monetary policy, it should be given the simpler task of concentrating on the long-run monetary requirements of a growing economy. The second argument would suggest that the central bank is especially equipped by tradition, experience, and institutional role to promote and police the development of the country's financial institutions and to maintain orderly conditions in its security markets— particularly to cushion the disturbing effects of governmental fiscal and debt operations. The third argument would suggest that the central bank can contribute most effectively to both short-run stabilization and long-run growth by following a definite, well-understood and publicized, consistent policy in its monetary operations, one to which it is committed sufficiently long ahead for borrowers and investors to be able to plan with confidence.

The difficulty with recommending that monetary policy be directed to creating and maintaining a stable long-run monetary environment is to give this recommendation a concrete content. Two concrete proposals have been advanced and canvassed in recent years. One is the Radcliffe Committee's proposal that monetary policy should seek to stabilize long-term interest rates at a level appropriate to the long-run balancing of savings and investment at a high employment level. The other is the proposal advanced by various American economists, that the money supply should be expanded at a constant rate based on the long-run growth rate of demand for money. The difference between the two proposals reflects partly a difference between the British and American institutional systems of monetary control—the British system concentrating on changing interest rates and the American on changing bank reserves and the quantity of money—and partly a difference in basic monetary theory, which resolves essentially into a difference over empirical facts. The Radcliffe proposal assumes either that fluctuations in the economy originate predominantly in changes in the demand for money that could be counteracted by changes in the amount of it supplied, or that the demand for output is insensitive in the short run to changes in interest rates; the alternative proposal assumes that fluctuations in the economy originate predominantly in changes in the demand for output that do not alter the demand for money, and that interest rates have a negligible influence on the quantity of money demanded. Since fluctuations may originate in both monetary and real disturbances, and both the demand for output and the demand for money are likely to be responsive to changes in interest rates to some extent, adoption of either proposal would entail some possibility of destabilization by comparison with an ideal stabilization policy. In the case of real disturbances, the Radcliffe proposal would eliminate both the stabilizing effects on expenditure of automatic increases in interest rates in booms and decreases in interest rates in depressions and the further stabilization that could be effected by countercyclical monetary contraction and expansion. The alternative proposal would eliminate the possibility of counteracting disturbances, and in the case of real disturbances would allow fluctuations in interest rates to induce increases in velocity in booms and decreases in velocity in depressions, these changes in velocity serving to accommodate a fixed stock of money to a varying level of output and activity. The destabilizing effects of either alternative, it can be argued, would be small by comparison with the destabilizing effects of active monetary stabilization policy as conducted in the past, and by comparison with the gains from a more stable monetary environment.[1]

The Radcliffe proposal was a recommendation to the central bank and the economic policy authorities; the American proposal is sometimes intended to be translated into legislation binding the central bank to expand the money supply at a specified rate. Such a statutory restriction on the central bank's freedom of action is alien to the tradition of British central banking, and presumably could not be contemplated; nor is the state of knowledge concerning monetary behaviour sufficiently advanced to permit the devising of a rule that would not run the risk of becoming inappropriate. The spirit of the two proposals could, however, be expressed in a recommendation to revise the Bank Act to make the Bank's primary responsibilities those of fostering the growth of the country's monetary and financial system, and maintaining a stable monetary environment in Canada, and to impose on the Bank the obligation not only to devise its policy with reference to those objectives, but to announce and explain publicly what its monetary policy is and will be for some reasonable time into

[1] The last half of this paragraph has been revised as a result of discussion with Alvin Marty.

the future. Whether the policy was to be expressed in terms of interest rates on certain government securities, or in terms of the rate of expansion of the money supply, could either be specified statutorily, or left to the Bank's discretion.[1]

IV. NEW CONTROLS OVER CREDIT

The preceding section dealt with three alternative approaches to the future use of monetary policy—acceptance of a lower expected standard of performance with respect to economic stabilization, determination to improve that performance in the future by reform of the system of monetary management, and alteration of the objective from economic stabilization to the creation of a stable monetary environment. Each of these approaches is consistent with the recommendation that the traditional techniques of monetary management be reinforced by the introduction of various kinds of selective controls over the granting and use of credit. It can be argued that even though the degree of stability achievable by monetary policy is not high, it would be higher if the monetary authority had the power to strike more directly at sources of instability, or that a more determinedly scientific approach to stabilization should be empowered to use techniques that analysis of the sources of instability suggests might be more effective than orthodox techniques; or that the use of selective credit controls could contribute significantly to stabilization without disturbing expectations and increasing uncertainty as much as would the use of orthodox monetary policy.[2]

The purpose of this section is to explore the merits and drawbacks of various types of selective control over credit. Such

[1] The recently revived technique of a fixed Bank rate is a device for committing the Bank to pursuing a stable policy in the very short run, and changing it only at intervals and by degrees to which the money market is accustomed. The position discussed in this subsection is essentially that a technique of this kind should be developed on a time-scale appropriate to the financial planning of the productive sector of the economy.

[2] The argument here would be that the use of selective methods explicitly recognizes that the circumstances are abnormal, and therefore minimizes the disturbance to long-run expectations. The validity of this argument clearly depends on selective controls being used infrequently and for short periods; if they become a permanent feature of the economic environment, their use for economic stabilization could raise the same problems as the use of monetary policy.

selective controls can be divided for discussion into four types—
'moral suasion', controls over bank behaviour, controls over
other credit institutions, and controls over particular types of
borrower. Since the use of selective controls in any form raises
some issues of a general nature, and since this paper cannot
embrace a discussion of all the specific kinds of selective control
that might possibly be considered, discussion of the four types
of selective control just mentioned is preceded by a brief statement of some of the general issues.

A. *Some General Issues*

Any attempt to use control of the money supply and credit
conditions to stabilize the economy, whether the method
employed is 'general' or 'selective', must necessarily operate
indirectly. What matters for economic activity is the level of
spending, not of borrowing in general or in certain specific
forms, and monetary or credit control must operate through
whatever influence the quantity of money, interest rates, or the
availability of credit in general or in certain selected forms has
on the level of spending. This means that selective credit
control can only be effective to the extent that would-be
spenders cannot resort to alternative financial institutions or
alternative sources of finance than those over which control
is exercised; and a primary question about any proposed
device of selective credit control is the extent to which it can
control actual spending, as distinct from merely altering the
form in which spending is financed. The answer to this question
obviously depends not only on the particular device under
consideration, but also on the length of time over which the
device is intended or required to be effective. Over the course
of time, would-be borrowers deprived of access to their customary sources of finance will learn to resort to alternative
sources, or to manage their affairs so as not to be dependent
on their previous sources; similarly, competition among lenders
will in the course of time develop substitutes for institutions
and types of lending resort to which is restricted by selective
control.[1] Thus heavy and sustained reliance on selective controls

[1] For example, the pressure of rising interest rates against legal limits on the
interest rates payable on deposits and chargeable on loans has led the chartered
banks to develop new deposit instruments and loan forms that enable them in
fact to exceed these limits. At the same time, these and other restrictions on the

may be self-defeating, and may have the long-run consequence of reducing the efficiency of the financial system and the economy by fostering the substitution of inherently less efficient for inherently more efficient financial institutions and practices.

Because the efficiency of selective controls depends on their frustrating the plans of would-be spenders who are dependent for finance on the specific credit institutions or forms of credit subjected to control, selective controls are inherently discriminatory between spending units. Should this consideration be a matter for serious concern? It can be argued—the contention that 'general' monetary control is non-discriminatory to the contrary—that 'general' monetary policy is equally discriminatory, since it in fact operates in part through the rationing of credit among borrowers by banks and other lenders. It can also be argued that any policy of economic stabilization is inherently discriminatory in the sense that it will entail frustrating the plans of some economic units (consumers or firms), and that the distribution of frustration among the units will necessarily be to some extent fortuitous. The practical question therefore is whether the inequity involved in any particular device of selective control is tolerable, in conjunction with the contribution to stabilization it makes.

To put the argument of the two preceding paragraphs a rather different way, the important economic fact is not so much that selective controls discriminate against some types of economic units, as that they discriminate against established efficient methods of financing. And the important economic question is not so much whether they are effective enough to justify their inequity, as whether the leverage gained by discriminating occasionally against efficient financing methods is worth the possible long-run loss of economic efficiency that this discrimination may produce.[1]

The possible long-run distorting effects of the discrimination

banks' freedom to compete in the deposit and loan market have fostered the growth of other deposit-taking and loan-making institutions, such as the trust companies and the finance companies.

[1] There is a close analogy between the use of selective controls on credit and the intermittent use of specific taxes such as capital levies or tariff surcharges. Both raise questions of equity, which have to be resolved by reference to established standards of equity, and both, if frequently resorted to or prolonged, may distort the economy into an inefficient structure.

implied by selective controls are particularly important in the case of selective methods of control applied to the operations of the chartered banks. In effect, the obligation imposed on chartered banks to maintain a minimum non-interest-yielding cash reserve in the form of Bank of Canada notes and deposits constitutes a tax on the chartered banks, levied in return for the privilege of conducting a banking business. Other restrictions on the chartered banks' freedom to determine the composition of their assets, such as the minimum liquidity ratio and other proposed devices to force chartered banks to hold government debt, constitute additional taxes—as do legal restrictions on the rates banks may charge. The use of such restrictions and variations in them to assist stabilization policy may in the long run retard the development of the banking system and foster the development of other less efficient institutional arrangements for conducting business the banks are best equipped to handle. In a concentrated banking system like the Canadian one, the use of selective controls directed at the banks may also encourage the banks to develop arrangements among themselves similar to those of cartels and combines, and oblige the central bank to accept such arrangements, as compensation for the loss of profit opportunities resulting from selective controls. Thus the distortions resulting from discriminatory treatment of banks may be aggravated by the distortions resulting from monopolistic practices.

One further comment is in order. Since discrimination is generally regarded as ethically undesirable, there is a natural tendency to condone or recommend it particularly in cases where the activities or economic units against which it is directed can also be considered as ethically or morally undesirable. Specifically, there is a strong tendency in discussions of selective credit controls to favour controls on the finance of speculation in stocks and real estate, on the grounds that speculation is a morally reprehensible activity, and on consumer finance, on the grounds that it is immoral for wage and salary earners to pledge their future earning power. Both types of financing can in fact be defended as rational activities which can contribute to the improvement of economic efficiency and welfare in the same way as any other kind of borrowing— speculation by leading to a more efficient allocation of assets among uses, instalment buying by leading to a more efficient allocation of consumption over time. If nevertheless it is considered that they should be restricted on moral grounds, the presumption should be that they are equally immoral whether the economy is booming or slumping, and should be dealt with by permanent measures.[1] The only possible economic argument for countercyclical selective control of them is that they contribute extraordinarily to economic instability. This cannot be readily demonstrated for speculation in stocks and real estate, which involves trading in existing assets; though it can be argued in the case of consumer credit, which finances the purchase of goods.

B. *Moral Suasion*

For the purposes of this paper moral suasion has been classified as a type of selective credit control. Actually it occupies an awkward middle ground between the unobjectionable straight-forward provision of information by the central bank about its own analysis of the economic situation and the best interests of private enterprises, and the use of explicit selective controls on credit, since it attempts to persuade economic decision-takers by one means or another voluntarily to take actions that the central bank wants them to take but cannot force them to take. Since the actions involved generally amount to some form of rationing of credit, and since the persuasiveness of the central bank ultimately derives from its powers of control over the money supply, moral suasion can however be assimilated more closely to selective credit control than to the proffering of disinterested objective advice.

The use of moral suasion by the central bank inevitably involves some conflict with the immediate economic self-interest of the institutions at which it is directed, which institutions must be persuaded to comply either on the general ground of responsibility to the community at large or on the narrower

[1] One important reason for the condemnation of speculation, in addition to the usual sober citizen's dislike of seeing someone else get something apparently for nothing, may be the realization that present tax laws give the speculator an enormous differential advantage over the citizen who earns his income by regular work. The appropriate remedy is not to try to hamper the speculator, but instead to remove the tax advantage by treating speculative capital gains as income.

ground of good relations with the central bank. The extent to which institutions can be persuaded to act against their immediate self-interest on these grounds obviously depends on a variety of factors, including the extent to which they can afford the loss of profits or of goodwill (in the first case) and the extent to which the central bank has power to discipline them (in the second case). It follows that moral suasion is more likely to be effective when directed at the chartered banks and other heavily concentrated sectors of the financial system and the economy than when it is directed at sectors characterized by keen competition among a large number of small firms. The more monopolized a sector is, the more dependent it is on governmental goodwill, and the more its activities are prominent in or open to public discussion, the more amenable it will be to control by moral suasion.

These considerations suggest the first reservation about the use of moral suasion. Its effectiveness depends on the extent to which economic decisions are concentrated in the hands of a few units, which consequently can afford to allow what are essentially political considerations to override economic calculation. Correspondingly, reliance on it implies at least tacit approval of concentration of economic activity in a few decision-taking units, and assumption of some governmental responsibility for rewarding compliance with moral suasion by favours of some kind. The recognition of responsibility is usually a reciprocal relationship. It may be considered only realistic to recognize that economic control in Canada is concentrated; and it may even be argued that such concentration is desirable on various economic grounds. But it should be recognized that the use of moral suasion does raise the question of whether economic concentration is desirable, and that this question is a controversial one.

A second question relates to the objectives at which moral suasion is likely to be directed. Judging by past experience in Canada and elsewhere, moral suasion is likely to be directed at or canalized into restraining types of lending or spending that according to conventional financial thinking are unsound or morally somewhat shady, such as loans for speculative purposes or for consumer spending. Restraint of this kind may have little effect in controlling the true sources of instability, which often are simply excessive spending on thoroughly respectable projects. More generally, moral suasion raises the question of how far the monetary authority, in collaboration with responsible financial institutions and leading corporations, is competent to judge better than the competitive market process (or possibly an economic planning agency) what types of expenditures are in the national interest and what types are not.

A third question relates to the time lag inevitable in the use of moral suasion. For moral suasion to work, not only must the monetary authority and the government be persuaded that the economy is getting out of hand, but the financial and business community to which moral suasion appeals must also be persuaded. This presupposes that the need for action is apparent to all concerned; and this in turn ensures that action will only be taken with an appreciable lag.

On the other hand, there are two considerations favouring the use of moral suasion. One is based on the assumption that private enterprises, both financial and non-financial, are poor forecasters and poor interpreters of their own economic interests, and moreover react to economic changes with considerable inertia. Consequently, it can be argued, the adoption by the monetary authority of a definite simple line on the nature of the contemporary economic situation and what action it calls for will be welcomed by the financial and business communities, and will speed up the change to policies that private-enterprise institutions would willingly follow if they were better informed and more flexible. This consideration amounts to accepting the proposition that in a complicated world, salesmanship has to substitute for perfect knowledge and wisdom, and assumes that imperfect guidance is better than none. The second consideration is based on the assumption that financial institutions are involved in intricate professional-client relationships with their customers, and that corporation management is built on a delicate balance of power among different departments, so that the application of the correct economic decisions is greatly facilitated if reference can be made to the overriding authority of the central bank's opinion. For example, it is frequently asserted that a directive or policy statement from the central bank makes it easier for commercial

H

banks to refuse their customers loans while retaining their goodwill; and it is conceivable that the financial-planning departments of big corporations may be similarly strengthened in their resistance to over-optimistic expansion plans emanating from the production and sales departments. These considerations, of course, implicitly assume that the judgment of the monetary authority is both reasonably reliable, and expressed in terms that both are plausible and can readily be translated into action by the relevant private-enterprise institutions. Clearly, these assumptions limit the extent to which moral suasion can be relied on to improve the performance of economic-stabilization policy.

C. *Control Over Chartered Banks*

One of the reasons why orthodox monetary policy operates slowly and imperfectly in restraining a boom is that at the start of the upswing the chartered banks are typically holding a relatively high proportion of government debt and a relatively low proportion of loans. As the upswing proceeds, and the demand for loans grows, the banks can satisfy this demand even though monetary policy is restraining the growth of their total assets, by running off their holdings of government debt in order to finance the expansion of loans. In effect, this process transforms idle bank deposits into active deposits, owners of idle balances being persuaded by a rise in interest rates to surrender these balances to the banks in exchange for government securities formerly held by the banks, and the banks relending the balances to borrowers who wish to spend them. In a different terminology, restriction of the money supply by monetary policy is partially offset by an induced increase in the velocity of circulation.

It can be argued that the effectiveness of monetary policy would be significantly increased if the central bank had the power to prevent the banks from running off their holdings of government securities, for example by being empowered to impose a variable minimum ratio of 'more liquid assets' to deposits, or a variable maximum ratio of general loans to deposits. Since the use of such powers would involve obliging the banks to hold more government securities than they would otherwise choose to hold, it could be argued that the granting of them would have the additional advantage of helping to keep down the cost of the public debt by partially insulating the government-securities market from the effects of restrictive monetary policy.

The quantitative magnitude of the influence on both aggregate spending and interest rates achievable by use of such powers depends on the extent to which spenders who normally finance themselves by bank loans have access to other sources of finance, or possess assets that can be sold or pledged to finance spending. The restraining effect on expenditures (and interest rates) would be greatest if everyone refused a bank loan had no alternative but to cancel his spending plans; even in this case some of the effect would be offset by the influence of lower interest rates in inducing larger expenditures by spenders not dependent on bank loans. The restraint on expenditures (and interest rates) would be virtually zero if all potential borrowers from banks had the alternative of financing expenditures by selling off holdings of government bonds. In general, the restraint achievable depends on the deterrent effect on would-be borrowers from banks of the higher cost of alternative means of finance. It is generally agreed that some groups of would-be spenders—notably small businesses and consumers—are sufficiently dependent on bank finance for the denial of bank loans to force them to cancel or curtail their spending plans. Thus, providing the banks do not channel their loans to such groups at the expense of other groups having access to alternative sources of finance, the powers of control under discussion could increase the effectiveness of stabilization policy to some significant extent.

Assuming that this kind of selective control of chartered-bank lending could contribute to stabilization, whether it should be employed depends on three sets of considerations. First, its use is an alternative to more vigorous and alert use of monetary restraint; instead of preventing the banks from lending as large a proportion of their total assets as they wish, the monetary authority could achieve the same effect on loans by restricting total bank assets more severely. Preference for the selective over the general method of control of bank loans must therefore be derived from an empirical judgment that the central bank cannot or will not apply general monetary restraint quickly and subtly enough—that is, it cannot anticipate the banks' switch from government securities to loans—or from the view that a more active monetary policy would have undesirable destabilizing effects on the economy, or from the judgment that the government-debt market should be protected so far as possible from the impact of monetary restraint. In the second place, the concentration of the restrictive effect on spenders who are dependent on bank finance may be regarded as both unfair and economically undesirable. In particular, it is frequently argued that restriction of bank loans bears unduly heavily on small businesses, with effects deleterious to economic growth and favourable to economic concentration and monopoly and the control of Canadian enterprise by American capital. These effects, so far as they can be demonstrated to exist and to be avoidable by other methods of stabilization, have to be weighed against the improvement in stabilization achieved by selective control of bank lending. Finally, forcing the banks to hold more government securities and less loans than they would like amounts to imposing a special kind of tax on bank earnings; whether this tax amounts to a net burden or not depends on whether it is assumed that total bank assets would be the same with or without the selective controls, or that in the absence of controls the central bank would restrict total bank assets more severely. In either case, some intricate questions about the effects on the banks' earnings and competitive position are involved.

Essentially similar considerations to those last mentioned are involved in proposals to supplement existing methods of control over bank deposits by giving the central bank power to alter the reserve ratio the chartered banks are obliged to maintain, either by direct variation of the required ratio or by requiring the banks occasionally to hold additional reserves in the form of 'special deposits', on which interest may or may not be paid.

In a modern central-banking system, the required reserve ratio serves two functions. First, it fixes the 'expansion multiplier'—the number of dollars by which the commercial-banking system can expand deposits on the basis of a dollar increment to reserves. Second, it imposes a tax on the commercial banks, equal to the loss of interest on the portion of reserves they would not hold if they were not obliged to. This tax, whose burden rises and falls with the general level of interest rates, can be regarded as the price the banks must pay to the central bank, and indirectly to the government, for the services of the central bank and the privilege of operating a banking business. Its level influences in the short run the division of bank earnings between the banks and the government, and in the long run the allocation of resources to the provision of banking services.

The use of variable reserve ratios rather than open-market operations with a fixed ratio to control the volume of bank credit can accordingly be recommended on two grounds. The first is that the central bank's control over bank deposits is closer, the higher the reserve ratio; and that close control is more desirable, and the burden of a higher reserve ratio on the banks more bearable, in the boom than in the slump. This argument assumes, plausibly, that banks will work closer to the minimum reserve ratio the higher that ratio is. The second argument is that raising required reserves in a boom will tend to restrain the growth of bank loans and the rise of interest rates in the same way as would requiring the banks to hold government debt directly, since reserves are an indirect form of public-debt holding. The factual assumption here is questionable, since taxing the banks by forcing them to hold larger reserves may increase their desire to hold loans rather than securities. On either argument acceptance of the recommendation involves the same considerations as before, a balancing of likely effectiveness in stabilization against considerations of equity and economic efficiency.

There is, however, a special set of circumstances in which the power to vary reserve requirements or to require the banks to hold special deposits may have particular advantages. A country on a fixed exchange rate may easily experience a rapid inflow of short-term capital; if the monetary authority wishes to prevent such a capital inflow from generating a multiple expansion of the domestic money supply, it may have considerable difficulty in doing so by open-market sales of securities, since the sales required may be extremely large. The desired insulation of the domestic monetary system could be secured more readily by requiring the banks to hold additional deposits at the central bank as reserves against the increase in foreign-owned deposits—in effect, the multiple-expansionary effect of an acquisition of foreign assets by the central bank would be offset by an increase in reserve requirements.

D. *Control over Other Credit Institutions*

In the past seven or eight years the argument has commonly been advanced that monetary control of the economy has been weakened by the development of financial intermediaries which offer the asset-owner assets which are close substitutes for bank deposits. The presence of these intermediaries, it is argued, means that an effort to tighten credit conditions simply leads asset owners to transfer their assets from the form of bank deposits into the form of substitutes for bank deposits; since the liabilities of financial intermediaries are backed by a fractional reserve of bank deposits, the effect is an increase in the total of money and close money substitutes that can be provided on the basis of a given amount of chartered-bank reserves provided by the central bank, so that the intentions of monetary control are frustrated, whether monetary control is conceived of as working through the total amount of money or through the amount of credit extended by financial institutions. Consequently, it is argued, effective monetary control requires that these financial intermediaries should be subjected to the same kind of cash-reserve requirement as are the commercial banks.

The importance of this argument depends on how far in fact monetary restriction leads to a transfer from bank deposits to the liabilities of financial intermediaries rival to banks. The empirical evidence produced so far does not suggest that such shifts are an important cause of frustration of monetary policy, or that the presence of financial intermediaries is a source of instability. To this proposition there is one important exception: the finance companies. In boom times the demand for instalment credit is so great, and so insensitive to the cost of instalment credit, that finance companies can offer very high yields to attract funds from alternative forms of liquid investment; by so doing, they provide finance for consumer purchases that add to the pressure of demand on available productive resources and so contribute to economic instability. Finance companies, however, are not generally considered to be close rivals to commercial banks in the same sense as other savings and deposit-accepting institutions; and proposals for controlling their activities are usually directed at controlling the terms of instalment finance, rather than the lending capacity of the companies. For this reason, such proposals are dealt with in the following subsection, on control of specific types of borrowing.

So far as other financial intermediaries are concerned, there would seem to be no empirical case for empowering the central bank to exercise control over their activities similar to that exercised over the chartered banks. There may, however, be a case on grounds of equity or financial efficiency for subjecting near-bank institutions to reserve requirements similar to those now imposed on chartered banks. The purpose of such a change would not be to improve the central bank's power to pursue economic stabilization—as already mentioned, there is little reason for believing that the central bank's control is weakened by the presence of financial intermediaries, and indeed so long as the public does not switch easily from bank deposits into close substitutes the presence of intermediaries may on the contrary increase the leverage of the central bank on economic activity.[1] On the contrary, the purpose would be to burden the intermediaries with the same taxation as the minimum cash-reserve requirement now places on the chartered banks. Whether this would constitute an improvement in equity and efficiency is a controversial question. As already mentioned, in return for this taxation the chartered banks receive certain services from the central bank, and enjoy the privilege of conducting a banking business. How far the services and the privilege are worth the tax paid for them is an extremely intricate question, as is the question of what equal conditions of competition between banks and near-banks would entail.

[1] The presence of financial intermediaries supplying assets very similar to bank deposits and holding a fractional reserve in the form of bank deposits means that the economy's total stock of 'liquidity' or 'money services' rests on a smaller fractional base of central-bank liabilities than it would if these intermediaries were not present. Consequently, so long as the public's division of its monetary assets between the various alternative forms, and the cash ratios observed by banks and competitive financial intermediaries, are reasonably stable, a given change in the central bank's liabilities will produce a larger absolute change in the public's stock of monetary assets when financial intermediaries are present than when they are not.

E. *Controls over Specific Types of Borrowing*

The foregoing subsections have been concerned with controls over specific types of lending institutions. This subsection is concerned with the alternative type of selective credit control, which is directed at specific types of borrowing, rather than at lending by particular institutions. The argument for controls of this type is that certain kinds of borrowing finance types of expenditure that are of especial importance in the causation of economic instability; and the case for such controls must rest on demonstration that instability can be reduced—that is that instability of the relevant types of expenditure can be reduced— by controls on the financing of such expenditure. Given that certain types of expenditure can be identified as contributing to instability, the problem raised by such proposals is how far control of the finance of such expenditure can mitigate instability. This problem is a serious one, because on the one hand there is no sure way of identifying a dollar of borrowing with a dollar of expenditure, and on the other hand the same expenditure can be financed in a variety of ways, some of which may be difficult to control. Specially, an individual or enterprise with a wide enough variety of assets or activities can always find a legitimate way of raising borrowed funds, regardless of the purpose for which the borrowing is intended; and similarly, if the demand for credit for some purpose is keen enough, the financial system can, given some time, always find a legitimate way of satisfying the demand.

Three main types of borrowing are commonly assigned a special role in the generation of economic instability: instalment borrowing, particularly consumer instalment finance; borrowing for new capital investment; and borrowing for stock-market and real-estate speculation. Accordingly, it may be argued that economic stabilization could be more efficiently secured by empowering the central bank, or some other governmental agency, to control the terms on which consumer instalment credit is available, to license borrowing for new capital investment, and (or) to prohibit borrowing for speculative purposes or to control the terms of such borrowing.

So far as consumer instalment credit is concerned, it can be argued on the basis of the evidence that consumer purchases financed by such credit have been a destabilizing factor in recent economic fluctuations. It can also be plausibly argued that consumer instalment buying is relatively insensitive to changes in the rate of interest incorporated in instalment-credit terms, but is sensitive to the down payment required and the period over which repayment is spread (as incorporated in the amounts of the instalment payments). Finally, it can be argued that the inequity and economic inefficiency involved in curtailing consumers' ability to pledge their future earning power are of a lesser order of importance than the inequity and inefficiency of similar restrictions applied to productive enterprises. Consequently, it can be argued, control of the down-payment and maturity terms of consumer instalment credit offers the prospect of a significant contribution to economic stabilization at a relatively small cost in terms of inequity and inefficiency.

On the opposite side, it can be argued that the use of controls over the terms of instalment finance places an inequitably heavy burden on the members of the community who are dependent on the earning power of their labour, as contrasted with those who possess property on which they can borrow, or whose prospective earning power is sufficiently high and certain to enable them to borrow on their personal credit from a bank. It can also be argued that any substantive use of such powers of control will foster evasion either directly or through the development of techniques for renting the services of consumer durables rather than selling the goods themselves on credit; this has in fact been the American and English experience with controls on instalment finance. Finally, there is the possibility that the control of purchases of consumer durables through control of the terms of instalment credit will set up replacement or 'echo' cycles in the purchase of such goods, which will aggravate the problems of the authorities concerned with economic stabilization in future.

According to accepted economic theory, the main source of fluctuation in economic activity is fluctuations in the volume of business investment, and one promising way of promoting economic stabilization is to stabilize the level of business investment. A possible approach to stabilizing business investment is to try to stabilize the amount of new borrowing for the purpose of business investment, by controlling access to the new capital market by the licensing of new capital issues, as was done in the United Kingdom for a long period.

Capital-issues control as a means of controlling new investment is however severely limited, especially in a country like Canada where firms have ready access to foreign capital markets. From a broad economic point of view, of course, the effect of control over access to the domestic capital market in inducing would-be borrowers to borrow abroad is not in itself objectionable, since restraint on new domestic capital issues would usually be introduced when the supply of domestic savings fell short of the demand for them, and foreign borrowing would tap foreign supplies of savings; still, the need to resort to foreign borrowing might unduly favour foreign control of Canadian enterprises. If, on the contrary, capital-issues control comprised both domestic and foreign flotations, it would raise problems both of interference with the activities of subsidiaries of foreign companies and of handicapping Canadian enterprises competing with foreign enterprises in the domestic and world markets. The main problem with capital-issues control, however, is that control of new capital issues is a remote and doubtfully effective way of controlling investment expenditure: the modern corporation can both finance itself by appropriations of current earnings, and plan its external financing to maximize its freedom with respect to the timing of its investment expenditures. It is probably safe to say that capital-issues control in the United Kingdom had little substantive influence on investment once physical controls over materials were abandoned, and that in fact it was never a major influence on investment, but only a device for ensuring orderly queuing of new issues in the capital market. More generally, capital-issues control is not a very promising device for control of investment, though it can be a useful financial adjunct of investment planning enforced by other means.

The third type of control over specific types of borrowing commonly recommended is control over borrowing for speculative purposes, especially stock-market and real-estate speculation. As previously argued, it is extremely difficult to establish that such speculative borrowing contributes to economic instability, since it involves the purchase of existing assets and not of currently produced goods. The most that can be argued is that the expenditure of speculative profits by speculators who sell out to more optimistic speculators contributes to aggregate demand, and that a bull market for equities may cheapen the cost of new capital to corporate enterprises and stimulate new investment. How far the excessive optimism of the boom is fostered by increases in stock and real-estate prices caused by purchases financed on credit is an unresolved question; so is the question of how far it is possible to restrain increases in aggregate demand by impeding speculation through restricting the availability of credit to finance it. Anyone with assets can speculate without the assistance of loans from a bank or a broker, and anyone with personal credit can obtain funds that can in fact be used for speculation. There is therefore considerable doubt whether control of loans for stock or real-estate speculation can either prevent speculation, or even if it can do so, contribute much to economic stabilization.

The case is different with speculation in stocks of physical goods, and a somewhat better case could be made out for selective control of loans to finance the accumulation of inventories. Unfortunately, speculative inventory accumulation is difficult to distinguish from the increases in inventories necessary to efficient production at a higher level; and in any case inventories can be financed by other means than borrowing.

IV.   CONCLUDING OBSERVATIONS

This paper has had two major purposes: to survey the alternative positions that may be taken with respect to the future conduct of monetary policy and the types of recommendations to which they lead, and to examine the possibility of increasing the power of monetary stabilization policy by the adoption of various types of selective credit control. Three alternative positions on future monetary policy have been distinguished: acceptance of a lower standard of performance, recommendation of changes designed to make monetary stabilization policy more effective, and recommendation of abandonment of short-run monetary stabilization policy in favour of creation of a stable monetary environment. In the author's own judgment, the third alternative has the most to commend it; however, if Canada remains on a fixed exchange rate the limitations on the freedom of domestic monetary policy which that entails probably will necessitate the adoption of the first alternative, or at best a mixture of the first and second alternatives. A variety of selective credit controls has been examined. Given the concentration of control in the Canadian financial system and economy, more intensive use of moral suasion might help stabilization policy, and the granting of powers to the central bank to control the more liquid assets or loans ratio of the chartered banks might also be useful and defensible. The author, however, has a prejudice against extension of the central bank's authority in these directions, on the grounds that it involves increased dependence on the central bank's judgment of complex economic problems, and tends to support economic concentration and monopolistic practices in the financial sector and in the economy generally. Turning to controls over specific types of borrowing, a reasonably good case can be made out for empowering the central bank to fix the down-payment and repayment terms of consumer instalment-credit contracts. While an even better case could be made out for regularizing the flow of private-investment expenditure, it is extremely doubtful that capital-issues control could be used effectively for this purpose. Finally, it is in the author's judgment highly questionable whether controls on borrowing for stock-market and real-estate speculation could contribute anything significant to economic stabilization.

CHAPTER VII

MAJOR ISSUES IN MONETARY AND FISCAL POLICIES IN THE UNITED STATES*

It is a long established tradition of monetary economics in the United States that discussion of major issues in monetary and fiscal policies should be restricted to the domestic aspects of the subject and should take the international environment as given. I find such a constraint, however, intolerably confining and inappropriate to the present circumstances of the United States.

In my opinion the major issue in monetary and fiscal policy in the United States at the present time is the shape that the international monetary system should take. Furthermore, the decisions—or failures to take decisions—on this subject that have emerged from the deliberations of the International Monetary Fund [1] and of the Group of Ten [2] are bound to constitute a source of future difficulties for US monetary and fiscal policy.

I. INTERNATIONAL MONETARY ISSUES

A. *The Deficiencies of Fixed Exchange Rates*

The classical debate on the issue of fixed versus floating exchange rates, which took the existence of the nation-state for granted, produced a theoretically overwhelming case for floating exchange rates, given the initial assumption that national policy-makers can be trusted to pursue domestic objectives in

---

* Presented at the 1964 Conference of Professors of Monetary Economics, sponsored by the American Bankers Association; reprinted from *The Federal Reserve Bulletin*, November 1964, pp. 1400–13. It may be of interest to record that this was the first such paper by an outsider ever to be published in the *Bulletin*.

a sensible fashion. The classical statement of this case is Milton Friedman's essay on the subject [3].

More recent works by Robert A. Mundell [4] and Ronald I. McKinnon [5] have abandoned the earlier identification of a nation with a particular currency area and have posed the question of fixed versus floating exchange rates as a problem of choosing the optimum currency area. These authors have raised important questions about the assumptions of the earlier analysis, notably with respect to the diversity of the economy and the internal mobility of its factors of production, the degree of involvement of the economy in international trade, and the relation of the 'moneyness' of the national currency to the international mobility of capital.

In spite of the questions it has raised, this new theorizing has strengthened the reasons for believing that the United States should have a floating exchange rate for the dollar in relation to other major world currencies. It has done this by calling attention to the importance of internal mobility of factors of production for the facility of adjustment under floating rates; to the effects of a low ratio of international trade to national income—such as we have in this country—in reducing the impact of changes in exchange rates on the domestic price level, and so in minimizing the conflict between the balance-of-payments objective and the price-stability objective of economic policy; and to the effects of a diversified domestic economy in encouraging capital to flow internationally in response to changes in exchange rates and to the effects of such changes on the profitability of investment.

Nevertheless, the United States has become increasingly committed to the present system of fixed rates of exchange between the various currencies and a fixed price of gold. These rates are alterable only in circumstances of 'fundamental disequilibrium', and for the major countries at least, the circumstances that would seem to reflect such disequilibrium have been redefined down to the vanishing point. This system of international monetary organization, under present conditions and given the policy objectives of the major nations, is seriously defective in a variety of respects.

Current analysis has come to list these deficiencies under three major headings: (1) The long-run liquidity problem. This is associated with the present level of the price of gold and with the inadequacy of new monetary supplies of that precious metal. (2) The confidence problem. This arises from the scarcity of gold, the use of the dollar as a substitute reserve, and the international mobility of capital that has developed, particularly since the European currencies became convertible and the United States became a chronic deficit country. And (3) the problem of adjustment to international desequilibria [6].

B. *The Mechanism of International Adjustment*

In this paper I shall not be concerned with the first two of these problems since they do not pose direct and concrete problems for fiscal and monetary policy. This statement needs to be qualified, however. That is, one must recognize that the confidence problem imposes restraints on the freedom of the United States to follow any policies that would be expansionary for the domestic economy if such policies would have adverse effects on the balance of payments. The reality and irksomeness of such restraints are evident from James Tobin's recent article in the *Review of Economics and Statistics* symposium in honour of Seymour Harris [7]. Also, the confidence problem obliges the US monetary authorities to pay particular attention to outflows of US short-term capital, in order to avoid alarming foreign central banks.

Under the gold standard system of immutably fixed exchange rates propounded in textbooks, adjustment of international payments disequilibria would occur automatically. It would be brought about by changes in domestic expenditures and prices, induced by contraction of the money supply in deficit countries and by expansion of the money supply in surplus countries. Such monetary changes would be initiated automatically by international gold flows, and reinforced by domestic monetary policies rigidly governed by national gold reserves.

Under the present system the operation of this mechanism is impeded in two ways. One impediment is the downward inflexibility of wages and prices—the recognition of which in the 1930's led economists to denounce the gold standard. The other is the unwillingness of governments—motivated by the objectives of price stability, full employment, and economic growth—

to tolerate and pursue the adjustment processes required by the system. Deficit countries are reluctant to deflate, and surplus countries reluctant to inflate, as the adjustment processes require. Adjustment of disequilibria, in the fundamental sense of the term 'adjustment', has therefore come to depend on two crucial factors.

The first is the inability of the countries concerned to achieve their stated policy objectives: specifically, the inability of deficit countries to pursue the goal of full employment, or their willingness to accept a performance short of that desired, for the sake of improving their balances of payments; and the inability of surplus countries to prevent their surpluses from generating domestic inflation, contrary to the objective of price stability.

The second factor is the response of the competitive system to the existence of disequilibrium and to the residual deflationary and inflationary pressures allowed by the incomplete fulfilment of policy objectives. Note that I have described this factor in such a way as to allow for processes of adjustment that do not depend on direct aggregate demand pressures; these processes may involve such elements as productivity-increasing innovations prompted by the micro-economic pressures of competition that are not allowed for in macro-economic models. Note also that the competitive response may involve perverse elements, particularly the tendency for private capital to flow from depressed to prosperous economies.

Dependence on these factors means that the adjustment of fundamental disequilibria is bound to be a slow process. The experience of the dollar-shortage period and of the ensuing dollar-glut period, combined with the projections of the Brookings Report [8], suggests that an adjustment period might run from 10 to 15 years.

An adjustment period of this prospective length poses extremely serious problems for the formation and execution of economic policy. In the first place, it requires a much longer perspective than democratic governments are equipped to adopt, bound as they are to seek electoral approval every 4 or 5 years, and focusing as they must on short-run economic developments. Much of the confusion, misunderstanding, and mutual recrimination that has impeded improvement in the international monetary system and in international economic relations in the postwar period can be attributed to the persistent but mistaken belief that problems of international monetary disequilibrium could be remedied by appropriate policies in a brief space of time.

In the second place, the financing of deficits cumulated over such long periods of time requires massive transfers of capital among countries. The usual facilities of central banks are not adequate to handle such large transfers, so it becomes necessary to arrange them by intergovernmental negotiation. And this raises a variety of difficult political problems for which solutions must still be found. While events in recent years have been pressing toward the use of inter-governmental transfers of long-term capital explicitly for the financing of international disequilibria, such transfers have not yet been recognized officially as essential to the logic of the system. I should note, in passing, that a system of slow international adjustment supported by large-scale transfers of capital from surplus to deficit countries raises some obvious questions about the efficiency of the resulting international allocation of capital.

C. *Policies for International Balance*

In Mundell's terminology the present international monetary system is, in fact, a 'disequilibrium system' [9]. The attempt in such a system to devise policies that will aid in the pursuit of the accepted policy goals—price stability, full employment, and growth—has led policy-makers and theorists alike into new and more complex ideas as to how policy should be conducted. These ideas are concerned with achieving the semblance of balance of payments adjustment in the short run, with the hope that in the long run a real adjustment will be brought about through the automatic competitive processes previously mentioned.

One method of achieving this effect—and this has already been referred to—is through negotiated intergovernmental transfers of longer-term capital.

Another method, which has become increasingly respectable in recent years, is to vary the degree of government interference in international trade and payments. For the deficit country— to wit, the United States—this method comprises the tying of foreign aid and military expenditures and the introduction of the interest equalization tax on the payments side; on the receipt side, it includes the negotiation of military sales to allies and envisages a variety of special incentives to increase exports.

For surplus countries seeking balance of payments adjustments through policies affecting trade and payments, it is recommended that resistance to the inflationary consequences of surpluses be sought in a liberalization of import policy rather than by tightening the supply of money. The appeal of this recommendation is usually enhanced (as in the Report of the Council of Economic Advisers submitted in January 1964 [10]) by a deliberate refusal to endorse the converse proposition for deficit countries, or even to recognize that the policies actually followed by the United States do represent its converse.

The third method is to select a combination of fiscal and monetary policies that will permit a high level of employment without aggravating the balance of payments situation. In terms of the simplest Keynesian theory of economic policy, if fiscal expansion is not accompanied by monetary expansion, the current-account balance will tend to worsen because rising income will increase the demand for imports. But at the same time the balance on capital account will tend to improve because rising income will tend to raise interest rates and attract capital inflows or discourage outflows. Monetary expansion will tend to worsen the balance on current account through its effect on income and to worsen the capital-account balance through its effect on interest rates, whereas monetary contraction will tend to improve the balance of payments on both accounts. Hence it should be possible to combine fiscal expansion with monetary policy in such a way as to raise income while improving the capital account enough to offset the adverse effect of higher income on the current account.

The required monetary policy will probably be a contractionary one, involving either an actual reduction in the quantity of money, or a slower rate of growth of the money supply than normal. It is possible, however, that this policy would be expansionary if the income effect of the fiscal expansion on the current account fell short of its interest effect on the capital account. In any case it would have to be 'contractionary' in the different sense of involving an increase in interest rates.

It is important to notice, for future reference, that the theory leading to this combination of policies for internal and external balance rests on very simple and possibly questionable Keynesian assumptions: specifically, if an increase in the level of income were to raise prospects for profits, monetary expansion could lead to a rise rather than a decline in interest rates. If so, it would have effects on the two parts of the balance of payments similar to those associated with fiscal expansion.

The policy analysis I have just outlined suggests fiscal expansion combined with monetary restraint for countries with deficits in their balance of payments, and fiscal restraint combined with monetary expansion (or at least not monetary restraint) for countries with surpluses. The fact that such a recommendation was made explicit to surplus countries in the 1964 report by the Council of Economic Advisers [10] no doubt stems in part from the reaction of the European central banks to the increase in US interest rates early in the summer of 1963, when there was still some tendency to assume that the European countries would respond passively to the US policy actions.

A further wrinkle of the analysis, which in US policy predates the argument outlined, recommends that the deficit country use monetary policy in such a way as to raise short-term rates relative to long—that is, to 'twist' the rate structure—with the purpose of attracting short-term capital inflows or inhibiting outflows while not discouraging long-term domestic investment. So far as I am aware, this part of the analysis has not been crystallized into a policy recommendation for surplus countries, though in some cases their policies have been designed to discourage short-term capital inflows by equivalent means.

The policies of fiscal expansion combined with higher interest rates in deficit countries and of fiscal contraction combined with lower interest rates in surplus countries just described are not fundamentally designed to restore international equilibrium. Rather they are designed to induce whatever transfers of capital are necessary for financing the deficits or surpluses associated with the pursuit of full employment and price stability in an environment of disequilibrium in exchange rates to pass through the private capital accounts of the balance of payments. In this way they seek to relieve the strains on the international monetary system and on intergovernmental relations that financing by central bank accumulations of the currencies of the deficit countries or by negotiated intergovernmental capital transfers entail.

The utility of such policies is conditional on the presence of a competitive adjustment mechanism working steadily (if slowly) behind the scenes. Their use is not only open to the questions about efficiency of capital allocation mentioned earlier but also conditional on their not impeding the underlying adjustment mechanism. The danger that they may impede adjustment is, of course, reflected in concern about the possibility of inflation; in wishful (and wistful) contemplation of an income policy (wage and price guideposts); and in government actions aimed at offsetting the influence of disequilibrium in exchange rates on the country's international competitive position by subsidies to productivity-increasing activities and by export promotion.

In one important sense, indeed, these balance of payments policies may work directly to aggravate international imbalance: for in so far as tight or loose monetary policies have an influence on domestic rates of growth, this method of preserving the semblance of international balance will accelerate the growth of the surplus countries and will retard that of the deficit countries. And in so far as international competitiveness is dependent on growth rates, it will tend to promote imbalance rather than balance.

The two connections assumed here, however, are doubtful: for fiscal policy can be designed to discriminate between investment and consumption, while the effects of growth on international competitiveness depend on the outcome of income and substitution effects.

To my mind, one of the major issues with respect to fiscal and monetary policies in the contemporary world concerns how far the two in combination can be used to operate the international disequilibrium system without aggravating and prolonging the disequilibria, and without indirectly fostering the need for, and the growth of, interferences with both international trade and payments, and domestic wage and price determination.

II. DOMESTIC ISSUES IN MONETARY AND FISCAL POLICIES

A. *The Shift to Fiscal Policy*

Having said this much about the international monetary system and the problems involved in the use of fiscal and monetary policy to operate it, let me turn to the consideration of monetary and fiscal policy from the domestic point of view.

The emergence of the United States as a reserve-currency country with a chronic balance of payments deficit has forced a major change in the conception of the respective roles of fiscal and monetary instruments in carrying out US economic policy. This change is more apparent in the successive annual reports of the Council of Economic Advisers than in the views and attitudes of the general public. At some cost in terms of longer-run historical accuracy, notably with respect to the early 1930's, it can be said that the United States in the past has relied in large part on monetary policy as its major instrument for achieving price stability and high employment. While fiscal policy has been used from time to time since the beginning of the New Deal, and especially during World War II, for the pursuit of macro-economic objectives, the prolonged period of dollar shortage prevented any serious conflict between the objectives of internal and external balance and made it unnecessary to work out a coherent and publicly accepted philosophy of the coordinated use of fiscal and monetary policy. In particular, it was not necessary to educate the public, including the legislators, in the use of fiscal policy to achieve short-run economic stability.

But with the appearance of a chronic deficit and balance of payments problem, it was no longer possible to use monetary policy for purely domestic purposes. Instead, monetary policy has had to be governed increasingly by the requirements of the balance of payments, and especially by the need to control international capital movements. Correspondingly, it has become necessary to put increasing emphasis on fiscal policy as the primary instrument for accomplishing domestic objectives.

B. *Problems and Requirements of the Transition*

The transition has not been without strain. Nor is it yet complete. One aspect of the strains involved has been the continued criticism of Federal Reserve policies by economists and others who have been dissatisfied with the performance of the domestic economy but who have been unwilling—or have refused—to recommend alternatives to monetary stringency as a way of coping with the balance of payments deficit. In other words, many professionals have continued to think of monetary policy as a purely domestic instrument in circumstances in which it cannot be so.

A more important aspect was the long delay in getting the tax cut through Congress and the need ultimately to sell it by the promise of government economy, both of which reflected the attachment of important sections of the public and of the Congress to orthodox notions of the necessity of balanced budgeting. While it is true that the apparent success of the tax cut has enabled the President to promise further tax cuts in the near future without exciting anything like the degree of opposition encountered before the recent tax bill was passed, there is certainly no proof that the country has mastered and accepted the theory of counter-cyclical fiscal policy.

I would maintain, on the contrary, that one of the major issues in monetary and fiscal policy in this country at the present time is the development of conscious public acceptance and official use of fiscal policy as a countercyclical device. It is one thing to concur in a tax cut after years of preaching by a conservative press that taxes are too high, and to do so after paying appropriate lip-service to the need for economy in government spending. It is quite another to set up machinery allowing the administration to cut taxes without a gesture in the direction of cutting spending, and to allow the administration to do so on the basis of its own judgment of what the economy requires. And it would be a still more demanding test to empower the administration to raise taxes when it felt that fiscal restraint was necessary to prevent inflationary developments.

To put the problem in another way, the tax cut has been only a first, and a relatively easy, step toward the efficient use of fiscal policy as a major instrument of domestic economic stabilization. The next step required is one that would give the budgeting authority discretionary control of fiscal policy. Such control would be comparable to the discretionary control that the monetary authority has long enjoyed over the money supply. This will be a difficult step. One reason is that it will be necessary to establish the idea of countercyclical fiscal policy as an operating principle of public finance. Another is that the step will require either a surrender of some congressional control over the taxing power or a revolutionary change in the methods by which Congress conducts fiscal business.

The former appears to be the more probable avenue of change. At the technical level, it would require the selection of those taxes whose variation will have the most predictable and substantial effects on expenditures—a matter important both for the use of tax variation as a policy instrument and for the feasibility of transfer of power over taxes from legislative to executive control—and the framing of rules for discretionary variation in tax rates that would be adequate to the needs of policy-making without departing too far from the principle of separation of powers in the Government of the United States.

As a preliminary, it would probably be necessary—and would be desirable on other grounds—to effect the rationalization of the tax structure that the experts have been urging for years but that was sacrificed in the pursuit of over-all reduction in taxes. It would also be helpful to keep the macro-economic impact of the tax-expenditure structure in the forefront of the discussion, as the Council of Economic Advisers did in its report for January 1964 [10], with a view to more frequent adjustment of tax rates to the increasing yield potentials created by the growth of the economy.

C. Specific Issues of Monetary and Fiscal Policy

General Effectiveness. Let me now turn from the broad issues raised for the deployment of the instruments of fiscal and monetary policy by recent changes in the world monetary environment and the international position of the US economy to some of the more specific issues that have been raised by the use of these instruments in recent years.

It will be generally agreed, I think, that one issue has been conclusively settled by recent experience. This is the capacity of fiscal and monetary policy, in co-operation, to raise the level of economic activity and to reduce the level of unemployment. The current expansion has continued longer than any previous expansion in this century. Indeed, it shows no clear indications of an early relapse, but rather of continuation at least into 1965. It has truly confounded those who believe that a 'natural' business cycle is inevitable and that economic policy can exercise no major influence over it. The expansion has exceeded the forecasts. It has reduced the budget deficit below the level that had been predicted. And it has permitted the administration to hold out the promise of further tax cuts next year, earlier than could have been expected.

The unemployment rate has fallen to 4·9 per cent, and this without any serious upward pressure on prices. This last fact is of special importance, in view of the hypothesis so widely advanced in recent years that economic policy has been faced with an entirely new problem—that of structural unemployment caused by automation. Traditional macro-economic policies, it was alleged, were incapable of coping with this problem. The evidence presented in support of this hypothesis was usually no more than the observation that a rise in unemployment has a differential impact on different sectors of the labour force, and it should be noted that empirical research on the problem has tended to reject the hypothesis as uncorroborated by the evidence [11].

The recent reduction in the unemployment rate provides much more direct and convincing evidence against the hypothesis. But it is not likely that this evidence will convince those who are overly impressed by the labour-saving effects of technical progress and who are unable to appreciate the capacity of a buoyant labour market to reabsorb displaced labour: indeed, a group calling itself the Ad Hoc Committee on the Triple Revolution has been making a great splash in Chicago recently with the notion that cybernation—not automation; that term is old-fashioned—threatens unemployment in the near future on a scale so great as to demand both the public provision of incomes to a large part of the labour force and the redefinition of the term 'work' to include education, voluntary political activity, and social welfare work [12].

To argue that the recent reduction in the unemployment rate

demonstrates the efficacy of macro-economic policies is not, of course, to argue that the present level of unemployment is satisfactory. Still less does it imply that there is no need for policies to improve the mobility of labour, if lower levels of unemployment are to be achieved with reasonable price stability. Nor does it imply that unemployment policy will be free of problems in the future, especially those associated with the impending flood of new entrants to the labour market; however, it does suggest that macro-economic policy, properly managed, can make a greater contribution to the solution of those problems than most non-economist commentators on automation, education, and related phenomena seem to believe. Finally, it does not imply that we have no need for a programme to deal with problems stemming from poverty, since the roots of most poverty lie in one form or other of incapacity to participate in the labour force, or to provide labour services valuable enough to earn a socially decent wage.

Relative Effectiveness: Fiscal Versus Monetary Policy.

While recent experience demonstrates the efficacy of fiscal and monetary policy in stimulating aggregate demand and employment, it raises the issue of the relative contributions of fiscal and monetary policy to the expansion. And this issue in turn involves perennial and deeper questions concerning the importance of money and the effectiveness of monetary policy.

A variety of factors make it difficult to interpret the experience of the past few years. One of these relates to the changes in Regulation Q in 1962 and 1963. These changes, designed to allow rates on time and savings deposits to rise enough to attract and hold short-term capital, caused these deposits to rise much faster than demand deposits and currency. The possibilities of substitution between demand and time deposits on the one hand, and between time and savings deposits and competing savings media provided by other financial intermediaries on the other hand, in response to the rise in deposit rates, make it impossible to determine exactly how expansionary monetary policy has been over the period, according to quantity theory standards. Such a determination would require a more detailed analysis of the magnitudes of the relevant cross-effects than is currently available.

If the question is approached in terms of movements in interest rates, other complications are encountered. One of particular relevance is the effect of the new depreciation guidelines and investment tax credit adopted in 1962 in raising the net return on investment, and so in effect making any given level of long-term interest rates less restrictive than before. E. M. Bernstein has estimated the effects of these changes as equivalent to a reduction of 1 percentage point in interest rates.[1]

Another is the standard point that the restrictiveness of a given level of interest rates varies with the circumstances. The importance of this point has been emphasized in certain theoretical papers that have reached me recently in advance of publication and that have been written with the current policy situation in view.[2]

Essentially, these papers question the standard diagrammatic assumption that the investment-saving (IS) curve slopes downward, so that monetary expansion necessarily reduces interest rates. The contrary assumption that the IS curve slopes upward can be reached by a variety of routes: (1) an income–investment relation stronger than the income–saving relation; (2) a static translation of the accelerator; (3) the application of marginal productivity theory to the effects of increased employment on the marginal productivity of capital in an aggregated Keynesian model; (4) the application of the relation between relative production quantities and factor prices in a two-goods model on the assumption that the capital goods sector is capital-intensive. And this assumption implies both that monetary expansion will raise interest rates and that the effort to stabilize interest rates in the face of shifts in the IS curve will be destabilizing.

Even without the assumption of an upward-sloping IS curve, the effort to stabilize rates may involve substantial expansion of the money supply, depending on the interest-sensitivity of the IS curve. And it may well be that both the critics and the defenders of recent monetary policy, in their concentration on interest rates, have been misled into understating the expan-

---

[1] This information was obtained in private conversation with Mr Bernstein.
[2] The authors in question are David Meiselman, R. A. Mundell, and Arnold Collery.

siveness of monetary policy and overstating the restraints imposed on it by balance of payments considerations.

In explaining changes in the US economy in recent years, the 1964 report of the Council of Economic Advisers [10] gives the impression of assigning relatively greater weight to tax reductions and a lesser and complementary role to monetary policy conducted, as it has been, within the limits set by the policy of raising short-term rates and twisting the yield structure to reduce outflows of short-term capital.

Milton Friedman, on the other hand, in reporting on his research in the 44th annual report of the National Bureau of Economic Research [13], demonstrates that in the period 1957–63 there was a fairly close connection between rates of change in the money supply (on the standard and his own definitions of money) and subsequent rates of change in the index of industrial production, when the changes in each series were calculated for homogeneous subperiods. This demonstration indicates that the otherwise mysterous slackening of the pace of economic expansion in the latter part of 1962, which is difficult to explain in terms of fiscal developments, appears to have been linked to a reduction earlier that year in the rate of growth of the money stock. The comparative timing of these changes also makes them difficult to explain in terms of a response of the money supply to prior changes in income.

In view of this evidence, of the considerations previously outlined, and of a variety of other evidence not worth citing in detail, I am inclined to attach a greater importance to monetary policy in generating and sustaining the expansion than the Council does, though I would not be prepared to accept the monetary explanation of growth in economic activity to the point of denying that fiscal policy was an important influence on income and employment. But while I believe that monetary policy was an important influence, I am not convinced that the monetary stimulation that has occurred has been fully intended. There is reason to suspect that it has been, to some extent, the unintended consequence of a policy intended to be modestly restrictive in the sense of raising the level of interest rates, but one that actually turned out to be quite expansionary in its effects on the money supply.

Effectiveness of the 'twist'. A related but subsidiary question about recent monetary policy relates to the effectiveness of the policy of twisting the rate structure. This issue involves the broader question of the empirical validity of the liquidity-preference theory. When this policy was initiated, the results of contemporary research suggested that changes in the composition of the public debt would have relatively trivial effects on interest rates. In fact, David Meiselman's work on the expectations theory of term structure implied that it would be negligible [14]. Meiselman's work has since been found defective by R. Kessel [15] and John H. Wood [16], who have discovered some evidence of liquidity preference.

Meanwhile, the twist policy has apparently had more influence on the rate structure than was earlier predicted for it. A recently completed doctoral dissertation by Neil Wallace [17], which attempts to combine term-structure theory with liquidity preference in a more general theory of forward interest rates, finds that the term structure has been twisted to a greater extent than the liquidity-preference element in his formulation would predict. As a result of the balance of payments problem, this question of the manipulability of the yield structure has gained new significance, and further research is evidently called for. A plausible line of explanation, but one difficult to explore, is that Federal Reserve policy pronouncements have a direct effect on the market's expectations.

D. *The Performance of the Federal Reserve: Independence and Competence*

The issues just discussed relate to the potency of monetary policy as an instrument, first, for controlling aggregate demand, and second, for achieving differential effects on the pattern of interest rates. Issues of quite a different kind have been raised by the performance and pronouncements of the Federal Reserve in the period since 1957. These issues relate to the control over the monetary instrument, as contrasted with the control of that instrument over the economy, and are concerned with two broad questions, which may be loosely described as the external and the internal aspects of control over monetary policy.

By the external aspect I mean the question of co-ordination

of monetary policy with the other instruments of policy—fiscal policy and debt management. This is really a question of the external relation of the Federal Reserve System to the other agencies of economic policy-making and more broadly to the political processes of government. By the internal aspect I mean the question of the efficiency with which the Federal Reserve manages monetary policy in pursuit of the objectives of that policy. This is really a question of the internal organization and operating procedures of the System.

The former is in essence a political problem or a problem in political organization. The latter is a problem on which economic theory and scientific economic research can be brought to bear—and in fact have recently been brought to bear. But it too is ultimately a political problem—or perhaps it would be more accurately described as a sociological problem. The economist does not have the skills to provide the answers to these problems, but in view of his alternative role as a political economist, he is naturally concerned with them.

These issues became active as a result of the Federal Reserve System's adoption of a sharply contractionary monetary policy in 1959–60 and of the resulting premature choking-off of the recovery from the 1957–58 recession. At that stage, I think it is fair to say, the major part of the professional comment was directed at the first issue. The Federal Reserve was widely criticized for being too concerned about resisting inflation and for having too little concern for promoting full employment and growth. And it was generally believed that the constitution of the System needed to be revised to give the administration a stronger and tighter control over the formulation and conduct of monetary policy.

While some commentators directed their criticisms at the System's methods rather than at its objectives, they were very much in a minority. And it was the majority view that found expression in the report of the Commission on Money and Credit [18]. The report's discussion of the potentialities of monetary policy was bland and conventional; and the report made extensive recommendations for reforming the constitution of the Federal Reserve System, without paying much attention to how the System actually operates policy.

The issues have recently been thrashed out again, in the

Hearings before the Sub-Committee on Domestic Finance of the Committee on Banking and Currency of the House of Representatives on 'The Federal Reserve System After Fifty Years' [19]. These *Hearings* were in many respects an odd production, in which the popular concern about the monopoly power of the money trust inherited from the late nineteenth century confronted the mid-twentieth century professional economists' concern about the failure of the country's central banking arrangements to apply sophisticated new developments in monetary theory. The two concerns found very uncertain common ground in an onslaught on the independence of the Federal Reserve in the Governmental structure and on its organization and methods of performing its functions.

In contrast to the proceedings of the Commission on Money and Credit, the purpose of the *Hearings* has been deliberately to encourage the airing of criticisms of the Federal Reserve— and criticisms have been recorded in abundance. The Keynesians have had their revenge on the System for the monetary policies of 1959–60. And the quantity theorists have had their revenge on both the System and the Keynesians for past insults and neglect.

Moreover, the quantity theorists' attack has been extended beyond past charges of ignorance of how money influences the economy—charges based on recent research on the theory of the demand for money—to charges of ignorance of how the System itself influences money. These charges are based on still more recent research on the theory of the supply of money.

Here I refer not to the *Hearings* themselves, but to the staff study by Karl Brunner and Allan Meltzer on 'The Federal Reserve's Attachments to the Free Reserve Concept' [20]. This study follows earlier works by Alexander J. Meigs [21] and William G. Dewald [22], which pinpointed the fallacies of the theory of monetary control originated by Burgess and Riefler [23] and underlined the inadequacies of this theory as a guide to the conduct of monetary control.

The result of the *Hearings* has been to dramatize both the unpopularity of the Federal Reserve System and its methods with a large number of monetary economists and the extent to which it has lost touch with new developments in monetary theory and new empirical research on monetary phenomena.

The report of the Commission on Money and Credit [18] and the discussions of monetary policy surrounding it had already revealed the gap between the Federal Reserve and the academic economists. But the *Hearings*—and especially the threat of legislation emanating from Representative Patman's Committee —are undoubtedly the main influence behind the efforts that Chairman Martin has recently initiated to modernize the Federal Reserve System.

As already mentioned, there are two distinct issues involved here, the external and the internal. So far as the first is concerned, I would judge that few economists now would be prepared to advocate an 'independent' central bank, as propounded in the literature published between the two World Wars; that is, a bank whose first duty is to protect the value of money against the inflationary propensities of the elected politicians. Such a function is consistent with neither political democracy nor modern concepts of the economic responsibilities of government. And even if it were, the historical record provides little evidence of the capacity of central banks to perform it wisely [24]. However, there are some subtle issues relating to precisely how the central bank should be integrated into the organization of the Government's economic policy-making, and specifically whether the central bank should be co-ordinate with the Treasury under the executive department, or should be subordinate to the Treasury.

In Canada this issue was recently decided in favour of making the Governor of the Bank responsible to the Minister of Finance, with the latter determining the broad outlines of monetary policy. This is the system that has ruled in England since 1945. Such a system of organization assumes that the Treasury makes macro-economic policy.

In this country, however, there is historical reason to fear that the Treasury might be excessively concerned with minimizing the interest cost of the public debt. This problem is part of a larger problem mentioned earlier: the need to develop among our people, including the legislative and executive branches of government themselves, a better understanding of the techniques and implications of fiscal policy.

With regard to the second issue—the application of modern economic theory and scientific research methods in the conduct of monetary policy—it is worth making the obvious point that the problem is not to get the central bank to employ and use economists. The Federal Reserve has done that for a long time, as have most other central banks. The real problem, which has close analogies with the problem of the use of scientists in industry, or of economists in economic planning, is to establish and maintain an organizational structure within which a scientific and research-oriented approach can be maintained in the face of the continual pressure of decisions that must be made on matters only remotely connected with scientific fundamentals.

A central bank operates in the markets for credit, and there is an inevitable tendency for it to conduct its analysis and formulate and rationalize its policies in terms of how they affect credit markets. There is an equally inevitable tendency for economists who get involved in central bank policy-making to think and talk in the same terms, if only to be able to communicate and command attention. As the Brunner–Meltzer study shows, for example, the prevalence of the free-reserve concept in Federal Reserve thinking is intimately associated with the necessity of formulating and communicating decisions to be implemented by the Manager of the System Open Market Account.

What internal institutional arrangements in the central bank would suffice to prevent this I cannot say: any major improvement in the theory of policy adopted by the bank is likely to harden into a dogma offensive to subsequent theorists, as indeed happened to the Burgess–Riefler theory. Perhaps the best that can be hoped for is that more active and sustained criticisms by academic economists will accelerate the rate of adoption of theoretical innovations.

REFERENCES

1. *International Monetary Fund, 1964 Annual Report*, Part II (Washington, D.C., 1964).
2. *Ministerial Statement* of The Group of Ten and *Annex* Prepared by Deputies, reprinted in *Federal Reserve Bulletin* (August 1964).
3. M. FRIEDMAN, 'The Case for Flexible Exchange Rates', *Essays in Positive Economics* (University of Chicago Press, Chicago, Ill., 1953).

4. R. A. MUNDELL, 'A Theory of Optimum Currency Areas', *American Economic Review* (September 1961).

5. R. I. MCKINNON, 'Optimum Currency Areas', *American Economic Review* (September 1963).

6. F. MACHLUP and B. G. MALKIEL (editors), *International Monetary Arrangements: The Problem of Choice*, report on the deliberations of an international study group of 32 economists (Princeton University Press, Princeton, N.J., 1964).

7. JAMES TOBIN, 'Europe and the Dollar', *Review of Economics and Statistics* (May 1964).

8. W. S. SALANT, et. al., *The United States Balance of Payments in 1968* (The Brookings Institution, Washington, D.C., August 1963).

9. R. A. MUNDELL, 'The International Disequilibrium System', *Kyklos* (1961).

10. *The Economic Report of the President Together With the Annual Report of the Council of Economic Advisers* (Government Printing Office, Washington, D.C., January 1964).

11. A. REES, 'The Dimensions of the Employment Problem Now and for the Foreseeable Future', remarks before a Symposium on Employment Sponsored by the American Bankers Association, Washington, D.C., February 24, 1964.

12. 'Conversation on "The Triple Revolution: Cybernation, Weaponry, and Human Rights",' *Chicago Perspective* (September 1964).

13. M. FRIEDMAN, 'The Monetary Studies of the National Bureau', *The National Bureau Enters Its Forty-Fifth Year* (National Bureau of Economic Research, 44th Annual Report, New York, June 1964).

14. D. MEISELMAN, *The Term Structure of Interest Rates* (Prentice-Hall, Englewood Cliffs, N.J., 1962); see, however, J. H. Wood, 'The Expectation Hypothesis, the Yield Curve, and Monetary Policy', *Quarterly Journal of Economics* (August 1964).

15. R. KESSEL, 'The Cyclical Behavior of the Term Structure of Interest Rates', unpublished MS., National Bureau of Economic Research, New York, 1962.

16. J. H. WOOD, 'Expectations, Errors, and the Term Structure of Interest Rates', *Journal of Political Economy* (April 1963).

17. N. WALLACE, 'The Term Structure of Interest Rates and the Maturity Composition of the Federal Debt', unpublished Ph.D. dissertation, University of Chicago, 1964.

18. *Money and Credit*, the report of the Commission on Money and Credit (Prentice-Hall, Englewood Cliffs, N.J., 1961).

19. U.S. Congress, House. Banking and Currency Committee, Subcommittee on Domestic Finance, *Federal Reserve System After Fifty Years*, Vols. I and II, 88th Cong., 2nd sess. (Government Printing Office, Washington, D.C., 1964).

20. U.S. Congress, House. Banking and Currency Committee, Subcommittee on Domestic Finance, 'The Federal Reserve's Attachment to the Free Reserve Concept', a Staff Analysis by Karl Brunner and

I

Allan Meltzer, 88th Cong., 2nd sess. (Government Printing Office, Washington, D.C., 1964).

21. A. J. MEIGS, *Free Reserves and the Money Supply* (University of Chicago Press, Chicago, Ill., 1962).

22. W. G. DEWALD, 'Free Reserves, Total Reserves, and Monetary Control', *Journal of Political Economy* (April 1963).

23. W. R. BURGESS, *The Reserve Banks and the Money Market* (Harper and Bros., New York, 1927); W. W. Riefler, *Money Rates and Money Markets in the United States* (Harper and Bros., New York, 1930).

24. H. G. JOHNSON, statement made February 25, 1964, before the House Banking and Currency Committee, Subcomittee on Domestic Finance, Vol. II, pp. 969–1020, cited in item 19 above. Statement includes on pp. 975–1016 a reprint of H. G. Johnson, 'Alternative Guiding Principles for the Use of Monetary Policy', *Essays in International Finance* (No. 44, November 1963) in which the role of monetary policy in general economic policy is discussed, (reprinted above as Chapter VI).

PART THREE

MONETARY AND FISCAL PROBLEMS
OF DEVELOPING COUNTRIES

CHAPTER VIII

FISCAL POLICY AND THE BALANCE OF PAYMENTS IN A GROWING ECONOMY*

I. INTRODUCTION

Any attempt to discuss the relation between fiscal policy and external economic relations as a separate aspect of governmental financial policy for economic development necessarily involves a somewhat severe abstraction, since for the purpose of analysing the growth process and the contribution that fiscal policy may make to it, economic relations with the rest of the world ought to be regarded merely as an extension of domestic economic activity. Concentration on the balance of payments as the aspect of external economic relations with which fiscal policy is or should be concerned involves a further abstraction, and a rather dangerous one, since the balance-of-payments, position of a country depends at least as much on another instrument of economic policy—exchange rate policy—as it does on fiscal policy. Not only must the relevance of exchange rate policy be kept constantly in mind, but also the temptation to stop analysis short at the balance-of-payments effects of alternative fiscal policies must be avoided, if the international economics of fiscal policy are to be examined scientifically. Accordingly, this paper begins with a general discussion of the international aspects of economic development, proceeds to an examination of the tendency of countries pursuing planned economic development to suffer chronic balance-of-payments problems, discusses the implications of this tendency for

* A paper prepared for the Third Study Conference on Problems of Economic Development of the Organization for Economic Co-operation and Development, on 'Government Finance and Economic Development', Athens, December 12–19, 1963. *Malayan Economic Review*, Vol. IX, no. 1, April 1964, pp. 1–13; *Government Finance and Economic Development*, edited by A. T. Peacock and Gerald Hauser, O.E.C.D., Paris 1965, Chapter 9, pp. 157–69.

economic policy in general and fiscal policy in particular, and concludes with some observations on import-substitution policies, and on policy towards private foreign investment.

II. EXTERNAL ASPECTS OF ECONOMIC DEVELOPMENT

From the analytical point of view, the availability of economic relationships with the rest of the world facilitates economic development in two major ways. First, at the macro-economic level, the rest of the world furnishes a source of savings additional to what is forthcoming, or can be extracted, from the domestic economy. The central difference between domestic and foreign sources of savings is that domestic savings can be augmented by taxation, whereas foreign savings must be obtained at the volition of foreign governments and international institutions and of private foreign investors. Foreign official capital is obtained by governmental negotiation and is not a variable controlled by fiscal policy as such; rather the general conduct of fiscal policy is constrained by the terms imposed by the official suppliers of foreign capital as a condition of development assistance, while fiscal policy must aim to make effective use of the extra resources provided by foreign financial assistance and to provide for interest and amortization payments on it. Private foreign capital, on the other hand, is a variable subject to direct influence by fiscal policy in three major ways: through the influence of the tariff structure (and other barriers to trade) in creating an incentive for foreign enterprises to establish productive facilities in the country rather than export to it; through the influence of the general system of corporate income taxation, special investment incentives and subsidies, and so forth on the private return to investment; and through the influence of special incentives or disincentives to the investment of foreign, as contrasted with domestic, capital.

Second, at the micro-economic level, the opportunity to exchange goods in the world market both enables the developing country to obtain more cheaply than it otherwise could the technologically advanced types of capital equipment and materials required for raising its level of productivity, and permits it to achieve a higher return from its development investment than it otherwise could, either by allowing it to specialize on the production of goods in which it has a potential comparative advantage in the world economy, or by giving it access to a market large enough to yield the full advantages of economics of scale. From the standpoint of establishing a self-sustaining process of economic growth, the latter consideration is probably more important than the former. In practical development planning and discussions of it, however, major emphasis is laid on import-substitution rather than export development; the reasons for this are partly that the objective of economic development planning is usually industrialization and imitation of more advanced countries rather than raising productivity and the standard of living as such, partly that for reasons discussed below the balance of payments appears as a special problem of underdeveloped countries which it is easier for policy to tackle by import-substitution than by export-promotion.

When foreign trade is conceived as extending the market opportunities of the domestic economy and so permitting more profitable investment of development resources, the problems of fiscal policy with respect to foreign trade and to domestic trade are essentially the same—to raise revenue for development and to spend it in ways that minimize private disincentives to growth and the distortion of the economy away from an efficient production pattern. From this point of view the chief fiscal problem in development planning stems from the traditional dependence of public finance in under-developed countries on taxes on international trade, especially import duties. In an underdeveloped economy with only a rudimentary domestic industrial sector, taxes on exports and imports probably affect mainly the distribution of income, rather than the allocation of resources. But as the economy develops, the allocative effects of taxes on trade are likely to become increasingly important, so that for efficiency the emphasis of fiscal policy must shift towards direct taxation, and types of indirect taxation that do not discriminate between domestic and foreign markets or sources of supply—except to the extent that such discrimination is itself a deliberate aim of development policy, or justified by its explicit contribution to economic growth.

III. BALANCE-OF-PAYMENTS PROBLEMS OF DEVELOPING COUNTRIES

The external aspects of planned economic development typically appear as an overall problem of keeping the balance of payments of the developing country in balance (or not too disastrously in deficit), with the availability of foreign exchange appearing as a constraint on development policy additional to the constraint set by the scarcity of resources. Hence arises the typical concern of fiscal policy, and of extra-budgetary policy, with the balance of payments as such, rather than with the more fundamental incentive and allocative problems discussed in the previous section.

According to familiar analysis, a chronic balance-of-payments deficit may be due to either a chronic state of excess demand, or to an overvalued exchange rate in the absence of excess demand. Both conditions tend to be characteristic of underdeveloped economies applying programmes of planned economic development, the latter increasingly so with the passage of time.

The initiation of planned economic development is itself likely to make the pre-existing exchange rate overvalued. Planned development implies both an increase in the level of domestic activity and hence in the aggregate demand for imports (and possibly also a reduction in the supply of exports), and a shift of demand towards capital goods, which have to be imported. To maintain equilibrium in the balance of payments, some reduction of domestic prices relative to world prices would be necessary, to induce shifts of resources from the domestic sector into the international sectors of the economy (the sectors producing exports and import-substitutes). Given the inflexibility of resource allocation generally assumed to prevail in underdeveloped countries, the required relative price adjustment might be substantial, involving substantial income redistribution from consumers to producers of internationally traded goods.

Governments are understandably and naturally reluctant to contemplate such relative price adjustments and income redistributions, for reasons ranging from a specific unwillingness to reduce overtly the real incomes of the urbanized professional, mercantile, and administrative classes to which the policy-makers belong and of the members of the extant industrial labour force on which they depend in part for political support, to a more general unwillingness to accept the writing-down of the real value of national resources that devaluation would entail. Instead, they are prone to seek an alternative solution by direct action on the import side of the balance of payments, by means of exchange controls, quantitative import restrictions, or higher import duties, justifying these policies by reference to social priorities and to the alleged inelasticity of foreign demand for (traditional) exports and of domestic demand for (non-priority) imports.

Such actions have the effect, intended and unintended, of shifting resources into the import-substitution sector, and in part they achieve covertly the necessary reduction of real incomes in the domestic sector; but to the extent that they constitute a tax on real incomes in the export sector they indirectly aggravate the balance-of-payments problem by impeding rather than fostering the growth of export supply. This effect is typically reinforced by deliberate policies of increasing taxation of exports, through export taxes, discriminatory exchange rates, marketing board surpluses, and so forth. Such policies are justified either by the traditional reliance on the export industries as a source of revenue or by the argument that either the demand for these exports, or the supply of them, or both, are extremely inelastic. Thus the effort to cope with the balance-of-payments problem by other means than devaluation may result in large part in a wasteful re-deployment of resources from the exporting to the import-substituting sector (wasteful because the resources are shifted from indirect production of importable goods to direct production at a higher real cost), when what is required is an expansion of both of the international sectors.

Not only is the initiation of planned economic development likely to result in the exchange rate being *de facto* overvalued, but the degree of overvaluation is likely to increase over time, as a result of the inflation of domestic wages and prices generated both by the tendency of economic planners to plan for an excessive level of demand, by taking overly-optimistic views of the potential savings forthcoming and the potential levels of agricultural output and increases in productivity, and by the natural tendency of wages and prices to rise in an economy operating at a higher level of activity than usual, and transforming its economic structure at the same time. The usual consequence is chronic and increasingly serious difficulty with the balance of payments, and an eventual switch of international economic policy from import-substitution to export-promotion, this policy being implemented by export-subsidies, foreign exchange 'bonuses' or favourable exchange rates for export proceeds, tax incentives for export-promotion or expansion, and the like.

At this stage, the country will have achieved the equivalent of a *de facto* devaluation, in the sense of a similar increase in the prices of both exports and imports relative to prices in the domestic sector. The important difference from explicit devaluation is that the degree of implicit devaluation will differ among the categories of internationally traded goods, and between commodities and 'invisible' items in the balance of payments such as capital movements, tourism, and emigrants' remittances, depending on the precise nature of the policies of foreign exchange conservation and augmentation adopted. At some later stage, either the increasing difficulty of administering an increasingly complex set of interventions in trade and payments, the main purpose of which is increasingly clearly to compensate for the overvaluation of its currency, or pressure brought to bear by the sources of external development aid (on which its balance-of-payments difficulties will make it increasingly dependent), will force the country to simplify the situation by explicit devaluation of the currency.

IV. IMPLICATIONS FOR DEVELOPMENT POLICY AND FISCAL POLICY

The foregoing idealized account of the balance-of-payments problems and policies of underdeveloped countries that adopt programmes of planned economic development is derived largely from the experience of underdeveloped countries in Asia and Latin America. It is perhaps of less immediate and direct relevance (though it is certainly not irrelevant) to the underdeveloped countries of the Mediterranean area. At any rate, let it serve as a cautionary tale from which to begin a discussion of fiscal policy and the balance of payments in a process of planned economic development. From the standpoint of formulating and conducting development policy, three major points emerge from the consideration of experience.

The first and most obvious point is concerned with exchange rate policy rather than with fiscal policy, though it has an important bearing on the objectives of fiscal policy and the restrictions that may be imposed on its use for promoting development. An underdeveloped country on a fixed exchange rate which undertakes a development programme and for this purpose employs the accepted techniques and instruments of planning will inevitably develop a balance-of-payments problem. If it adheres tenaciously to its exchange rate, it will equally inevitably find itself forced to use its fiscal and other control instruments to compensate for the inappropriateness of its exchange rate. Further, once balancing the balance of payments becomes firmly established as an object of policy, and economizing on foreign exchange an objective conditioning its use of its planning instruments, it is virtually certain that it will come to follow policies that are different from those it would adopt if the balance of payments as such were not a pressing problem, policies that will militate against achievement of the nominal objective of economic growth. With respect to items in the current account, the country's policy is likely to put excessive emphasis on import-substitution, both because imports are easier to control than exports and because the development of import-substituting industries gives the superficial appearance of economic development even if great waste of resources is involved, and insufficient emphasis on export-promotion, for a variety of reasons discussed in the previous section. Further, the criteria of saving or earning foreign exchange are likely to dictate a different choice of international sector industries for development promotion than would a calculation of comparative advantage based on relative real costs. With respect to the capital account, the balance-of-payments problem is likely to lead the country into excessive 'distress' borrowing from foreign countries and financial institutions, and may lead it either to impede private foreign investment in the country by placing restrictions on the remission of profits and capital, or at the other extreme to provide excessive inducements to private foreign investment that promises to save foreign exchange.

To avoid having its development programme fall into the balance-of-payments trap, a country ideally should adopt a floating exchange rate. The argument commonly advanced against adoption of a floating rate is that it encourages resort to inflationary means of financing development, and will therefore result in a continual depreciation of the exchange rate. The weakness of this objection, however, is that countries planning economic development by that very fact are under strong pressures to resort to inflationary financing, and that if they adhere to a fixed rate in these circumstances they will have to combat the resulting balance-of-payments problems by direct or fiscal means that are certain to introduce significant distortions in the allocation of resources. The choice is therefore not between price stability and inflation but between two methods of offsetting the adverse effects on the country's international competitive position of the domestic inflation that accompanies development planning. A floating exchange rate achieves this offsetting automatically, without interfering with the allocation of resources according to comparative advantage as modified by development planning. By contrast, under a fixed exchange rate the offsetting must be accompanied by piecemeal measures that inevitably introduce allocative distortions.

If a country nevertheless chooses to adhere to the fixed exchange rate system, its policy-makers should remain on the alert for the development of significant overvaluation of the currency, and be ready to correct it by timely devaluation and to repeat the devaluation when overvaluation reappears, rather than resist devaluation to the last ditch, defend the exchange rate by using all the available instruments of intervention in the balance of payments, and be forced eventually into a drastic devaluation accompanied by the sweeping fiscal and monetary reforms that are almost invariably insisted on by the International Monetary Fund in such cases, and which usually eventuate in a prolonged period of domestic deflation and heavy unemployment.

To the extent that a country does commit itself firmly to its existing exchange rate, and makes the maintenance of that rate a primary objective of economic policy, this commitment imposes the restraint of avoiding domestic inflation in its development programme. Since this restraint implies maintaining sufficient slack in the economy to prevent inflation, it is a restraint that no country consciously planning economic development is likely to comply with to the extent necessary. The policy problem therefore becomes one of choosing a development programme whose inflationary consequences on the balance of payments can be contained within reasonable limits by the available policy instruments.

In the actual conduct and formulation of policy, the chief problem for the policy-makers is to remain aware of the fact that these policy instruments are being used to offset an inappropriate exchange rate, and to design their use with reference to the underlying real economic situation rather than with reference to balance-of-payments considerations as such. For this purpose, the notion of the 'shadow' exchange rate as a guide for decisions involving foreign and domestic alternatives is an essential concept for intelligent economic planning. In particular, fiscal policy affecting the production and marketing of internationally traded goods should be guided by the principle that in general the domestic prices of internationally traded goods should differ from their foreign prices by the same proportion, specifically by the proportion by which the shadow exchange rate diverges from the actual exchange rate. In other words, exports should be subsidized and imports taxed to offset the effects of overvaluation; and if the balance of payments threatens to deteriorate as a result of domestic price inflation, the policy-makers should increase the incentives for both exporting and import-substitution proportionally, rather than concentrate on increasing the incentives for import-substitution alone, as they usually do.

Deviations from the principle that exports should be subsidized and imports taxed at the same rate require economic justification on other grounds (economic development grounds) than balance-of-payments considerations. Such justifications are, at the level of abstract theory, confined to variations of the optimum tariff argument; the other arguments for protective policies that have been advanced in recent years (external economies, non-economic wage differences between industry and agriculture, the infant industry argument) on closer

consideration lead to the recommendation of taxes and subsidies directed at domestic production, consumption, or factor
use. The strength of the optimum tariff argument for protection
of domestic industries or taxation of export industries in underdeveloped countries has been greatly exaggerated in theory and
application, since it must depend on low elasticity of demand
for the country's exports, and demand for any one country's
products is likely to be elastic in the long run due to the elasticity
of supply from competing sources. In reality, optimum tariff
reasoning is more likely to apply to two other current account
items—tourism, and emigrants' remittances—than to commodity trade. The other arguments for protection in underdeveloped countries, as already mentioned, are logically not
arguments for protection but arguments for some other form
of intervention; but the budgetary problem of financing
subsidies, or of achieving the effect of a subsidy on one activity
by imposing taxes on the alternatives, may in practice make a
divergence of domestic from foreign relative-price relationships
the second-best policy solution.

The other two points that emerge from consideration of the
experience of development planning concern the detailed
policies countries follow in attempting to keep the composition
of the balance of payments in conformity with the requirements
of economic development. These policies involve primarily
the use of some combination of direct controls on and taxation
of trade to restrict the overall volume of imports and to give
priority to 'essential' over 'non-essential' imports. The 'essential'
imports include foodstuffs, raw materials, and capital goods,
the 'non-essentials' being 'luxury' consumption goods and the
machinery and materials for making them. The theory underlying this kind of policy is the valid principle that if the country
is to make a major effort at economic development it must
restrict its real consumption—which in equity implies particularly restriction of consumption of luxury goods by the
higher-income groups—and invest the resources so obtained
in the accumulation of capital equipment. Where the policy
errs, with effects generally inimical to efficient development, is
in attempting to implement this principle through action
directed at the availability of imported supplies of the goods in
question, in addition to or in place of action directed at the

distribution and disposition of income, which determine the demand for such goods.

If a country seeks to make the composition of its imports conform to the pattern appropriate to a rapidly developing economy by rationing its scarce supply of foreign exchange so as to favour imports of essential food and materials and capital goods and inhibit imports of luxuries, it is likely to impede its economic development in two major ways. Such a policy involves an implicit subsidy on imports of the essential goods, and tax on imports of the non-essential goods, by comparison with a situation of no controls on imports coupled with an equilibrium exchange rate. By relying on foreign exchange rationing instead of imposing an explicit tax on imports of non-essentials, the policy-makers miss the opportunity to appropriate the scarcity value of non-essential imports created by rationing. Instead of adding to the tax revenue available for development, the scarcity rent is allocated to the recipients of import licences (from whom it may be passed back as bribes to government employees), or, if domestic prices of imported goods are controlled to prevent abnormal profits, diffused among the consumers of the goods in question. This is the first deleterious effect of exchange rationing on the rate of economic growth—the sacrifice of an opportunity to raise tax revenue. This sacrifice can be quite substantial, as is evidenced by the very high domestic prices (relative to foreign) of foreign-produced goods frequently observable in countries practising exchange control. If exchange control or import restriction were replaced by exchange auctioning or tariffs, the government could obtain the same effects on the pattern of imports while increasing the revenues available for financing development. This is the second major point that emerges from the experience of planned economic development: that fiscal policy methods are superior to direct control methods for shaping the balance of payments to conform to the requirements of an economic development policy.

The other adverse effect of foreign exchange rationing on economic development is one that is common with, and cannot be avoided by, the use of taxes on imports to discourage consumption. This effect occurs because a restriction or tax on imports gives an incentive to resort to substitution for imports from domestic supplies, either by giving an inducement to domestic production of the same or similar goods or by encouraging the substitution of domestic goods serving similar purposes. For example, prohibition or heavy taxation of imported items of conspicuous consumption such as large private automobiles may foster either the establishment of a local automotive industry or the development of conspicuous expenditure on large private residences and extensive personal services. In a very underdeveloped economy, taxation of imported luxuries may approximate closely to taxation of luxury consumption, and even restrictions or prohibitions on the importation of luxuries may reduce the consumption of higher-income groups to the benefit of savings. But as an economy develops and becomes more differentiated, these measures are likely to become decreasingly effective as a source of development revenue (directly, or indirectly by increasing saving) and increasingly protective in effect. Similarly, the subsidies to certain types of imports implicit in unrestricted entry are likely increasingly to divert domestic resources away from the production of close substitutes, such as domestic food production or capital goods production. The consequence is that policies intended to influence the pattern of domestic expenditure, and specifically to facilitate an increase in saving and investment at the expense of consumption, come to exercise an important effect on the allocation of resources, diverting resources towards production of goods the importing of which is discriminated against, and away from production of goods the importing of which is implicitly subsidized.

This unintended and presumably undesirable allocative effect would not occur if taxes (or rationing, though rationing is a less efficient technique because it wastes taxable capacity) were directed at the consumption of non-essential goods rather than at the importation of them—in other words, if the primary emphasis of fiscal policy were laid on shaping income distribution and demand, rather than the balance of payments as such, to conform to the requirements of economic growth. Instead, taxation of consumption of non-essentials regardless of origin would be conducive to efficient allocation of resources in production, since the relative production costs of goods would be the same at home and abroad. But taxation of goods at different rates to the final purchaser would entail some allocative inefficiency in consumption, especially in a tax system relying heavily on high rates of tax on a few major items, since it would induce substitution of lightly-taxed for heavily-taxed commodities in consumption and so promote purchases of goods having relatively high alternative opportunity costs to the economy (that is, high ratios of real cost to the country to money price to consumers). Hence there is a case for shifting from reliance on excise and import taxation of a few items to reliance on income taxation, a general sales tax, or possibly an expenditure tax as the economy develops. This is the third major point that emerges from analysis of the balance-of-payments problems of developing countries—the desirability of employing fiscal methods of operating on the composition of the balance of payments that do not discriminate or discriminate as little as possible, between foreign and domestic sources of supply and among different items of consumption.

The principle of non-discrimination advanced here may seem at first sight to conflict with the earlier recommendation of a combination of import-substituting and export-promoting policies in the case of overvaluation. But in fact there is no conflict between the two. In the earlier case, the apparent money costs of imports and returns from exports diverge from their alternative opportunity costs as a result of overvaluation, and export-promotion and import-substitution (in parallel) are required to offset this monetary distortion of resource allocation. In the present case, taxation of imports introduces a divergence between the social opportunity costs of domestic and foreign supplies of the taxed commodities, which would be removed by taxing purchases of these commodities regardless of source. To put the point another way, overvaluation gives the country an apparent comparative disadvantage in internationally traded goods in which it has a real comparative advantage, and taxation or restriction of imports gives it an apparent comparative advantage in import-substitution where it has a real comparative disadvantage; in both cases, policy should aim at making apparent and real comparative advantage and disadvantage correspond.

V. SOME ASPECTS OF IMPORT-SUBSTITUTION

There are a variety of reasons for expecting that the economic development of a hitherto underdeveloped country will entail the development of domestic production of import-substitutes, strictly in accordance with the principle of comparative advantage. Economic development involves the accumulation of material capital, the acquisition of skills on the part of the labour force, and the introduction of modern technology, and also enlarges the extent of the domestic market. It thus involves the overcoming of initial comparative disadvantages of the underdeveloped country in relation to the advanced countries of the world, which make the former dependent on the latter for supplies of advanced types of consumers' and producers' goods. Import-substitution of this type may, further, have to be a deliberate objective of economic development policy, both because economic planning is necessary to ensure the efficient development of the economy and because the effects of the characteristic overvaluation of the currency previously discussed have to be counteracted by conscious economic policy.

Unfortunately, both the tendency of policy-makers to translate propositions that are valid subject to careful qualification and quantitative evaluation into simple slogans and rules of thumb, and the pressure of the balance-of-payments problem associated with an overvalued currency, typically result in import-substitution becoming an objective of development policy for its own sake, rather than a corollary of efficient allocation of development resources. The pursuit of import-substitution as an objective can result in extremely expensive misallocation of resources, the costs of which to the economy are not readily apparent, and the effects of the protective policies used to encourage import-substitution on market structure and competitive conditions may be contrary to what is required for the establishment of self-sustaining economic growth. These effects are relevant to the efficient design of fiscal policy, in so far as import-substitution is implemented by tariff and taxation policies, or by direct methods (import-restriction, government investment in import-substituting industries) that could be replaced by fiscal measures that would achieve the same effect.

The cost of import-substitution to the economy can be measured by the excess of the cost of domestic production of import-substitutes over the cost of importing the same goods (corrected if necessary for the change in the exchange rate necessary to keep the balance of payments in balance); alternatively it can be measured by the subsidy given to the domestic producers of import-substitutes. The existence and the magnitudes of these subsidies are disguised by the fact that they are customarily given in forms that do not pass through the budget. A tariff, for example, in so far as it protects domestic production amounts to an extra-budgetary tax on consumers and subsidy to producers, collected directly from the consumers by the producers. A tax concession to firms producing import-substitutes, or government investment in producing import-substitutes that yields a rate of return on the capital less than the normal rate of return gross of taxes on private investment, is a subsidy at the expense of the community at large, which must pay more taxes or receive less benefits from public expenditure than it otherwise would.

A further factor which disguises the magnitudes of the subsidies offered for import-substitution is associated with the complex input-output structure of modern industry and the practice of differentiating in import-substitution policies between final assembly or manufacturing processes and the production of raw materials and components. Import-substitution policies typically concentrate on securing the establishment of domestic facilities for final manufacturing processes, and to this end both impose barriers to the importation of the finished products and facilitate the importation of components and materials. The effect of the latter practice is to make the effective subsidy offered to final manufacturing stages much higher than is indicated by the excess of the domestic price of the finished commodity over its price in the world market. Suppose, for example, that a country has a 30 per cent tariff on fabricated copper products, that raw copper accounts for 50 per cent of the (foreign) cost of production, and that raw copper is allowed free entry. In effect, the fabrication process is being protected at the effective rate of 60 per cent, and if this degree of protection is necessary to permit domestic fabrication to compete with imports, the country is incurring an excess cost of fabrication of 60 per cent. This percentage also represents the excess resource cost per unit of foreign exchange expenditure saved, and the implied degree of overvaluation of the currency (measured by the excess of the implied 'shadow' price of foreign exchange over the official exchange rate). The effective degree of protection in this example is twice the degree implied by the tariff rate; much higher ratios of effective to nominal degrees of protection can easily result from combinations of incentives to import-substitution each of which by itself may appear modest and indeed only reasonable.

The purpose of the two preceding paragraphs is to point out that the excess cost of production of import-substitutes induced by import-substitution policies is both difficult to evaluate and easy to underestimate. The implication for fiscal policy is that fiscal incentives to import-substitution need to be carefully appraised, to determine the magnitude of the rate of subsidization implicit in them and whether the results are likely to justify subsidization at this rate. Even if import-substitution is desired for its own sake, regardless of its effect in increasing the real cost to the economy of the goods in question and reducing productivity, there must obviously be some limit to the rate of subsidization that is justifiable; and rational policy-making should evidently attempt both to prevent the rates of subsidization offered to particular import-substituting industries from exceeding a tolerable level, and to equalize the rates of subsidization offered to the various claimants for fiscal assistance. This last proposition is frequently expressed in the recommendation that a developing country should impose a uniform (and moderate) tariff rate on imports; but this prescription is far too simple to provide a guide through the complexities of input-output relations among industries and the effects of tax policies and concessions on the profitability of production.

A second effect of import-substitution policies frequently overlooked or underestimated in economic development planning and policy is the influence of protection of the domestic market on the market structure and competitive practices of the protected import-competing industry. Such protection provides a foundation for the development of oligopolistic market structures, characterized by non-price competition among a small group. The tendency is reinforced when, as is frequently the case, protective policies encourage the establishment in the country of branch plants and subsidiaries of the giant corporations of the advanced countries, since these corporations characteristically transplant with them both the technology of production and the marketing practice of their home countries, neither of which is well adapted to the factor availabilities and market size and standard of living of the developing countries. The consequence is likely to be both that the underdeveloped economy will suffer the 'wastes of imperfect competition' (which may not be wastes, but rather a reflection of consumer sovereignty, in the advanced countries) and that the protected industries will not become a dynamic source of technical progress and improving productivity, but instead will play a parasitical role in relation to the economy at large. These possibilities have no direct implications for fiscal policy for economic development, though they provide a counter-argument to the 'external economies' and 'infant industry' arguments generally advanced in support of the use of fiscal measures to promote the establishment of import-substituting industries, and suggest the desirability of caution in offering fiscal inducements to import-substitution. Also, they suggest that such inducements should be so designed that they can be partially or wholly withdrawn if they appear to be supporting monopolistic practices; and that the problem of undesirable effects on domestic market structure could be minimized by concentrating fiscal inducements on exporting rather than import-competing industries.

VI. SOME OBSERVATIONS ON POLICY TOWARDS PRIVATE FOREIGN INVESTMENT

Underdeveloped countries pursuing planned economic development, and indeed all countries which suffer from a scarcity of domestic capital for investment in economic growth, typically have ambivalent attitudes towards the investment of foreign private capital in them, and especially towards direct foreign investment. On the one hand, such investment contributes to the country's growth and economic development, not only by providing scarce capital but by serving as a medium for the transmission of modern technology; recognizing these benefits, underdeveloped countries are frequently prepared to offer special tax and other concessions to foreign enterprises willing to establish productive facilities within their borders. On the other hand, national sentiment is disturbed by contemplation of the profits earned by foreigners on these investments, and also by the fact that direct investment gives foreigners 'control' over parts of the national economy. Consequently, economic policy usually seeks to exercise control over such investment and its rewards, by such means as insisting on resident participation in the investment, seeking to have the capital provided as fixed-interest rather than equity investment, and so forth.

The economic policy issues raised by private foreign investment are complex, and extend well beyond balance-of-payments considerations into the fiscal treatment of private investment in general. Only a few brief observations on it will be offered here.

In the first place, a country is virtually certain to derive a substantial net benefit from foreign private investment in it. The reason is that the social benefit from such investment exceeds the private benefit to the investor not only by the theoretically important but difficult-to-quantify effects of investment in raising the marginal productivities of co-operant domestic factors of production and raising the productivity of all factors by increasing the scale of the economy, but also by the tangible and directly observable increase in direct and indirect tax revenues generated by the investment. Foreign private investment in a country, in other words, raises its national income by the value at market prices of the marginal product of the capital and the increase in value at market prices of the marginal products of the domestic factors it employs, whereas the foreign investor receives the value of the marginal product of this capital at factor cost (net of indirect taxes) less the direct taxes he has to pay to the country's government (corporate income tax, non-resident withholding tax). Cases in which a country loses by foreign investment in it are extremely difficult to construct: the main possibilities are that foreign investment in an export industry may increase supply sufficiently to lower the price of the export in the world market enough to reduce domestic real income, and that the profits of the foreign investor may be obtained by exploiting a monopoly position in the domestic market created by the import-substitution policies of the country invested in. The former requires a rather special set of conditions; the latter is within the control of domestic economic policy.

It follows from the general net social profitability of private foreign investment in an underdeveloped country that, on the one hand, restrictions placed on such investment can involve substantial economic loss for the country, and that, on the other hand, there is considerable scope for a country to gain economically by offering special inducements to private foreign investors to invest in it, in the form of lower taxes than are imposed on resident capital. The rationale of discriminating in favour of foreign investors is that resident capital can be taxed regardless of where it is invested, and can be forced into investment within the country, whereas foreign capital can only be taxed if its owners can be induced to invest in the country.

In the second place, from the point of view of dealing with the balance-of-payments problem, there are various reasons for preferring direct investment to fixed-interest investment by foreign capitalists. Apart from the facts that direct investment brings technology and training with it, and that a substantial fraction of the profits it earns is likely to be re-invested in the country more or less automatically, the profits from which earnings are remitted will tend to vary with the level of activity in the country, which in turn will reflect to some extent the strength or weakness of its balance-of-payments situation. Hence the burden on the balance of payments of transferring payment for the services of foreign capital will tend to adjust itself automatically to the capacity to bear it, when foreign capital takes the form of direct investment, whereas the burden of fixed-interest charges on borrowed capital is inflexible. In addition, if the country gets into balance-of-payments difficulties, devaluation will lighten the burden of transfers of income on direct investments, but will not affect the foreign exchange burden of fixed-interest obligations (assuming that capital and interest are denominated in foreign currency).

Thirdly, the fear of foreign 'control', and the desire to prevent it or modify it by insisting on resident participation in the ownership and management of foreign enterprise, would seem in most cases to be concerned with a spurious problem, and the policies to which it gives rise likely to have a nuisance value far in excess of any positive advantages to be derived from them. On the one hand, foreign enterprises are economic organizations, and their profit-maximizing endeavours are likely to serve the national objective of promoting economic efficiency and growth. On the other hand, there is little reason to think that participation in the ownership of foreign enterprises will help to develop domestic entrepreneurial talent or improve the economic performance of the enterprises in question, and some reason to fear that it will have the contrary effects.

CHAPTER IX

IS INFLATION THE INEVITABLE PRICE OF RAPID DEVELOPMENT OR A RETARDING FACTOR IN ECONOMIC GROWTH?*

The question posed in the title of this essay is an apparently simple one, demanding a choice between two widely-held views of inflation. This apparent simplicity, however, is deceptive, and the necessity of choice invalid; for the question exploits the fact that both the word 'inflation' and the word 'development' (or 'growth') have multiple meanings in current discussion. In particular, both may be used to refer either to economic facts or to economic policies; and indeed the first half of the question uses the word 'inflation' to refer to a fact and the second half uses it to refer to a policy (or the outcome of other policies). Furthermore, inflation, defined broadly in the factual sense of an upward trend of prices, includes the possibilities of both mild and rapid, and steady and erratic, upward price movements; and each of these distinctions is connected with important differences in the economic consequences of inflation. It is therefore neither necessary nor correct to regard the two propositions of the question as exclusive alternatives; on the contrary, the two can be discussed virtually independently. In this essay, it will be maintained that a moderate degree of inflation—specifically, inflation at an annual percentage rate that can be counted on the fingers of one or at most two hands— is likely to be an inevitable concomitant of a development policy that seeks efficiently to mobilize an economy's resources

* This paper was prepared for the Third Rehovoth Conference, on Fiscal and Monetary Problems in Developing States, held in Israel in August 1965. It is to be published in the Proceedings of the Conference, and has also been published in *The Malayan Economic Review*, Vol. XI, no. 1, April 1966, pp. 21–28.

for economic growth; but that a policy of deliberately promoting development by inflationary means, though it has theoretical and practical attractions, is likely in fact to retard rather than foster economic growth.

Before entering on these arguments, however, it seems desirable to discuss briefly the naïve interpretation of the question, according to which the problem is whether inflation is associated with rapid or with slow economic growth. The available historical and comparative evidence on this point is fairly conclusive: there is no convincing evidence of any clear association, positive or negative, between the rate of inflation and the rate of economic growth. This is particularly true of the longer-run historical evidence; an impressive contribution in this respect is provided by the recently-published *Monetary History of the United States*, by Friedman and Schwartz,[1] which finds that the United States has grown at relatively high or low rates in periods of both deflation and inflation. Comparative studies based on shorter periods of experience, such as that of the *Commission on Money and Credit*,[2] have tended to find at most a slight inverse association between the rate of economic growth and the rate of inflation *or* deflation among countries, for rates of inflation or deflation lying outside a modal range of zero to low rates of inflation.

The absence of any marked historical association between observed rates of growth and of inflation is only to be expected. In the longer run, one would expect an economy to adjust to whatever rate of monetary growth it experiences largely through price movements, or conversely to adjust its monetary growth to its growth and price trends, depending on whether its exchange rate is variable or fixed. Moreover, it has become increasingly clear that the main determinants of economic growth are to be found in the growth and application of knowledge, through technical and managerial change and the improvement of human capacities, rather than through the saving and investment of capital in the narrow sense. These are aspects of economic life over which monetary developments exercise little

[1] M. Friedman and A. J. Schwartz, *A Monetary History of the United States, 1867–1960*. A study by the National Bureau of Economic Research. (Princeton University Press: Princeton, N.J., 1963.)

[2] Commission on Money and Credit, *Money and Credit: Their Influence on Jobs, Prices and Growth*. (Prentice-Hall: Englewood Cliffs, N.J., 1961.)

direct and obvious influence, except when monetary disturbance —either deflationary or inflationary—disrupts the system of economic organization. For the same reasons one would expect differences between countries to be dominated by social and cultural differences, and cross-country comparisons to provide little clear-cut evidence on the relation between inflation and economic growth, except again for experiences dominated by monetary disturbances.

Historical experience is, however, not a very useful or relevant guide to the issues under discussion, since that experience predominantly reflects the influence of chance or natural developments, whereas contemporary concern with these issues is prompted by the deliberate adoption of policies of manipulating the economic environment so as to mobilize resources for and foster the achievement of economic growth. To be relevant, therefore, historical and comparative analysis would have to go beyond the simple correlation of growth rates and rates of price change, into an analysis that would seek to isolate the influence of inflation on growth from other contemporary growth-promoting or growth-inhibiting influences. In the absence of detailed empirical analysis of this kind, it is necessary to resort to theoretical analysis combined with empirical observation. This is the approach employed in the remainder of this essay.

The first question to be discussed is whether the mobilization of an economy's resources by development policy inevitably involves inflation. It is contended here that some degree of inflation—but a moderate degree only—is the logical concomitant of efficient economic mobilization. The argument rests on two propositions. One is that, so long as inflation proceeds at a rate low enough not to disturb seriously the general confidence in the stability of the value of money, its effects are primarily to redistribute incomes, and to do so to an extent that does not involve serious social consequences, rather than to produce significant misallocations of resources, such as occur when people come to expect inflation and seek to protect themselves from it by holding goods instead of money and by using political means to safeguard their real incomes. The other proposition is that, owing to the various rigidities and immobilities characteristic of any economy, but particularly of underdeveloped economies, upward movements of wages and prices can help to reallocate labour and resources and to draw labour out of traditional or subsistence sectors into the developing sectors of the economy. It is important to notice that this proposition, like the first, presumes a general expectation of stability in the value of money, as a precondition for the offer of higher wages and prices to serve as an inducement to mobility.

The second proposition implies that some inflationary pressure in the economy will assist the task of mobilizing resources for development; the first implies that such inflationary pressure will not introduce offsetting distortions causing significant real losses to the economy as a whole, but will instead mainly involve transfers of income within the economy, the social consequences of which will be small enough to be acceptable. Efficient policy-making will therefore involve arriving at a 'trade-off' between the mobilizing and redistributive effects of inflation that will involve some positive rate of inflation. The indicated optimum rate of inflation is likely to be significantly higher for an underdeveloped than for an advanced economy, for two reasons: first, the sophisticated financial system of an advanced economy provides many more facilities for economizing on the use of money in face of expected inflation; and second, the superior mobility of resources of an advanced economy implies that the increase in total output achievable by inflationary means is relatively much smaller. Thus one might expect that whereas 'tolerable' price stability in an advanced economy is frequently defined as a rate of inflation of no more than one to two per cent a year, the tolerable degree of stability for an underdeveloped economy might be in the range of a four to six per cent annual rate of price increase. (My colleague Arnold Harberger has suggested that a 10 per cent annual rate of inflation represents the outside limit of inflation justifiable by this line of argument.)[1] This analysis, of course, relates to purely domestic considerations and ignores the balance-of-payments or exchange-rate implications of internal price trends.

The foregoing remarks relate to the question of inflation as a

---

[1] Arnold C. Harberger, 'Some Notes on Inflation', in *Inflation and Growth in Latin America*, edited by Werner Baer and Isaac Kerstenetzky. (Irwin & Co.: Homewood, Ill., 1964.)

consequence or aspect of economic development policy, and to the argument that some degree of inflation is the necessary price of rapid development. It has been argued that a modest rate of inflation is a logical part of an efficient development policy, in the sense that the 'price' may purchase gains in efficiency of resource allocation and utilization that outweigh the costs. The argument now turns to the second problem raised by the question, the effectiveness or otherwise of inflationary financing of development programmes.

The deliberate use of inflationary policies to promote economic development has been recommended on theoretical grounds by certain economists; and the fact that many underdeveloped countries have for one reason or another resorted to such policies has led a number of other economists to condone or find merit in inflation as a means to economic development. This paper will not attempt to survey all the theoretical arguments—in particular, it will not go into the structuralist *v.* monetarist debate over inflation in Latin America—but will instead outline the major theoretical and practical arguments for inflation as a means to development, and discuss the major defects of inflationary development policy in practice.

The main theoretical arguments for inflationary development policies derive from two systems of economic thought, the Keynesian theory of income and the quantity theory of money. The Keynesian approach to the question (which derives from the Keynes of the *Tract* and the *Treatise* as much as from the Keynes of the *General Theory*) argues that inflation will promote growth in two ways: by redistributing income from workers and peasants, who are assumed to have a low marginal propensity to save, to capitalist entrepreneurs, who are assumed to have a high marginal propensity to save and invest; and by raising the nominal rate of return on investment relative to the rate of interest, thus promoting investment. Neither of these arguments, however, is either theoretically plausible or consistent with the facts, at least so far as sustained inflationary processes are concerned. Both rest on the arbitrary and empirically unsupported assumption that entrepreneurs realize that inflation is occurring, whereas the other members of the economy do not, or not fully. As to the first, the theoretical prediction is that all sectors of the economy the prices of whose services are upwards-flexible will come to anticipate inflation, so that no significant redistributions of income will take place; and this prediction accords with the mass of the available evidence. As to the second, the theoretical expectation is that free-market interest rates will rise sufficiently to compensate holders of interest-yielding assets for the expected rate of inflation; this expectation also accords with the mass of the available evidence. This argument for inflation, therefore, is valid only in two possible sets of circumstances: first, in the early stages of an inflationary development programme, while the mass of the population (especially the workers and the savers) still has confidence in the stability of the value of money; and secondly, when inflationary financing is accompanied by governmental policies of holding down the wage and interest costs of business enterprise. Such policies would generate distortions in the allocation of resources, which might offset any benefits to growth from the inflationary policy; in particular, the contrary view has been argued that inflation will discourage the supply of saving for investment.

The quantity theory approach, on the other hand, adopts the more realistic assumption that in a sustained inflationary process the behaviour of all sectors of the economy will become adjusted to the expectation of inflation, and that consequently the effect of inflation will be to redistribute income, not from workers or savers to capitalist entrepreneurs, but from the holders of money balances—who are the only losers from an inflation that is anticipated—to the monetary authorities who issue money the real value of which steadily depreciates. Inflation imposes an 'inflationary tax' on holdings of money, which consists in the real resources that the holders of money have to forgo each period in order to restore the real value of their money holdings. The presence of this tax, in turn, encourages the public to attempt to evade the tax by reducing their real holdings of money, by shortening payments periods, holding inventories of goods instead of cash, and so forth; these efforts involve a waste of real resources and a reduction of real income, the 'collection cost' of the inflationary tax. On the other hand, the real resources collected by the inflationary tax are available for use in the development programme; and if they are used for investment, the inflationary policy may accelerate economic growth. It should be noticed, however, that in the transitional stages of an inflationary development policy, or in the process of acceleration of such a policy, whatever contribution to growth there is may be outweighed by the increased waste of resources produced by the increase in the inflationary tax.

In practical experience, resort to the inflationary tax as a method of financing economic development is generally prompted by the inability of the developing country to raise enough revenue by taxation and by borrowing from the public to finance its development plans—either as a result of the low income and taxable capacity of the economy, or more commonly as a result of inability to command the necessary political consensus in support of the necessary sacrifices of current income. Unfortunately, the same characteristics of underdevelopment that limit the capacity to finance development by orthodox fiscal methods also place rather narrow limits on the possibility of financing development by inflation. Especially, underdevelopment implies a relatively smaller use of money than is common in advanced countries, and therefore a relatively smaller base on which the inflationary tax can be levied.

Before discussing this point in detail, it is appropriate to refer to a related question that figured large in the development literature of about a decade ago, the question of the extent to which development can be financed by monetary expansion without producing inflationary consequences. The answer, clearly, is that such financing can be safely pursued up to the limit set by the growth of demand for money consequent on the expected growth of the economy at stable prices, plus the growth of demand for money associated with the monetization of the subsistence sector (where relevant), minus the portion of the growth in the money supply that must be created against private debt. The magnitude of the resources that can be made available for financing development by this means, however, depends on the magnitude of the absolute increase in the money supply permitted by these factors, or to put it another way on the rate of growth of the demand for money, the ratio of money to income, and the portion of the additional money that can be used to finance public spending. Thus, for example, with a rate of growth of demand for money of 6 per cent, half of which can be used to finance public spending, the budget deficit financed by monetary expansion would be 3 per cent of the initial money supply. If the ratio of money supply to national income were in the neighbourhood of 2/5, as is common in advanced countries, this would make 1·2 per cent of national income available for development investment; if, on the other hand, the ratio of money supply to national income were in the lower neighbourhood of 1/5, as is common in under-developed countries, only one half of one per cent of national income would be available for development investment.[1] The difference in the order of magnitude of the money-to-income ratio explains both why budget deficits in underdeveloped countries are more frequently associated with inflation, and why in such countries inflationary financing of development is more frequently resorted to, than in advanced countries.

In the same way as it limits the scope for non-inflationary deficit financing of development, the restricted use of money in underdeveloped countries limits the extent to which inflation can make resources available for economic development through the inflationary tax. Ignoring the possibilities of non-inflationary financing by monetary expansion due to the growth and monetization of the economy, the yield of the inflationary tax as a proportion of national income will be the product of the money-to-income ratio, the rate of inflation, and the proportion of the increase in the money supply captured for financing development. Thus, with the assumed money-to-income ratio of 1/5 and capture rate of 1/2, a 10 per cent rate of inflation would secure 1 per cent of national income for the development programme, and so on. The money-to-income ratio, however, is not insensitive to the rate of inflation, but is on the contrary likely to decrease appreciably as the rate of inflation rises, thereby setting limits to the possibilities of development finance by these means. (Note also that in so far as development financing depends on a growth of demand for money resulting from monetization of the economy, inflation is likely to reduce that growth by inhibiting monetization, so

[1] The illustrative numbers used are derived from J. J. Polak, 'Monetary Analysis of Income Formation and Payments Problems', *International Monetary Fund Staff Papers*, VI, no. 1 (November 1957), pp. 1–50, Table on p. 25.

further reducing the net amount of resources gathered for development finance through inflation.)

In a recent article, Professor R. A. Mundell has used a simple model of inflation, economic growth, and the demand for money to estimate the contribution that inflationary financing might make to economic growth.[1] His results, which are based on rather generous assumptions about the magnitudes of the determinants, designed to produce a maximum estimate, show a maximum inflationary tax yield of 3 per cent of national income and maximum increase in the growth rate of 1·50 per cent on one formulation of the influence of the rate of inflation on the demand for money, and a yield of 3·2 per cent of national income and increase in the growth rate of 0·8 per cent on another.

Contrary to Mundell's own judgment, these are not negligible figures, when compared with the savings ratios and growth rates characteristic of underdeveloped countries. But they are extreme estimates, and likely to exceed substantially the contribution that inflation could make under even the most favourable circumstances.

The circumstances in which inflation is resorted to in underdeveloped countries, however, are far from the most favourable conceivable; and their inflations are extremely likely to proceed in such a way, and to be accompanied by such other economic policies, as to exercise a serious retarding influence on economic growth. Specifically, inflationary financing may impede growth in three major ways, each contrary to the assumptions of the 'inflationary tax' model.

In the first place, contrary to the assumption that prices throughout the economy adjust freely to inflation, the government of a developing country employing inflationary development policies is likely to be under strong political pressure to protect important sectors of the community from the effects of inflation, through control of food prices, rents, urban transport fares, and so on. Such controls inevitably distort the allocation of resources within the economy, and particularly their allocation to private investment in growth. Fixing of low prices for food inhibits the development of agricultural produc-

---

[1] R. A. Mundell, 'Growth, Mobility, and Inflationary Finance', *Journal of Political Economy*, LXXIII, no. 2 (April 1965), pp. 97–109.

tion and the improvement of agricultural technique; control of rents, on the other hand, may unduly foster the construction of new housing to accommodate those who cannot find rent-controlled housing or to enable landlords to evade rent controls. All three policies tend to promote urbanization, which involves expenditure on social overhead and may increase the numbers of the urban unemployed. Moreover, control of prices of food, and particularly of fares on state-owned transport facilities, may involve the state in explicit subsidies on the one hand and budget deficits on the other, so that the proceeds of the inflationary tax are wasted in supporting the consumption of certain sections of the population rather than invested in development. Such phenomena are widely observable in the underdeveloped countries of the world. (They are also observable in advanced countries, but the latter can more easily afford the wastes of resources involved.)

In the second place, contrary to the assumptions of the 'inflation tax' model, inflation typically does not proceed at a steady and well-anticipated rate, but proceeds erratically with large politically-determined variations in the rate of price increase. These variations in the rate of inflation divert a great deal of the effort of private business into forecasting and speculating on the rate of inflation, or hedging against the uncertainties involved. They also destroy the possibility of rational calculation of small margins of profit and undermine the incentives to strive constantly to reduce costs and improve performance, which striving is the key to the steady increase of productivity in the industrially advanced nations.

Finally, the inflation tax model assumes either a closed economy or a country on a floating exchange rate system. In reality, countries—especially underdeveloped countries—are exposed to competition in and from the world economy, yet they display a strong propensity to maintain fixed exchange rates and to defend them to the limit of their exchange reserves, borrowing powers, and ability to use exchange controls. In this kind of setting inflation introduces a progressive tendency toward exchange rate overvaluation, balance-of-payments difficulties, and resort to increasing protectionism, which in turn results in the diversion of resources away from export industries and toward high-cost import-substituting industries, and a consequent loss of economic efficiency. While the appearance of growth may be generated by the establishment of import-substitute industries, the reality may be lost in misallocation of resources produced by protectionism and the inefficiency of exchange control procedures. Moreover, eventually the increasing overvaluation of the currency is likely to force a devaluation, coupled with a monetary reform involving drastic domestic deflation. This experience, in addition to the immediate disturbing effects of deflation in interrupting the growth of the economy, has the long-run effect of damaging the stability and confidence of expectations on which the process of investing in the growth of the economy depends.

To summarize, this essay has argued the following propositions. First, an efficient development policy should plan on some modest degree of inflation as a means of more fully mobilizing the economy's resources; in this limited sense, inflation is an inevitable price of rapid development. Second, while a policy of financing development by deliberate inflation has strong attractions theoretically and politically, the possibilities of stimulating economic development by this means are quite limited. Third, inflationary development policies in practice are unlikely to achieve this stimulating effect, but on the contrary likely to retard economic growth, by distorting the allocation of resources and wasting the inflation-gathered development resources on consumption, by increasing uncertainty and reducing incentives for innovation and improvement, and through their balance-of-payments effects by fostering the inefficiencies of protectionism and exchange control.

CHAPTER X

INTERNATIONAL MONETARY REFORM AND THE LESS DEVELOPED COUNTRIES*

I. INTRODUCTION

The connection between the well-functioning or malfunctioning of the international monetary system and the ease or difficulty of the process of development of the less developed countries is remote, and hence is rarely appreciated by those directly concerned with development problems. On the other hand, the notion that the creation of money entails someone getting something for nothing is only too readily grasped, with the consequence that the growing recognition of the need for reform of the present international monetary system has evoked a host of proposals for such reform designed to capture the 'something for nothing' as additional development assistance for the less developed countries. This essay seeks to contribute to a deeper understanding of the issues involved in international monetary reform as they bear on the problems of the less developed countries. To this end, Section 2 discusses the general interest of the less developed countries in a properly functioning international monetary system, Section 3 describes the nature of the present problem of international monetary reform, and Section 4 analyses various proposals designed to link international monetary reform with the provision of increased development assistance to the less developed countries. Section 5 presents a critical evaluation of the most far-reaching of such proposals, the Hart–Kaldor–Tinbergen proposal for an inter-

* Reprinted from *Economic Policies Towards Less Developed Countries* (Washington; The Brookings Institution, 1967) with the permission of the Brookings Institution Publications Department. An early draft was published in the *Malayan Economic Review*, Vol. XI, no. 1, April 1966, pp. 1–20.

national commodity reserve currency; the amount of space devoted to this scheme is accounted for by the professional eminence of its proponents and the publicity the plan has attracted, and not by any likelihood of its being adopted.

II. THE INTEREST OF THE LESS DEVELOPED COUNTRIES IN A PROPERLY FUNCTIONING INTERNATIONAL MONETARY SYSTEM

A properly functioning international monetary system may be described as one that provides a combination of international liquidity and adjustment mechanisms adequate to permit rectification of balance-of-payments disequilibria without imposing the necessity of severely deflationary policies on the deficit countries or obliging them to resort to balance-of-payments restrictions on current and capital account transactions, and over the long run provides a rate of increase of international liquidity adequate to support a steady growth of world production, trade and payments at levels as close to 'full employment' of world resources as possible. The establishment of such an international monetary system would contribute substantially to the promotion of the economic development of the less developed countries, and particularly to their growth through trade, in two major ways: first, by modifying or removing the need for various balance-of-payments motivated policies of the developed countries that currently impede the development of the less developed countries, and secondly by establishing an international monetary framework within which the natural processes of diffusion of economic development throughout the world economy could operate with maximum force.

Many of the trade and aid policies of the developed countries that impede the efficient development of the less developed countries are directly or indirectly the result of the concern of the former with actual or potential balance-of-payments deficits, a concern aggravated by the deficiencies of the present international monetary system. The outstanding example is the tying of aid to expenditure in the donor country and the various inefficiencies it produces: in the case of the United States, the progressively restrictive tying of aid that has occurred in the past several years has been the direct consequence of the Administration's concern to remedy the country's chronic deficit; in the case of the other donor countries, the protectionist motive for aid-tying probably predominates over the balance-of-payments motive, though the latter motive was strong in the European countries during the dollar-shortage period and probably continues to be influential, especially in the cases of the United Kingdom and France. Apart from motivating the tying of development aid, balance-of-payments considerations undoubtedly operate to reinforce the unwillingness of all the developed countries to expand the scale of the foreign aid they provide to the less developed countries, so that the defects of the present international monetary system may be held partially responsible for the problem of the 'external resources gap' with which UNCTAD was concerned.

Under the present rules governing international economic relations, embodied in GATT and the IMF Charter, protection is to be implemented solely by tariffs; but quantitative import restrictions are sanctioned in cases of balance-of-payments deficits.[1] While GATT principles call for such restrictions to be applied in as non-discriminatory a fashion as possible, and to be removed as soon as the need for them has passed, and GATT has striven with considerable success for the implementation of these principles and particularly for the elimination of European quantitative restrictions established during the dollar-shortage period, there is a strong tendency for such restrictions to be influenced by protectionist considerations and to be perpetuated for the same reason. The use of quantitative restrictions for the correction or prevention of balance-of-payments deficits under the present international monetary system is likely to be especially disadvantageous to the less developed countries for several reasons: first, because in so far

[1] In fact, as evidenced by the vociferous protests evoked by the use of temporary tariff surcharges by Canada in 1962 and Britain in 1964, the paradoxical principle has been established that only tariffs are to be used for permanent restriction of imports, and only quantitative restrictions for temporary restriction of imports. On the face of the matter there is no obvious reason for believing this to be the most efficient deployment of the two instruments for achievement of the relevant policy objectives: temporary tariff surcharges have the advantage over quotas of being more quickly applicable, and of automatically tending to exercise deflationary pressure on the domestic economy through the additional tax revenue collected.

as protectionist considerations influence the design of such restrictions they are likely to be directed against imports in which less developed countries have an actual or potential comparative advantage;[1] second, because such restrictions usually base import quotas on past trade, and so discriminate against new and rapidly expanding sources of supply; and third, because the disruption of trade and the uncertainty associated with the imposition of quantitative restrictions are likely to bear especially heavily on less developed countries owing to their lower degree of diversification with respect to both variety of products and range of alternative markets for particular products.

Balance-of-payments difficulties in the present international monetary system have increasingly generated a third type of governmental intervention in international transactions, in the form of controls over private international capital movements. In the case of the United States, deliberate exception has been made for capital movements to less developed countries, and similar discrimination probably characterizes the capital market policies of the European countries, at least with respect to investment in their former colonies, so that the net effects of the trend towards intervention in private international capital flows for balance-of-payments purposes may actually be to further rather than to impede the development of the less developed countries through private foreign investment. As a general proposition, however, it seems likely that the less developed countries as a group stand to lose rather than to gain from the trend towards reliance on capital market interventions as a means of dealing with balance-of-payments disequilibria, on the grounds that they are likely to lose by any fragmentation of the world economy by the erection of new barriers to international competition.

The considerations outlined in the preceding three paragraphs suggest that the less developed countries would benefit substantially from the establishment of an international monetary system that provided a more adequate combination of liquidity and adjustment mechanisms. The most important contribution that such a system could make would be to remove the inhibitions

[1] Unfortunately, it is very difficult to obtain concrete information on the discriminatory effects of quantitative restrictions, especially as between developed and less developed countries.

to expansion of aid generated by fear of consequent balance of payments difficulties, and to facilitate the untying of aid and the resultant increase in its efficiency. In addition, less developed countries would benefit significantly from the removal of restrictions on international trade and payments now motivated and justified by balance-of-payments difficulties, whose effect is frequently to protect production in the developed countries and to aggravate uncertainty in international trade.

The less developed countries have, however, a far more important interest in the establishment of an international monetary system that would operate in an expansive fashion to promote the growth of world production and trade at high levels of employment and activity, through providing an adequate secular expansion of international liquidity. As the classical economists demonstrated, a competitive international economic system contains various automatic mechanisms that tend to diffuse economic development from the primary centres of growth to the less developed periphery. These mechanisms, which involve the transfer of production of commodities requiring scarce natural resources and of products characterized by high labour-intensity and low technological sophistication from the centre to the periphery, operate with most efficiency—and least impediment from policies of resisting them adopted by the centre countries—in an environment of high employment and steady growth of productivity in the developed countries.

The transmission process is motivated by the pressure of demand in the developed countries and the availability of actual or potential lower-costs supplies in the less developed countries, based on natural resources or the abundance of low-wage labour. Political resistance to the transmission process, expressed in protectionist policies for domestic activities threatened by competition from the less developed countries, is motivated by aversion to loss of income and the costs and uncertainties of conversion of resources to higher-income activities. The maintenance of high levels of employment and activity in the developed countries facilitates the transmission process in two ways: by providing the maximum incentives to develop additional sources of supply in the less developed countries to relieve the pressure of scarcity in the developed countries, and by providing the maximum incentive and opportunity for resources in the developed country activities adversely affected by competition from the less developed countries to move into more lucrative alternative uses rather than to demand protection to reduce or eliminate the pressure for such movement. Conversely, an environment of generally slack demand reduces the incentive to develop new foreign sources of supply, reduces the ability of resources to move out of industries encountering difficulty in competing with foreign producers, and increases both the political pressure for and the political justifiability of protection of such industries.[1]

The less developed countries will obviously benefit from having the process of transmission of economic development operate as efficiently and rapidly as possible. They therefore have a strong interest in the establishment of an international monetary system conducive to the maintenance of full employment in the developed countries and the resolution of international disequilibria by expansion in the surplus countries rather than contraction in the deficit countries. Specifically, they have a particular interest in the establishment of an international monetary system that will expand international liquidity at a rate great enough to impart an inflationary bias to world economic development. This is so for two reasons: first, because (it is generally agreed) some moderate upward trend of prices in a developed country induced by demand pressure facilitates the reallocation of resources and the mobility of labour; and second, because the promotion of planned economic development in the less developed countries tends to generate inflationary price movements there, which price movements tend to cancel out their ability to export unless offset by price increases in the developed countries to which they export.

[1] In a full employment environment, resources tend automatically to move out of inefficient low-income industries, and the wasteful effects of protectionism become apparent to and are given political expression by the efficient high-income industries whose expansion is hampered by the general scarcity of resources; thus the demand for protection tends to be undermined both economically and politically. In an under-employed economy, by contrast, resources tend to stay in the inefficient low-income industries, providing economic justification for demands for protection, while the availability of resources to the efficient high-income industries gives the latter no reason to oppose demands for protection by the former.

III. THE PROBLEM OF INTERNATIONAL MONETARY
REFORM

The International Monetary Fund was intended by the planners of postwar reconstruction of the international economy to provide a monetary framework for a liberal international trade and payments system that would be free of the defects of the gold exchange standard of the interwar period that eventually precipitated the collapse of the international monetary system in the 1930's. Specifically, the International Monetary Fund was intended to supplement the world's inadequate supplies of monetary gold with international liquidity in the form of drawing rights on the Fund proportioned to the various countries' importance in international commerce; to provide an effective mechanism of international adjustment through internationally agreed and accepted changes in the exchange rates of countries suffering from 'fundamental disequilibrium' in their balances of payments; and to distribute the burden of adjustment more fairly between surplus and deficit countries by means of the 'scarce currency' clause, sanctioning discrimination by deficit countries against countries in chronic balance-of-payments surplus.

In the course of the postwar evolution of the international economy, however, the International Monetary Fund has been thrust from its intended central position in the international monetary system by the growing use of the US dollar as an international monetary reserve supplementary to gold, and the development of a dollar-exchange standard similar to the sterling-exchange standard that worked successfully up to the First World War only to collapse so disastrously in the interwar period. This development has been an unintended but natural consequence of the dominance of the United States in the world economy in the period since the Second World War, and particularly of the role of the United States in the prolonged period of dollar shortage as chief world trader and source of external capital for reconstruction and development.

With the emergence of the dollar-exchange standard and the establishment of the United States as the central reserve currency country of the international monetary system, the international liquidity provided through the International Monetary Fund has been relegated to a role secondary to *ad hoc* arrangements between the United States and the major European countries important in international finance; for a variety of reasons the other leading countries have become increasingly reluctant to contemplate altering their exchange rates, while the reserve-currency role of the dollar is assumed to preclude alteration of its exchange value, so that in practice the significant exchange rates have become rigid and alterations of them ruled out as a method of adjustment of balance-of-payments disequilibria; and the scarce currency clause has become a dead letter, while the appropriate division of the burden of adjustment between debtor and creditor countries has become the subject of increasingly acrimonious dispute among the countries concerned.

Like the sterling standard before it, the dollar standard in the postwar period has made an important contribution to the growth of the world economy by providing a reasonably stable monetary environment for the conducting of international trade and payments on an increasingly liberal basis. With the successful reconstruction of Europe, culminating in the establishment of the European Common Market, and the emergence of the United States after 1957 as a country in serious chronic balance-of-payments deficit, however, the dollar exchange standard has been increasingly subject to internal strains, which have led both academic observers and officials concerned with the operation of the system to fear that it may collapse in the same way as its predecessor gold exchange standard, to believe that the system is in need of fundamental reform, and to advance proposals for basic changes in international monetary organization.

It is commonly agreed by international monetary experts[1] that the present dollar exchange standard suffers from three major problems: the confidence problem, the liquidity problem, and the adjustment problem. The confidence problem derives from the fact that the use of the dollar as an international reserve in substitution for gold is currently conditional on its

[1] See especially Fritz Machlup and Burton G. Malkiel (eds.), *International Monetary Arrangements: The Problem of Choice*, report on the deliberations of an international study group of thirty-two economists (Princeton, N.J.: Princeton University Press, 1964).

convertibility into gold by central bank holders, and the likelihood that any large-scale attempt to convert dollars into gold would, by threatening the exhaustion of US gold reserves, precipitate a collapse of confidence in the dollar that would wipe out international liquidity and completely disrupt international trade and payments. The fact that the power to precipitate such a collapse lies in the hands of the central banks of countries other than the United States (and the United Kingdom, which plays a similar role as a secondary reserve-currency centre) has made the continued operation of the system dangerously dependent on voluntary co-operation among national central banks, and (especially since early 1965) vulnerable to tactics of non-co-operation designed to put pressure on the United States to follow balance-of-payments policies desired by the European surplus countries.

The liquidity problem is the problem of providing for the long-run stable growth of international reserves required to support the steady expansion of international trade and payments associated with the normal growth of the world economy. This problem has two aspects. First, if the required rate of growth of international reserves exceeds the rate of growth of monetary gold stocks provided by the mining of new gold, making up the difference by a more rapid expansion of outstanding holdings of the reserve currency implies either that the reserve currency country suffer a progressive reduction of the ratio of its gold reserves to the claims on those reserves held by other countries (in the form of reserve holdings of its currency) or that the other countries progressively increase the ratio of their reserve currency holdings to their gold reserves, or both. The former alternative involves a progressive weakening of the international liquidity of the reserve currency country and increasing danger of loss of confidence in the reserve currency; the latter alternative involves a progressive sacrifice of the monetary autonomy of the non-reserve-currency countries and acceptance of international monetary management by the reserve-currency country. Second, within limits set by the ability of the non-reserve-currency countries to discipline the reserves currency country by using their option to convert its currency into gold without precipitating a crisis of confidence, the rate of growth of international liquidity is governed by the balance-of-payments deficits of the reserve currency country, and (depending on that country's policies) may be too large or too small for stability and may fluctuate in a destabilizing fashion. This problem is especially acute when, as has been the case for the past eight years, the reserve currency country runs an abnormally large deficit: the international monetary implications of an unduly small deficit or a surplus could be counteracted by purchases of non-reserve currency assets by the central bank or Treasury of the reserve currency country.

The third problem of the present international monetary system is the adjustment problem: the problem of correcting, by automatic processes or policy measures, the economic forces that give rise to international monetary disequilibrium. This problem is essentially the other side of the coin to the confidence and liquidity problems, since the more promptly adjustment can be effected the less the danger of loss of confidence in the deficit country's currency and the less the need for liquidity to finance transitional deficits (and the less the need for growth of liquidity to finance prospectively larger future deficits). Fundamentally, adjustment of international disequilibria means the alignment of a country's prices and costs with those of other countries so as to make its products competitive enough with those of other countries in the world and its domestic market to enable it to finance its capital exports by a current account surplus or finance its current account deficit by normal capital imports.[1]

The rigidification of exchange rates under the present international monetary system, associated with the emergence of the dollar as central reserve currency, has ruled out the resort to exchange rate changes in cases of fundamental disequilibrium envisaged in the design of the International Monetary Fund. The effective alternatives are, first, the classical gold-standard mechanism of inflation in the surplus country and deflation in the deficit country, and second, the use of interventions in international trade and payments to suppress the manifestation

[1] Much analytical confusion has been engendered by the practice in international financial and policy-making circles of regarding both special intergovernmental capital transactions and interferences with private capital move-motivated by the existence of international monetary disequilibrium as measures of balance-of-payments 'adjustment'. Such measures are not 'adjustment', but stop-gaps for 'financing' disequilibrium pending its adjustment by other means.

of the need for adjustment in international monetary disequilibrium, pending solution of the adjustment problem by automatic forces coming into play with the passage of time, coupled with domestic measures to increase international competitiveness. The use of the gold-standard mechanism, however, is severely limited by the adoption in the major countries of the policy objectives of full employment and price stability, which leads deficit countries to resist deflation and surplus countries to resist inflation. The result is sharp controversy between the two parties to international disequilibrium over the equitable distribution of the burden of adjustment, a controversy exacerbated by the fact that in the disequilibrium of recent years the surplus European countries have had strong historical reasons for disliking inflation, while the deficit United States has had equally strong reasons for disliking abnormally high unemployment; both attitudes derive from interwar experience, and their effect has been to make each party unsympathetic to the policy restraints encumbering the other. In effect, adjustment under the present international monetary system depends on the inability of the policy-makers in the surplus country to resist inflationary pressure and of the policy-makers in the deficit country to maintain employment at the desired level. This mechanism of reluctant adjustment is bound to take considerable time and to generate continual mutual recrimination, while the size of the payments imbalances involved in the process of slow adjustment inevitably exerts pressure for the increasing use of interventions in international trade and payments to reduce the magnitudes of deficit and surpluses, and especially for the use of restraints and controls on private capital movements.

These defects of the present international monetary system have led both academic economic experts and public personages eminent in the international financial world to put forward plans for the reform of the system designed to cope with one or more of the major problems. Broadly speaking, these plans fall into two alternative categories: proposals to substitute for the present system an automatic self-regulatory system, either by returning to the classical gold standard or by adopting a regime of floating exchange rates, and proposals for reforming the existing system to improve its functioning. The former type of proposal has not received serious consideration and is unlikely to do so, even though early in 1965 President de Gaulle of France denounced the financial power that the present system gives to the reserve-currency countries and called for a return to the gold standard. Among the latter group of proposals, the two alternatives under active discussion are concerned with the reform of the provision of international liquidity, and hence with the liquidity and confidence problems; they are not concerned with improvement of the mechanism of international adjustment, except indirectly in so far as the crux of the debate between their proponents is the distribution of the responsibility for and burden of adjustment between deficit and surplus countries.

The two alternatives in question, favoured respectively by the United States and the United Kingdom and by the Common Market Countries (especially France), are to increase the powers of the International Monetary Fund to provide international liquidity, and to create a new type of international reserve asset outside the International Monetary Fund, in the form of a 'composite reserve unit' made up of the currencies of the major countries in fixed ratios, which these countries would be obliged to hold in a more or less fixed ratio to their gold reserves.[1] Both would diminish the reserve-currency roles of

[1] Under the former scheme, the confidence problem would be mitigated because the growth of reserves in the form of IMF liabilities rather than dollar and sterling balances would avoid the progressive weakening of the liquidity positions of the reserve-currency countries mentioned above; the long-run liquidity problem would be solved by regular increases in the Fund's liabilities. (Under the more sweeping version of this alternative advocated by some academic experts—to convert the IMF into a World Central Bank, the confidence problem would be eliminated by converting existing holdings of reserve currencies into liabilities of the International Monetary Fund, and gradually liquidating the corresponding dollar and sterling assets; the long-run liquidity problem would be taken care of by appropriate secular expansion of aggregate Fund liabilities through open market operations.) Under the latter scheme, the confidence problem would be eliminated by fixing the ratios to gold holdings of the various national currencies held as reserves, and the long-run liquidity problem would be dealt with by periodic increases in the amount of composite reserve units and in the ratio of these to gold reserves required.

Both proposals, by removing the confidence problem, would facilitate adjustment to international disequilibrium by means of exchange rate changes, especially by changes in the values of the present reserve currencies, the dollar and the pound. Such changes would merely require compensatory transfers of the currency whose value was changed to or from the International Monetary Fund or the holders of composite reserve units.

the dollar and the pound and 'internationalize' the use of credit money as a substitute for gold, the former indirectly by providing an explicitly international form of credit in substitution for or supplementation of dollars and sterling, the latter directly by sharing the role of international reserve currency between these currencies and the other major national currencies. The significant difference between the two proposals, a difference which reflects the divergent interests of their proponents, is that the former would entail an extension of international control of the international monetary system through the International Monetary Fund, which as presently constituted is dominated by the United States and in which the less developed countries have representation, whereas the latter would increase the dependence of the system on collaboration and agreement among the leading nations of the international economy, which would have to agree on the amount and rate of increase of the stock of composite reserve units and the ratio to gold in which they would be held. In particular, the need for agreement would enable the Common Market countries to insist on sufficient limitation of the stock of composite reserve units to force the deficit country (i.e., the United States) to assume the major part of the burden of adjustment by following deflationary domestic policies. (In European thinking, in fact, the composite reserve unit plan is envisaged as a way of raising the price of gold among the advanced countries—by tying the purchase of gold to a parallel purchase of composite reserve units—and restoring the discipline of the gold standard.)

The choice between these two alternatives is therefore effectively a choice between an international monetary system that places a major responsibility for adjustment on the surplus country, and one which places major responsibility for adjustment on the deficit country—essentially, a choice between a more expansive and a less expansive international monetary system than the present one. The choice evidently will be determined by negotiations among the developed countries, negotiations in which the less developed countries will have little or no participation and over whose outcome they can exercise little influence. Nevertheless, as explained in the preceding section, a decision to reform the international monetary system along the more expansive rather than the less expansive line could make a substantial difference for the prospects of economic growth of the less developed countries, and especially for their prospects of development through trade. This is—or should be—a relevant consideration for the developed countries engaged in the negotiation of international monetary reform.

IV. PROPOSALS FOR REFORMING THE INTERNATIONAL MONETARY SYSTEM IN WAYS THAT WOULD PROVIDE ADDITIONAL ECONOMIC AID TO THE LESS DEVELOPED COUNTRIES

The fact that both the need for reform of the international monetary system and the need of the less developed countries for increased external resources for development have simultaneously become increasingly apparent in the past six years or so has led a number of economists and international monetary experts to devise and recommend schemes for international monetary reform that attempt to solve both problems simultaneously, by channelling the real saving implicit in the expansion of international liquidity to the less developed countries. Frequently the recommendation of such schemes is based on the notion that it is somehow unfair to the less developed countries to reform the international monetary system without designing the reform specifically to benefit the less developed countries, on the implicit assumption or explicit assertion that such reforms benefit only the developed countries and even in some unspecified sense damage the less developed countries.

On the face of the matter, there is no obvious advantage, and much evident and avoidable complexity, in attempting to solve two different and incommensurable problems with one and the same institutional change; and there is good reason to suspect that the proponents of these schemes have essentially been attempting to use the need for reform of the international monetary system as a lever to obtain by subterfuge additional aid for the less developed countries that the developed countries would be unwilling to grant explicitly as such. Nor is the assertion that reforms that do not explicitly and directly benefit the less developed countries are inequitable at all convincing.

In the first place, while most people's ethics would protest a change that benefited the developed countries at the expense of the less developed, it is ethically far more debatable to protest a change that would benefit the developed countries without harming the less developed countries,[1] let alone one that would, as argued in the preceding section, benefit the less developed countries as well. In the second place, to judge plans for reform only on the criterion of direct contribution to the less developed countries is to confuse efficiency considerations with distributional considerations, and to ignore the fact that the economically most efficient solution to a problem will provide the maximum saving of resources and the maximum possibility of compensation to the less developed countries for any losses they might incur, or of additional transfers of external resources to them. In the third place, the question of direct benefit to less developed countries may be irrelevant or misleading, since if the developed countries so desired they could offset any such direct benefit by other policy changes, for example by reducing their bilateral or multilateral foreign aid or by increasing their trade barriers.

These proposals, therefore, merit consideration only on one of two alternative criteria: either that they represent a superior solution to rival reform schemes, judged from the point of view of the requirements of international monetary reform, or that they are more likely to be acceptable as means of providing additional external resources and other benefits to less developed countries than alternative direct schemes of achieving the same results. The second of these criteria involves the imponderabilities of political feasibility; but some analysis of the effectiveness of the schemes in achieving their objectives is possible.

The proposals in question fall into two broad classes: a variety of schemes for providing the additional liquidity required by an expanding world economy through loans to the less developed countries, so that the real savings involved in the growth of the international reserves of the developed countries would

---

[1] This statement needs qualification to the extent that less developed countries accumulate international reserves over time, and these reserves would be backed by liabilities of the developed countries; the magnitudes involved, however, are not such as to make this a significant source of inequity for the less developed countries.

be automatically channelled into external capital assistance for the less developed countries; and the Hart–Kaldor–Tinbergen commodity reserve currency plan, under which the real savings involved in the growth of international liquidity would be invested in the accumulation of stocks of primary products, mostly produced by the less developed countries. Unlike the first class of scheme, however, which simply attempts to graft a requirement of additional aid to less developed countries onto reform schemes of the kind that are currently being discussed, the Hart–Kaldor–Tinbergen scheme proposes a fundamental transformation of the present international monetary system rather than a modified version of the alternatives discussed in Section I, a transformation that is derived from fundamental monetary theory. For this reason, discussion of that scheme is assigned to a separate section.

Discussion of proposals in the first category is most conveniently approached by considering first the more imaginative and visionary proposals for international monetary reform proposed by non-official writers, and then the possibilities of the type of reform scheme actively under consideration by international monetary officials.

The objection to current reform proposals that underlies the advocacy of schemes of the first type is that these proposals would provide additional liquidity against assets consisting of the liabilities of the developed countries, so that the implicit savings would be channelled to the developed countries which would be accumulating the liquidity. This would be directly the case under the composite reserve unit plan, and would also be the case if additional Fund liabilities for use as reserve assets by the leading developed countries were created for them against deposits of their own currencies, as proposed for example in the Roosa plan.[1] It would also be likely to be the case, indirectly, under proposals for converting the International Monetary Fund into a world central bank operating on traditional central banking lines, since following sound banking principles such a bank would conduct its open market operations

[1] Robert V. Roosa, *Monetary Reform for the World Economy*, New York, Harper & Row [1965].

For a critique of this plan, see Harry G. Johnson, 'Roosa on International Monetary Reform', *The National Banking Review*, Vol. 3, no. 2 [December 1965], 182–92.

in the securities markets of the developed countries. To avoid this allegedly undesirable feature, this group of plans envisages creating international liquidity directly against loans or grants to the less developed countries.

An alternative and more illuminating way of putting the objection, which avoids the 'something-for-nothing' overtones of the concept of 'implicit savings' inherent in the creation of international reserves, and also explains why the developed countries concerned with international monetary reform have not found it particularly persuasive, is as follows. If the developed countries were to pool contributions of their own currencies to back a new international reserve unit (whether inside or outside the International Monetary Fund does not matter) and were then to withdraw amounts of the new reserve unit exactly equal to their individual contributions of national currencies, international liquidity would be created at no cost in real resources to, and with no need for real saving by, anyone. The 'implicit saving' involved in holding the additional international reserves would be exactly matched by the 'implicit dissaving' involved in creating the domestic currency for deposit in the pool. The objection consists in asserting that this procedure would be unfair to the less developed countries whose currencies are unacceptable to the developed countries as backing for the new international reserve unit, and that instead these countries should receive the new international money in the first instance (or the contributions of national moneys) so that the developed countries would be obliged to earn back the new liquidity from them through balance-of-payments surpluses. This would entail the necessity of real saving by the developed countries, to match the real investment by the less developed countries that would be financed by the new money creation. The schemes proposed aim in one way or another to achieve this result, by creating new international liquidity directly or indirectly against loans or grants to the less developed countries.

An early proposal along these lines was the first Stamp Plan,[1] according to which less developed countries would be given

[1] For description and discussion of this and alternative plans, see Herbert Grubel (ed.), *World Monetary Reform: Plans and Issues* (Stanford: Stanford University Press, 1963).

certificates representing purchasing power that could be used for development expenditures in the developed countries, which certificates the developed countries would agree to regard as international reserves for the purpose of settlement of payments imbalances among themselves. This plan had a number of obvious defects, stemming from ambiguity about which countries would have to agree to accept the certificates and whether they would be convertible into gold at the International Monetary Fund or not. Essentially, the certificates would have been a means of providing additional aid tied to purchase in the participating developed countries, or the equivalent of a grant of aid from the International Monetary Fund; in either case, the international monetary effects could have been achieved much more efficiently by other means, while the advantages to the less developed countries depended on the developed countries being willing to give aid in this form but not in others.

The proposal to convert the International Monetary Fund into a world central bank, advocated in various forms by a variety of writers, offers a much superior opportunity to channel additional liquidity into aid for the less developed countries. The extent of the opportunity would depend, however, on how far the liabilities of the world central bank merely supplemented in contrast to replacing gold as an international reserve money. If gold were to be completely replaced, and the world central bank's liabilities become the ultimate international reserve, there would be no economic restrictions on the assets that it could purchase to increase its liabilities,[1] and it would be free to lend or even make grants to the less developed countries as it desired. If, on the other hand, the liabilities of the World Bank were substitutes for gold, and countries were free to convert their holdings of these liabilities into gold if they so desired, the bank would have to manage its asset portfolio so as to maintain the confidence of its (national) customers in its liquidity. This would in all likelihood prevent it from giving

---

[1] Since an ultimate reserve money cannot be exchanged with its issuer for any other form of money, the issuer need hold marketable assets only to the extent that it envisages desiring to reduce the amount of its liabilities outstanding. The bank's management, however, might restrict its assets to particular types for political or conservative reasons, or be obliged to do so by the representatives of the national states on its directorate.

grants to the less developed countries (though it could probably get away with some concessional loans) and restrict its freedom to purchase the securities of less developed country governments. It could however probably invest a significant part of its funds in securities issued by the International Bank for Reconstruction and Development and by the growing number of regional development banks or by the International Development Association, as proposed by Stamp in a revision of his original proposal, and so long as it kept a substantial proportion of its resources in securities readily marketable in the developed countries it could channel much of the annual increment of its resources into external assistance for the less developed countries. This procedure is the one most commonly suggested by those who would like to combine international monetary reform with additional aid to the less developed countries. With international monetary reserves currently in the neighbourhood of $70 billion, an increase in international liquidity at the rate of 3 per cent per year could channel a maximum of $2·1 billion, and at the rate of 5 per cent a year $3·5 billion, of new loans to the less developed countries; these figures of course substantially overstate the net resource transfer involved, which would depend on the interest rate and repayment period of the loans.

The foregoing discussion, however, assumes that the aid policies of the developed countries are independent of the operations of the world central bank, so that whatever aid would be channelled by the latter to the less developed countries would be a net addition to their aid receipts. Since in the real world the left hand usually knows full well what the right hand is doing (though it may not admit it in public), this is an unrealistic assumption. A more realistic view suggests two points for consideration: first, if the management of the World Bank attempted to give more aid than the developed countries thought desirable, the latter could offset the efforts of the former by reducing the aid they contributed through other routes; and second, even if none of the annual increase in international liquidity was channelled to the less developed countries through portfolio investment by the world central bank, the latter could nevertheless play an important role in increasing the flow of aid by confining its security purchases to the public debt of developed countries that agreed to match such purchases by increasing their bilateral or multilateral aid to the less developed countries.

The proposals currently under discussion for expanding liquidity through the International Monetary Fund, however, stop far short of transforming that institution into a world central bank, and hence do not encounter the problem of whether or not the new reserve assets created at the Fund would constitute an ultimate reserve money or be convertible into gold and national reserve currencies. Instead, they envisage the creation of a carefully limited type of secondary international reserve asset, that would be either convertible at the Fund into currencies supplied to the Fund by participating developed countries under lines of credit, or transferable directly between participating countries within quantitative limits as to the amounts countries would be obliged to accept, or transferable in fixed proportion to other types of international reserve assets, on the lines of the composite reserve unit proposal. Under any of these alternative arrangements, the liquidity of the assets held by the Fund against the new monetary liability would be in principle a relatively unimportant consideration, and it would be quite feasible to invest a substantial proportion of these assets in development lending, either directly or through the World Bank.[1]

Like the more comprehensive plans for international monetary reform discussed above, however, a scheme to channel resources to the less developed countries in this way would be successful in increasing the overall flow of development assistance only if the developed countries participating in it were 'irrational', in the sense either of failing to appreciate that the scheme would impose on them a tax for the finance of development in no way necessary to the objective of increasing international liquidity, or in the sense of being willing to give in this covert form development assistance that they would not be

[1] A carefully considered proposal along these lines has been made by the expert group convened by the Secretary-General of UNCTAD in the autumn of 1965; the proposal envisages the creation of Fund Units against the deposit of national currencies, and the investment of the whole of the currencies so deposited in IBRD bonds. See 'International Monetary Issues and the Developing Countries,' United Nations Conference on Trade and Development, Doc. TD/B/C.3/6, November 1 1965.

willing to give overtly as bilateral or multilateral aid. Moreover, for reasons inherent in the secondary nature of the reserve assets in question, the amount of development assistance so made available might be both erratic and substantially smaller than might appear from prospective liquidity needs as they appear at present. The reason is that the amount of such new assets created would presumably be what was considered necessary to fill the gap between the growth of international liquidity requirements and the growth of the combined total of gold stocks and reserve currency holdings. Changes in confidence in the reserve currencies could make the gap to be filled vary erratically, while a recovery of confidence in the dollar and the pound consequent on the improvement of the balance-of-payments positions of the US and the UK could lead to a sufficiently rapid growth of holdings of reserve currencies to obviate the need for creation of supplementary new international reserve assets.[1]

V. THE COMMODITY RESERVE CURRENCY PROPOSAL

The commodity reserve currency proposal of Hart, Kaldor and Tinbergen[2] starts from a rejection of three alternative reforms of the international monetary system. Extension of the key-currency system is rejected on grounds of the difficulty of making additional reserves practically available[3] and the

[1] It is true, as the UNCTAD Expert Group argues in its Report, that erratic variations in the rate of creation of Fund Units could be smoothed out in the flow of development finance, and so need constitute no serious problem in that context. However, in so far as the purpose of the creation of Fund Units is to stabilize the growth of the world economy by stabilizing the rate of growth of its international money supply, stabilization of the rate of release of the national currencies deposited in exchange for Fund Units to the less developed countries could have destabilizing effects on world growth. These would result from the temporary sterilization of these funds when an abnormally large increase in secondary liquidity was required for world stability, and the release of previously sterilized funds when an abnormally small increase in secondary liquidity was required.

[2] 'The Case for an International Commodity Reserve Currency', United Nations Conference on Trade and Development, E/Conf. 46/P/7, February 17, 1964.

[3] The argument here relies on the 'dilemma-of-the-deficit' reasoning outlined in Section 1: that for its currency to be acceptable as an international reserve money a country's balance-of-payments position must be 'strong', yet for the

dependence of the system on confidence among the reserve currency countries in each others' domestic and balance-of-payments policies. Establishment of a credit-creating world central bank is rejected on the grounds that it would conflict with national sovereignty, both because countries would have to maintain confidence in each others' willingness to abide by the agreement setting up the bank and because the bank would have sovereign powers to place the real resources of one country at the command of another through its credit operations, and that therefore the bank would inevitably operate conservatively and for the benefit of the advanced industrial countries to the neglect of the less developed countries. Revaluation of gold is rejected on the usual grounds that it would have to be large to be successful, would increase the costs of operating the international monetary system, would shower uncovenanted gains on a few countries, and would not be justified because the price of gold is already maintained artificially.[1]

Instead of these three alternatives, the authors propose an ingenious scheme under which the International Monetary Fund would be converted into a world central bank whose liabilities would be backed (in addition to a fiduciary issue) by gold and by warehouse receipts for a bundle of primary commodities whose aggregate value (not the prices of the individual commodities) would be stabilized in terms of gold by the Fund's open market operations. Under the scheme,

available supply of its currency to expand its balance-of-payments position must be 'weak' (in the sense of requiring a deficit). This reasoning obviously applies only to a 'natural' development of a currency as an international reserve money, and the difficulty could be avoided by international agreement as in the composite reserve unit scheme, under which countries would simply swap their own currencies for an equal amount of reserves, with no effect or a strengthening effect on their balances of payments, depending on the accounting conventions used to define the latter.

[1] As Harrod in particular has pointed out ('A Plan for Increasing Liquidity: A Critique', *Economica*, Vol. XXVIII, no. 110 [May 1961], 195–202, a review of Robert Triffin, *Gold and the Dollar Crisis* [New Haven: Yale University Press, 1960]), many of these arguments are beside the point, in the sense that they object to features of the proposal that are incidental to its main purpose of strengthening the international monetary system; in addition, most of them —especially the cost of operation—apply with as much or greater strength to the commodity reserve currency plan, unless one shares the authors' view that uncovenanted and arbitrarily distributed benefits secured at considerable cost to the world as a whole are to be welcomed if the beneficiaries are less developed countries but not if they are gold-producing countries.

existing holdings of reserve currencies would be liquidated by sales of stockpiled commodities and gold by the reserve currency countries to the Fund, and all countries would therefore become free to alter the rate of exchange between their currencies and 'bancor' (the Fund's liability). The scheme would therefore contribute to the solution of the confidence and adjustment problems in the same way as the more orthodox proposal for a world central bank. The fundamental difference lies in the provision of liquidity, especially in the context of secular growth.

On behalf of the commodity reserve currency plan, as against the proposal for a discretionarily-managed world central bank, it is argued, first, that the automaticity of the plan would avoid the conflicts of national sovereignty with respect to the latter's credit operations mentioned above, and so presumably make the plan more acceptable to the developed countries; and second, that the stabilization of commodity prices in terms of gold would have great economic advantages to both the less developed and the developed countries.

The argument on the second score derives from a long-recognized feature of the gold standard, which has provided the rationale for commodity reserve currency schemes past and present: that any commodity reserve standard tends automatically to stabilize the prices of commodities in general, since a rise in such prices relative to the commodity tends to reduce production of the standard commodity, contract the money supply, and force down prices of other goods, and conversely a fall in such prices tends to be counteracted by the monetary expansion consequent on increased production of the standard commodity. This mechanism operates, it is important to note, in two ways: directly by affecting the generation of income through stimulating or depressing output of the standard commodity, and indirectly by affecting demand for output through alteration of the money stock; a credit-money standard operates only in the latter way, by discretionary management of the stock of money. The difficulty with the gold standard is that the existing stock is extremely large relative to the flow of new production and that non-monetary demand for current output is small relative to the monetary demand, so that the stabilization mechanism works extremely slowly.

The argument for broadening the gold standard to include a range of primary commodities important in world production and trade is that large current production relative to stocks, and large non-monetary demand relative to monetary demand, would make the stabilization mechanism operate rapidly.

To this consideration the authors add another argument, that the scheme would promote world economic growth. This argument rests on an asserted empirical asymmetry in the mechanism of world economic growth, and an assertion that the commodity reserve currency plan would overcome this asymmetry. The empirical proposition is that the rate of growth of world manufacturing production exerts a strong influence on the prices of primary products and hence on the rate of growth of primary production, but that there is no mechanism by which an increase in the rate of growth of primary production calls forth an increase in the rate of growth of industrial production: while an increase in primary production permits an expansion of industrial production, the resulting fall in primary product prices reduces demand for industrial products and on balance tends to depress the world economy and retard its growth. The commodity reserve currency plan would, it is argued, by maintaining primary commodity prices and thereby increasing the incomes of primary producers through stockpiling, inject the required additional demand for industrial products into the system and promote its growth.

In the contrary case in which commodity prices were rising and sales of primary commodities from stocks were depressing the world economy (a case which the authors regard as much less likely, and against which they provide certain safeguards by asymmetries in the rules governing eligibility of commodities for the plan),[1] the authors argue that the depressive effects could be avoided by devaluation of the currencies of the developed countries. The same remedy is recommended for an adverse movement of the terms of trade between primary products and manufactures produced by excessive wage increases in the developed manufacturing countries.[2]

[1] Especially, commodities whose prices rise more than 50 per cent above the initial standard price are automatically excluded from the reserve, while the prices of included commodities may fall indefinitely without leading to exclusion.

[2] The argument of the authors is marred here as elsewhere by a tendency to confuse money prices with relative prices, and to treat money wages in the

The empirical asymmetry on which this argument is based obviously assumes a naïve Keynesian model of the world economy in which less developed countries spend all they earn, whereas the developed countries allow their output of manufactures to respond passively to the demand for it. If the developed countries used fiscal and monetary policy to maintain full employment, adjusting their exchange rates as necessary to maintain international equilibrium, the asymmetry and its retarding effects on economic growth would not arise. The solution to the authors' problem is therefore to establish a properly functioning international monetary system as defined in the previous section, not necessarily to adopt their scheme for forcing full employment through the operation of the buffer stock. It is a striking pecularity of the authors' argument that they assume that developed countries will follow rational economic policies in the face of primary commodity prices rising due to excess demand or falling (relatively) due to excess wage increases in the developed countries, but will not follow a rational economic policy in the face of commodity prices falling due to excess supply.[1]

Leaving aside the question of promotion of world growth, on which the authors' arguments are not particularly persuasive, the commodity reserve currency plan is open to a number of well-known practical and theoretical objections.

developed countries as being determined autonomously without reference to productivity and the level of unemployment.

[1] The economic irrationality of the authors' world is further exemplified by their assertion (*op. cit.*, p. 34) that under their scheme devaluation would directly change the terms of trade between manufactures and primary products, whereas under the present system devaluation would leave unchanged the relation between primary product prices and industrial countries' wages. Neither proposition is in general correct. This scheme stabilizes the money prices of primary products, not the terms of trade between these products and manufactures; and while the devaluation of a manufacturing country's currency would initially lower the world-market price of its manufactures relatively to the average price of primary products, it might produce a subsequent inflation of domestic wages and prices sufficient to restore the previous terms of trade. Under the present system, such a devaluation would alter the relation between the devaluing country's wages and primary product prices in the world market, providing that a subsequent inflation of domestic wages sufficient to offset the devaluation did not occur. Note that the assumption of unchanged money wages in the devaluing country required to make the first proposition valid would invalidate the second proposition, while the assumption of a compensating wage inflation required to make the second proposition valid would invalidate the first proposition.

The first set of practical objections concerns the extent to which the scheme would really contribute to the welfare and development of the less developed countries. The scheme would stabilize the average money price of the commodities included under it; but it is self-evident that this is by no means equivalent to stabilizing either the average purchasing power of the commodities over manufactured goods, or the average money or real incomes of the producers or the export earnings of the producing countries. Moreover, since it is the average price of the commodities and not their individual prices that will be stabilized, by purchases or sales of commodities in the fixed ratios composing the bundle, the scheme could well destabilize the prices of particular commodities important to particular countries, that happened to be falling while the average price of a bundle was rising or vice versa. Further, the effects of open market operations on the prices of particular commodities would depend on the elasticities of demand for and supply of them, so that such operations might produce sharp variations in the pattern of commodity price relationships disturbing to their suppliers and users.

A particularly relevant point in this connection is that, since its aim is to stabilize money prices of commodities, the scheme would do little to counteract the alleged long-run tendency of the terms of trade to turn against primary products, which the authors imply is one of its purposes. Generally speaking, that tendency (if it exists) would merely assert itself in a long-run upward trend of the money prices of manufactures, instead of a downward trend of money prices of primary products. The only qualification would be that, since the commercial demand for primary products and the rate of growth of the monetary demand for stocks of primary products would presumably be related to the growth of the money value of total output, the rate of growth of total demand for primary products would be somewhat greater—and consequently the rate of fall of the relative prices of primary products somewhat smaller—than in the absence of the scheme.

A second set of practical objections concerns the cost of operating the commodity reserve scheme and the implications of the magnitude of its operations. The operating cost would include the resource cost of the required annual additions to the stock, the storage costs of the stock, and the costs of the buying and selling operations. The fact that commodities are not perfectly durable but deteriorate over time would require the management of the stocks to turn them over periodically, so that gross purchases and sales would be substantially larger than the annual net additions to the stocks, with correspondingly larger expenses for transactions costs. The turnover of stocks would make the International Monetary Fund a much larger participant in the world commodity market than the net annual acquisitions to stock would suggest, with corresponding power to dominate the market for good or evil.[1] It should be observed that, of the total costs of operation of the commodity reserve currency scheme, only a small fraction would directly benefit the less developed countries by increasing their export earnings: in the first place, much of the cost would be storage and transaction cost; secondly, a substantial part of the net additions to stocks would be supplied by developed countries.[2]

[1] H. G. Grubel, 'The Case Against An International Commodity Reserve Currency', *Oxford Economic Papers*, N.S. 17, No. 1 (March 1965), 130–5, calls attention to the size of these costs and their growth over time. He estimates that the resource cost (net annual addition plus 6 per cent operating cost) would rise from $3,918 million in 1973 to $12,384 million (at a 3 per cent growth rate) or $20,140 million (at a 4 per cent growth rate) in the year 2000; of these figures, $2,258 million, $5,032 million, and $9,038 million respectively represent the cost of net annual acquisitions. These figures may exaggerate the size and growth of resource cost, since his 6 per cent operating cost allowance is far above the Hart–Kaldor–Tunbergen estimate of 3–3·5 per cent, and makes no deduction for the storage and operating costs of existing stockpiles. Grubel reckons that the gross annual purchases for the stocks would rise from $11·5 billion (three year turnover period) or $7·8 billion (five year turnover period) to $45·9 billion or $29·5 billion (3 per cent growth rate) or $70·7 billion or $46·0 billion (4 per cent growth rate) in the year 2000. Such a vast participation in the market, he points out, entails a Hobson's choice between unwieldy rigid rules and undesirable discretionary power in operations in the market.

[2] For the thirty commodities included in the Hart–Kaldor–Tinbergen scheme, 58 per cent of world exports come from less developed countries. Applying this percentage to Grubel's figures for net acquisitions, making the extreme assumption that these purchases increase the total export earnings of the less developed countries by the same amount, and accepting Grubel's cost estimates, it appears that the scheme would expend $3,918 million to increase less developed countries' export earnings by $1,310 million in 1973, and $12,384 million or $20,140 million to increase their export earnings by $2,919 million or $4,882 million in the year 2000. The implied cost-benefit ratios are obviously extremely high. Using the authors' own much lower estimate of $200 million for net additional storage costs, it would cost $2,458 million to increase less developed countries'

It could be argued that the costs of the commodity reserve currency plan, high as they could be, would be of little importance if the plan actually secured a substantial improvement in the international monetary system. This question introduces the well-known theoretical objections to the commodity reserve currency standard.[1] These are, briefly, as follows. First, a partial standard of the kind proposed, which is to be grafted onto the international gold standard while allowing national autonomy in the creation of domestic credit money, is not truly a reform of the monetary standard but a scheme for price support of the commodities included combined with a cyclical deficit-surplus fiscal policy mediated through the commodity stocks.[2] Secondly, since the commodities suitable by reason of durability, marketability, and conditions of supply for inclusion in the scheme are bound to account for only a small part of world output and to be unrepresentative of aggregate output, their costs of production relative to other commodites are likely to change in consequence of uneven technical progress and new resource discoveries, so that stabilization of their money prices is likely to destabilize the general level of prices, perhaps even more than has occurred under the gold standard. Thirdly, because of the small share of these commodities in total output and the limited elasticities of supply and demand for many of them, the automatic stabilizing effects (through direct income effects on their production and indirect monetary effects of automatic variations in stocks) of the commodity reserve standard are likely to be small and consequently to take considerable time to be effective.[3] Finally, the scheme depends on persuading nations that have already largely abandoned the gold standard, in spite of the great

export earnings by $1,310 million in 1973: still a high cost-benefit ratio. Further, it must be remembered that the net transfer of external resources to the less developed countries is less than the value of the increased export earnings, owing to the resource cost of producing the commodities.

[1] For a full discussion, see Milton Friedman, 'Commodity Reserve Currency', *Journal of Political Economy*, LIX (June 1951), 203–32, reprinted in *ibid.*, *Essays in Positive Economics* (Chicago: University of Chicago Press, 1953), 204–50.

[2] See Friedman, *op. cit.*, p. 222. The retention of gold as the basis of the international monetary system under this scheme exposes it to the same possible danger of loss of confidence as might afflict a world central bank obliged to maintain convertibility of its liabilities into gold at a fixed price.

[3] These points are illustrated in the Mathematical Appendix.

320 ESSAYS IN MONETARY ECONOMICS

weight of the historical tradition and symbolism that have supported it, to adopt and live by an untested and unorthodox alternative of an equally arbitrary kind.

In view of all these considerations, and especially of the inefficiency of the plan itself in achieving worthwhile objectives and the deliberate reversal of the historical evolution from the gold standard to intelligent monetary management that it would entail, the commodity reserve currency plan appears to offer little to recommend it as a solution to the problem of international monetary reform. Less developed countries and their sympathizers would be better advised to press for as liberal a credit-based international monetary system as can be achieved, preferably an internationally-controlled world central bank.

MATHEMATICAL APPENDIX ON COMMODITY RESERVE MONEY

Consider first a static equilibrium system with a fixed nominal quantity of money M and a desired ratio of money to income k; in such a system the price level p is determined by the equation $M = kpY$, where Y is real output, and the effect of a change in k is $\dfrac{dp}{p} = -\dfrac{dk}{k}$. Now consider a similar system producing a commodity whose quantity is represented by C and whose price is fixed at one unit of money by a commodity reserve system, and another commodity whose quantity is represented by X and whose (variable) price is p. Let the desired ratio of money to income again be k, the desired money stock being $M^* = k(pX + C)$ where $pX + C = Y$ and initially $M^* = M$. The expenditure equation of the system is

$$Y = E + S = pX' + C' + S,$$

where E is total expenditure, S is saving (initially equal to zero), and primes denote quantities consumed (initially equal to quantities produced). Differentiating by p,

$$Xdp = X'dp + pdX' + dC' + dS$$

or
$$O = pdX' + dC' + dS$$
$$= -dC + dC' + dS$$

(since initially $X = X'$, p must change to make $dX' = dX$, and on the production side $pdX + dC = O$). The first term is a production substitution effect dependent on the change in p; the second term is a combination of two effects: the effect of increased saving in reducing expenditure on C, representable by a marginal propensity to consume, and a substitution effect dependent on the change in p. Hence the equation may be rewritten (using the fact that initially $C = C'$) as

$$O = (\epsilon + \eta)C\,\frac{dp}{P} + (1 - c)dS,$$

or (1)
$$\frac{dp}{p} = -\frac{1 - c}{(\epsilon + \eta)C}\,dS,$$

L

where ϵ and η are respectively the elasticity of supply of and (compensated) elasticity of demand for the commodity with respect to its own price.

To introduce monetary behaviour, assume that any disequilibrium between actual and desired money stocks is adjusted according to the equation

$$(2) \quad dS = a \, dM^*$$

$$= a \left[M \frac{dk}{k} + kp \, X \frac{dp}{p} \right]$$

Substituting in (1),

$$(3) \quad \frac{dp}{p} = - \frac{(1-c)aM}{(\epsilon + \eta)C + (1-c)akpX} \cdot \frac{dk}{k}$$

$$= - \frac{(1-c)ak}{(\epsilon + \eta)\bar{c} + (1-c)ak(1-\bar{c})} \cdot \frac{dk}{k}$$

where $\quad \bar{c} = \dfrac{C}{pX + C} = \dfrac{C}{Y}$

$$(4) \quad dS = aM \frac{(\epsilon + \eta)C}{(\epsilon + \eta)C + (1-c)akpX} \cdot \frac{dk}{k}$$

$$\frac{dS}{M} = \frac{a(\epsilon + \eta)\bar{c}}{(\epsilon + \eta)\bar{c} + (1-c)ak(1-\bar{c})} \cdot \frac{dk}{k}$$

From these equations it is evident that if $\epsilon = \eta = O$, $\dfrac{dp}{p} = - \dfrac{1}{1 - \bar{c}}$ $\dfrac{dk}{k}$ and $dS = O$, that is, the result would be the same as in the static system first considered except for the rigidity of the money price of the standard commodity. Any stabilizing effect on prices depends on there being some elasticity of demand for or supply of the standard commodity. It is obvious from inspection of (3) that the fall in the price of the non-standard good is smaller, the larger are the elasticities of demand for and supply of the standard commodity. It can also be verified that the price fall will be smaller, the larger is the marginal propensity to consume the standard commodity, and the smaller are the adjustment coefficient and the desired ratio of money to income (a and k). The magnitude of the price fall will vary inversely or directly with the share of the standard commodity in total output, depending on whether $\epsilon + \eta$ is greater or less than $(1 - c)ak$; the probable magnitude of the parameters make the former the more likely case. From inspection of (4), it is obvious that $\dfrac{dS}{M}$ will be closer to $\dfrac{dk}{k}$ (i.e., the addition to money stocks will be closer to the desired increment, and therefore the economy will be returning more rapidly to its initial price level) the larger are the average and marginal propensities to consume the standard commodity (the larger the ratio of production of that commodity to total output and the higher the marginal propensity to consume it), the higher the elasticities of demand for and supply of the standard commodity, the lower the desired ratio of money to income, and the higher the adjustment coefficient.

To obtain an impression of the stabilizing effect that might obtain in practice, one might plausibly assume that $c = \bar{c}$, and that $\bar{c}$ is in the neighbourhood of $0 \cdot 05$. η is likely to be under unity for primary products, probably in that neighbourhood of $0 \cdot 4$; given that many of the commodities covered in the proposed scheme are agricultural products, whose supply is fixed within the crop year, ϵ would be very small, probably no more than $0 \cdot 1$. More difficulty is encountered with k and a, which require specification of the period of the analysis; this might be taken as one year for $a = 1$, with k probably around $0 \cdot 05$ (given that it is international reserves and not money in the hands of the public with which the scheme is concerned). With these figures the results are:

$$(5) \quad \frac{dp}{p} = 0 \cdot 677 \, \frac{dk}{k}$$

$$(6) \quad \frac{dS}{M} = 0 \cdot 356 \, \frac{dk}{k}$$

These figures indicate a significant but not a very high degree of stabilization.

INDEX OF SUBJECTS

INDEX OF NAMES